The Kurds of Northern Syria

The Kurds of Northern Syria

Governance, Diversity and Conflicts

Harriet Allsopp and
Wladimir van Wilgenburg

Volume 2: "Governing Diversity: The Kurds in a
New Middle East"

I.B.TAURIS
LONDON • NEW YORK • OXFORD • NEW DELHI • SYDNEY

Bloomsbury Publishing Plc
50 Bedford Square, London, WC1B 3DP, UK
1385 Broadway, New York, NY 10018, USA

BLOOMSBURY, I.B. TAURIS and the Diana logo are trademarks of Bloomsbury
Publishing Plc

First published in Great Britain 2019
Reprinted 2019

Copyright © Iraq Institute for Strategic Studies (IIST) 2019

Harriet Allsopp and Wladimir van Wilgenburg have asserted their right under the Copyright,
Designs and Patents Act, 1988, to be identified as Editors of this work.

For legal purposes the Acknowledgements on p. x constitute an extension
of this copyright page.

Cover design: Adriana Brioso
Cover image: Kurdish people in Mursitpinar, Syria, 2014. (© RIS MESSINIS/AFP/
Getty Images)

A catalogue record for this book is available from the British Library.

A catalog record for this book is available from the Library of Congress.

ISBN: HB: 978-1-7883-1483-1
PB: 978-1-8386-0445-5
eISBN: 978-1-7883-1597-5
ePDF: 978-1-7883-1598-2

Series: Kurdish Studies

Typeset by Deanta Global Publishing Services, Chennai, India
Printed and bound in Great Britain

To find out more about our authors and books visit www.bloomsbury.com
and sign up for our newsletters.

أنجز هذا المشروع بأجزائه الخمسة بدعم مركز أبحاث التنمية العالمية، أوتاوا-كندا

The work involved in this and subsequent volumes was carried out with the aid of a grant from the International Development Research Center, IDRC, Ottawa, Canada Iraq Studies (IIST) معهد الدراسات الاستراتيجية – دراسات عراقية

Contents

Acknowledgements

This book is the product of a broad network of individuals, institutions and a team of dedicated researchers, experts and facilitators who have worked tirelessly to realize the aims and objectives of this project on identity and representation of the Kurds. The project was initiated by the Iraq Institute for Security Studies (IIST) Lebanon – by the late Dr Faleh A. Jabar, who worked unstintingly to achieve its aims. This book is dedicated to his memory and legacy.

The IIST and authors would like to extend their sincere thanks and appreciation to the International Development Research Council (Canada), which funded this project.

This book on Syria involved many people inside the country, who for reasons of security and safety remain anonymous. Not only translators, drivers, hosts, and reporters who provided assistance and, in some cases, risked their lives but also all those who participated in surveys and shared their experiences and opinions with us. Those individuals, organizations and institutions that we are able to name include Heybar Othman, Can Mirzo, Bashir Talati, Mohammed Hassan, Ekrem Salih, Redwan Bezar, Ehmed Shiwesh, Enwar Omer, Nuvin Ibrahim and reporters from NRT, KNN, Kurdistan 24, ARA news, and ARTA FM. Abdulrahman Dawud who helped distribute and translate surveys. Zuzan Hesen who helped conduct surveys in Kobani. Drivers, Fahad Fatah and Bahri Jammo; the Bali family in Kobani (Jamal, Mahmud and Mustafa Bali); the Kobani hotel and the Qasr Ani hotel for hosting our researcher and for their hospitality and support; all officials, NGOs and others who assisted in the research and surveys.

Field research would not have been possible without access to and freedom of movement within and across northern Syria and the willing cooperation and communication of officials and politicians from within the DAA governance structures, the Kurdistan Region of Iraq and from the political opposition in and outside Syria. Our thanks is extended to the members of the Kobani and Jazirah self-administrations that facilitated access across these two cantons, including Ranya Mihemed, head of media department in Kobani; Alan Osman (former head of media department in Cizere canton) and his successor Dilxwaz Xelil; Arsek Baravi, the head of the Jazirah canton's Media Council; PYD representatives Khaled Issa (France), Sheruan Hasan (Netherlands), Sihanok Dibo (Qamislo),

Gharib Hesso (KRG) and Salih Muslim; the Kurdish officials in Kobani: Ayse Efendi, Idris Nassan (now working with a NGO), Anwar Muslim, Ismet Sheikh, Emin Salih (now promoted as head of foreign relations of Kobani) and others; the Kurdish officials in Jazirah canton: Abdulkarim Omer, Abdulkarim Saroxan and Kanaan Berekat; the TEV-DEM and Syrian Democratic Council officials Ilham Ahmed, Hediya Yousef, Abdulsalam Ahmed, and Diyar Qamislo; the SDF and YPG officials: the late Abu Amjad, Sharvan Darwish, Abdulaziz Mahmud, Dr Nasr Haji Mansur, among others; the KNC officials Majdal Delli, Zara Saleh, Mohammed Ismail and others who helped organize meetings with KNC leaders in Syria and in the Kurdistan Region of Iraq and all those politicians and activists who shared their experiences with us; and Amjad Othman, member of the Syrian Democratic Council, and head of the Reform Movement. Thanks also to Nawaf Xelil, head of the Rojava Research Centre; Adib Abdulmajid, founder of ARA news who assisted with help from the Netherlands, and Rodi Naso who helped in Amude.

Maps

Courtesy of Aryan Nawzad (@AryanNawzad) and Eduardo Artika (@LCarabinier).

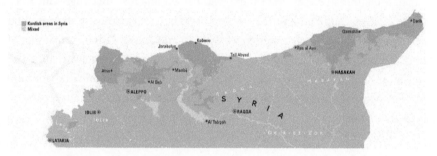

Map 1 The Kurdish demographic spread in northern Syria

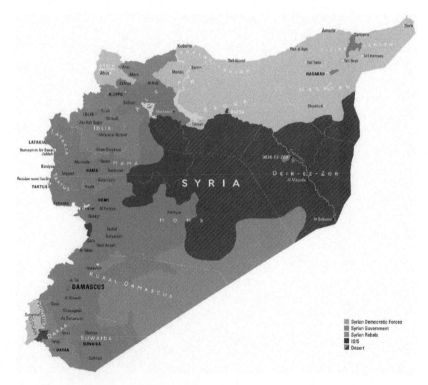

Map 2 Syria: Areas of control, June 2017

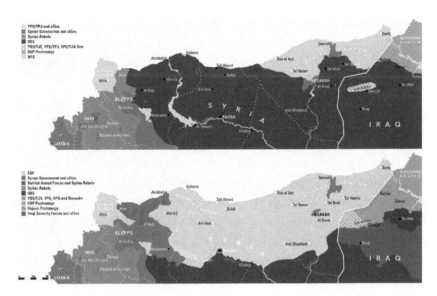

Map 3 Expansion of Kurdish control: December 2014–June 2017

Note on Transliteration and Bibliographic Referencing

This book draws on texts and interviews in English, Arabic, Turkish and in Kurmanji Kurdish. The geographic areas it concerns are also home to a variety of languages, some of which have been politicized due to proscriptions on their public use. Therefore, using one model of transliteration applicable to all place names and organizations has not been possible. As far as possible, places commonly referred to by their Arabic names have been transliterated according to a simplified use of the system employed by the *International Journal of Middle Eastern Studies* (excluding the use of diacritic symbols). However, common spellings are employed to promote ease of understanding, The spelling 'Kobani', based on the Kurdish name for the city and surrounding region, came into widespread usage during the siege on the city and is used in this book. It has also been spelt Kobane, and Kubani and referred to by its Arabic name, Ayn al-ʿArab. For consistency, place names which have a variety of spellings due to local language variations and differences in transliteration models, (such as the Jazirah region, which can also be spelt Jazira, Jezira, Jazeera, or in Kurdish, Cizîrê) the *IJMES* model of transliteration, above, is employed. Names of organizations are referred by their most commonly used name or acronym (see glossary of acronyms and abbreviations) so as to be most recognizable and understandable to the reader. Where necessary or appropriate, both Arabic and Kurdish names are given. Peoples' names are generally written as they, themselves, would have them transliterated.

Bibliographic References

Due to the current and changing subject matter, research for this book involved constant monitoring of events on the ground in Syria through field research, respondents and through live news and opinions published on the internet. As a result, several news resources have been cited in this work. Sources have been provided to verify facts which may not be widely known and to gauge as wide a possible impression of opinions of people in the regions. These sources have been corroborated as far as possible through field observations, interviews and other open source materials. News sources are cited within the footnotes, while other sources, including academic literature, publications by think tanks and organizations, political documents and interviews are listed in the bibliography.

List of Acronyms and Abbreviations

1957 genealogy of parties:
> the group of Kurdish political parties that trace their origins to the founding of the first Syrian Kurdish political party in 1957.

Asayish: *Asayîş.* The police force of the Democratic Autonomous Administrations (DAAs, also referred to as the cantons).

SCP: *Al-Hizb Al-Shuyu'i Al-Suriy,* The Syrian Communist Party, formed in 1944.

Democratic Autonomous Administrations (DAAs):
> Governance structures of the Afrin, Kobani and Jazirah cantons.

FSA: *al-Jaysh as-Suri al-Ḥurr*, the Free Syrian Army. Founded 29 July 2011 by officers who had defected from the Syrian Army. Aimed at removing the Syrian government through armed opposition. Consists of a variety of small and large military units.

Gorran: *Bizûtinewey Gorran*, Movement for Change, political party in the KRI.

HAT: *Hêzên Anti Teror,* Anti-Terror Unit affiliated with the DAA Asayish forces.

HPC: *Hêzên Parastina Cewherî*, Civilian Defence Forces of the DAAs.

HPG: *Hêzên Parastina Gel*, People's Defence Forces. Armed wing of PKK operating in Turkey.

HXP: *Hêzên Erka Xweparastinê*, Self-Defence Forces of the DAAs.

ISIS: Islamic State of Iraq and Syria, '*Daesh*' also known as the Islamic State of Iraq and the Levant (ISIL), or simply, the Islamic State (IS).

Jabhat al-Akrad:

Liwa' Jabhat al-Akrad l-Nusrah Sha 'bnā al-Sūrī, Kurdish Front Brigade to Protect the Syrian People. Part of the FSA.

Jabhat al-Nusra:

armed group in Syria affiliated to al-Qaeda.

KCK: *Koma Civakên Kurdistan*, Union of Communities in Kurdistan. Kurdish confederation for the PKK (Turkey), PYD (Syria), PJAK (Iran) and Kurdistan Democratic Solution Party or PÇDK (Iraq) and associated organizations.

KDP: *Partiya Demokrat a Kurdistanê*, Kurdistan Democratic Party led by Masoud Barzani, President of the KRG.

KDP-S: *Partiya Demokrat a Kurdistanê li Sûriyê*, Kurdistan Democratic Party of Syria. One of the larger Syrian Kurdish political parties belonging to the 1957 genealogy. Patronized by the KDP (Iraq) and part of the KNC.

KNAS: Kurdish National Alliance in Syria, formed on 13 February 2015 by five Syrian Kurdish political parties of the 1957 genealogy. The KNAS cooperated with TEV-DEM.

KNC/
ENKS: *Encûmena Niştimanî ya Kurdî li Sûriyê*, Kurdish National Council of Syria. Political coalition of some Kurdish parties belonging to the 1957 genealogy. Supported by the KDP of Iraq.

KRG: *Hikûmetî Herêmî Kurdistan*, Kurdistan Regional Government, Kurdistan Region of Iraq.

KRI: the Kurdistan Region of Iraq.

PCWK: the Peoples' Council of Western Kurdistan, *Meclîsa Gel a Rojavayê Kurdistanê*, (also known as MGRK). Established 16 December 2011 by the PYD and affiliated organizations. The PCWK became representative of the PYD-led administration in the Erbil power sharing agreements.

PÇDK: Kurdistan Democratic Solution Party (Iraq). Ideologically affiliated to Abdullah Öcalan. Member of the KCK.

Peshmerga: *Pêşmerge*, (literally 'one who confronts death'). KRG military forces operating in the Kurdistan Region of Iraq.

Pêşverû (Peshveru)/ PDPKS:
Partiya Dimoqrati Pêşverû Kurdi li Sûriyê, Kurdish Democratic Progressive Party in Syria led by Abdulhamid Haj Darwish.

PJAK: *Partiya Jiyana Azad a Kurdistanê*, Kurdistan Free Life Party, Iran. Ideologically affiliated to Abdullah Öcalan, supports the democratic autonomy project and is part of the KCK.

PKK: *Partiya Karkerên Kurdistanê*, Kurdistan Workers Party, Turkey. Founded by Abdullah Öcalan in 1978. Part of the KCK.

PUK: *Yekêtiy Nîştimaniy Kurdistan*, Patriotic Union of Kurdistan (KRI), Jalal Talabani.

PYD: *Partiya Yekîtiya Demokrat*, Democratic Union Party. Established in 2003. It formed the YPG, YPJ and TEV-DEM. It is part of the Syrian Democratic Assembly (SDA).

Qamh: *Tiyar al Qamh*. Wheat-wave Movement Law–Citizenship–Rights Movement (*qiyyam, muwatana, huqouq* QMH). Part of the Syrian Democratic Assembly.

Quwwat al-Sanadid:
Forces of the Brave. Arab SDF unit. Members were from the Shammar tribe in Hasakah/Jazirah.

Rojava Peshmerga:
Syrian Kurdish forces allied to the Kurdish National Council (KNC). Trained and based in the KRI.

SDC: Syrian Democratic Council. Founded on 10 December 2015 as the political wing of the Syrian Democratic Forces (SDF). Worked towards a secular, democratic and federalist system for Syria.

SDF: *Quwwat Suriya al-Dimuqratiya*, Syrian Democratic Forces. Formed 10 October 2015. A military alliance of Kurdish, Arab, Assyrian, Armenian, Turkmen, Circassian and Chechen armed groups, dominated by the YPG/YPJ and including *Jaysh al-Thuwar, Burkan al-Furat* (Euphrates Volcano), the

Syriac Military Council, *Quwwat al-Sanadid*. Supported by the international anti-ISIS coalition to dislodge ISIS from northern Syria.

SKC: Supreme Kurdish Committee, *Desteya Bilind a Kurd*. An administrative committee formed in accordance with the Erbil power sharing agreement of 12 July 2012. The PCWK and KNC were equally represented in the committee. The SKC became redundant after power sharing failed.

SNC: Syrian National Coalition of Syrian Revolution and Opposition Forces or the Syrian National Coalition, founded in November 2012. Political opposition coalition backed by Western powers and founded on the principle that the Assad government must leave power. The KNC became a member of the SNC in 2013.

SUP: Syriac Union Party. Part of TEV-DEM and part of the Syrian Democratic Assembly (SDA). Located in the Jazirah region.

Sutoro: Syriac security force affiliated to the SUP, which cooperated with the YPG and Kurdish Asayish forces.

Syrian National Council:
a political opposition council formed in 2011 in Turkey. Replaced by the SNC.

TEV-DEM: *Tevgera Civaka Demokratîk*, the Movement for a Democratic Society. The political coalition governing the Democratic Autonomous Administrations of northern Syria. Established by the PYD in 2011.

UAR: The United Arab Republic, the political union of Syria and Egypt 1958–1961.

Yekîtî: *Partiya Yekîtî ya Kurdî li Sûriyê*, Kurdish Union Party in Syria. One of the larger Syrian Kurdish political parties. A member of the KNC.

YPG: *Yekîneyên Parastina Gel*, People's Protection Units of the Democratic Autonomous Administrations (DAAs). Originally formed as the armed wing of the PYD, the YPG became the de facto army of the DAAs. The majority of its members were ethnically Kurdish, but the force also includes Arab and foreign fighters.

YPJ: *Yekîneyên Parastina Jin*, Women's Protection Units of the
             Democratic Autonomous Administrations (DAAs). The YPG's
             female brigade set up in 2012.

al-Wahda: the Syrian Kurdish Democratic Union Party (in Arabic, *Hizb
             al-Wahda al-Dimuqrati al-Kurdi fi Suriya* or, in Kurdish, *Partiya
             Yekîtî ya Demokrat a Kurdî li Sûriyê*). This party was the PYD's
             primary political competitor in Afrin Canton. Participated in
             municipal elections in this region. Part of the SDA.

YBS: *Yekîneyên Berxwedana Şengalê*, Sengal (Sinjar) Resistance Units,
             Yezidi militia, trained by the YPG/HPG. Formerly called the King
             Peacock Troop (Arabic: *Malik Al-Tawus*).

Introduction

Representation and governance of the ethnic, religious and cultural diversity in the Middle East region has been an enduring challenge to successive governments in its variety of states. For decades, attempts to unite diverse communities (many organized according to local identities and traditional sub-state representative channels) around a central state, and efforts to form cohesive nation states have relied on assertion of majority identities and have galvanized the population through rhetoric and policies constructed around external and internal threats. In Syria this practice, and the attachment of citizenship and nationhood to Arab ethnicity and Arabist policies, forged autocratic power relations that guaranteed control and stability rather than representation and participation. Stability came at a cost to freedoms of expression and thought and to the representation of ethnic and religious minorities and diverse social classes. The Kurds in Syria were one such collective. Kurdish identity and culture were forcibly assimilated to an Arab state identity or expression of it was criminalized. But, for decades, Kurds in Syria organized both politically and culturally, circumventing the state, to maintain and protect identity.

With the 'Arab Spring' of 2011, a wind of opportunity and change blew through Syria and long-standing taboos were shattered as an unprecedented protest movement spread in March. While the Arab street protests defiantly confronted corruption, authoritarianism and inequality in Syria, the Kurds protested in unison, but also found an opening to present their specific identity and demands and to call for greater representation. The involvement of foreign powers in the unfolding crisis and the militarization of the conflict, however, fractured any developing unity formed around common Syrian experience and interest in opposing corruption, increasing participation and economic equality. The resulting conflicts, sectarian violence, rise of Islamic political agendas and local power politics divided the Syrian peoples and the spirit of the 'spring' was marred by violence and destruction. Yet, within and despite the ensuing armed conflicts, Syrian Kurds embarked upon their first attempts at self-representation.

This book examines the development of far-reaching, quasi-autonomous governance structures, dominated by the (Kurdish) Democratic Union Party (PYD), in northern Syria. It does so within the analytical framework of identity and representation – an analysis contextualized also by the breakdown of the unitary Syrian state and uncertainty of the future. The content of the following pages is the result of extensive research in, and on, Syria, which was also part of a larger programme initiated and organized by the Iraq Institute for Strategic Studies and funded by the International Development Research Council (IDRC of Canada). Field surveys and interviews of particular groups in northern Syria are used to examine shifting political identities in a time of civil unrest and conflict. This book addresses, in particular, the political context existing at the time of research and writing in Syria, where the PYD-led administration held significant power in the northern areas, but in which the Syrian government still claimed a right to rule and central control and where the other opposition forces also attempted to claim rights of representation and legitimacy within the state system.

At the time of research and writing, Syria was still locked in a brutal and spiralling civil war, in which identity, loyalties and questions of representation proliferated. Radical groups had seized and monopolized services, distribution and political leadership, imposing highly ideological doctrines and systems of rule upon besieged or captive populations. The territory became an arena for complex, intertwining and conflicting proxy wars preventing resolution of core tensions that had arisen from basic inequalities and popular demands for democracy. With the descent into civil war, the weakening of the unitary state and increased intrigue in its internal affairs, Kurdish groups seized opportunities to increase their agency in domestic and international affairs and to pursue demands for equal representation and self-rule based on institutional and constitutional recognition of pluralism. Building on a history of social and political organization and pursuit of democratization, after 2011 Syrian Kurds emerged as an assertive force within a myriad of overlapping, conflicting and uncertain governance and power structures in Syria.

Interest in Syrian Kurdish issues swelled, yet, access to the areas became increasingly problematic when the military campaign against ISIS expanded. The dangers of field research inside Kurdish areas intensified and inter-Kurdish disputes complicated border crossings. Nonetheless, unparalleled field research for this book was conducted in northern Syria and it provides a unique view into the dynamics and processes of the breakdown and generation of representative and governance structures among Syria's Kurds, and of what might emerge or follow on from them. The research provides a window onto a particular moment in Kurdish, Syrian and regional history, which, as if seen from a moving train, was likely to gradually, or dramatically, change in appearance and character as we moved forward. As far as possible, we have attempted to make the analysis presented in this book relevant beyond the facts of the day – that is, to ground the analysis in the enduring and transforming social and political structures of Kurdish society itself rather than on the existing governance structures in Kurdish regions. Therefore, the Democratic Autonomous Administration (DAA) governance structures are problematized in the context of Kurdish identity in order to critically analyse its representativeness. We neither seek to unduly criticize the DAAs nor propagandize its successes. Rather, we have attempted to present both facts and opinions about identity and representation in a manner that allows them to speak for themselves.

The research concerns of this book were, first, to identify and examine the primary reference points for identity construction among Syrian Kurds and to understand why they are given importance over other possible determinants of identity. Second, to analyse the existing institutions and organizations capable of representing Syrian Kurds. And third, to assess the prospects for future representation in the Kurdish regions. These questions are addressed through six chapters: The first chapter introduces and provides an overview of identity and representation among Syrian Kurds before the start of civil unrest in Syria in 2011. It looks at the demographic foundations of the PYD-governance structures and at how identity in Kurdish areas was shaped by the state, by the existence of a trans-state Kurdish entity and by traditional sub-state socio-economic relations. Through this it demonstrates how political parties became the dominant, but not the only channels for representation of the Kurdish identity in Syria.

These political parties are examined in detail in Chapter 2. As the primary contenders for representing the Kurds, this chapter provides a comparison of the two main political blocs: that of the PYD and that of the Kurdish National Council (KNC). It looks at their ideologies, objectives, political practices and alliance formations within and outside Syria, and elaborates on the balances of powers between them. Through the analysis, where these political blocs converge or diverge is made clear, providing a basis for examining the representative structures available to Syrian Kurds and how they respond to identity.

The third chapter concentrates on the PYD-led administration in northern Syria. It looks at the structures of organization and representations within it and clarifies the changes in its structures and identity by connecting them to its gradual extension of political and military power. It unravels the overlapping structures of governance and security in the region, the move towards federalism and the challenges that the administration faced. The experience of DAA rule is expanded upon further in Chapter 4, which draws extensively on survey data to analyse opinion about identity and governance among Syrian Kurds. Looking at opinion about the DAAs, experiences of its model of direct democracy and at how, if and why ideas about identity have changed over the course of the crisis in Syria, this chapter provides a unique window into the DAAs and into Kurdish ideas about identity and representation at this time. Through it, the complex range of views about governance structures and prospects for self-rule in Syria are illuminated.

Moving away from a sub-state level of analysis, Chapter 5 spans outwards to look at the role of regional and international actors in shaping the form and legitimacy claims of organizations representing Syrian Kurds. It examines the impact of other Kurdish political parties in Iraq and in Turkey on identity formation and examines how regional and international states have affected the balance of powers within Syria; their impact on the governance of the Kurdish regions and their influence on the future representation of Kurds in Syria.

Finally, Chapter 6 turns to address the wider prospects for future representation of Kurds in Syria. By drawing together the analysis of previous chapters, possible scenarios are suggested and conclusions are drawn about the achievements and failings of the various representative organizations operating and structures present in Syria and about the challenges ahead.

Method and fieldwork

Although the need for this research was driven by the crisis in Syria and the development of quasi-autonomy in northern areas of Syria, the course of our fieldwork was not straightforward and drawing conclusions from it even more complicated. At the time of writing there were no accurate estimates of the death toll from the conflict. The protracted nature of the conflict and constant increase in the number of casualties had led most organizations to essentially stop counting. The last UN 'unrefined' estimate that more than 500,000 Syrians had been killed was based on data from 2014 but continued to be cited in 2018.[1] More than half the population of 21 million had been displaced from

---

[1] UN Special Envoy Staffan de Mistura gave the estimate of 500,000 in early 2016. Megan Specia 13/04/2018: 'How Syria's death toll is lost in the fog of war', *New York Times* (online), https://www.nytimes.com/2018/04/13/world/middleeast/syria-death-toll.html (last accessed 17/04/2018).

their homes. Life expectancy had been reduced by a staggering twenty years, 80 per cent of Syrians were deemed to be living in poverty, unemployment had increased to nearly 60 per cent, damage to Syrian infrastructure and revenues were estimated to amount to US $200 billion, 83 per cent of electricity had been cut[2] and the Syrian pound had soared from SP 44.57 to a dollar in October 2010 to SP 620 to US $1 on 11 May 2016.[3] Conditions in Syria were not conducive to a secure and normal life, let alone to posturing about ideal political outcomes. The ongoing conflict and involvement of foreign powers inside Syria as well as the shifting power relations and unresolved political issues meant that the situation was in flux and subject to dramatic substantive changes, as demonstrated by the rapid takeover of Afrin by Turkey in March 2018.[4] Yet, the establishment of a quasi-autonomous administration over Kurdish areas in northern Syria and the effective security mechanisms in place there meant that it was possible to begin to address these pressing questions concerning the future of Syria and the place of the Kurds within it.

The research for this book concentrated on the Syrian Kurdish population and the territory in which Kurds claimed a majority in northern Syria, and which were also controlled by the PYD at the time of writing (see maps). The territory itself was not defined or fixed and control over areas of it was disputed and subject to change. Likewise, the demography of the area was not homogenous and included various religious and ethnic sects as well as a growing population of refugees and internally displaced persons.

The relative stability and security of northern Syria compared to other areas meant that it was possible for our researchers to enter Syria to conduct field research between April and August 2016 in the Jazirah and Kobani regions. Gaining access to the region, however, was greatly complicated by mounting tensions between the PYD and the KDP, triggered by the PYD announcement of federalism earlier that year. After obtaining permission to travel to northern

---

[2] News.com 09/02/2016: 'Shocking figures that sum up the Syrian Civil War', *News.com.au*, http://www.news.com.au/world/middle-east/shocking-numbers-that-sum-up-syrian-civil-wa r/news-story/0361e487c319253b7703d7cc881cb2c8 (last accessed 15/04/2016); Jillian Kestler-D'Amours 12/03/2015: Chilling Syrian numbers: '83% of electricity cut, life expectancy drops 20 years', *The Star*, http://www.thestar.com/news/world/2015/03/12/chilling-syrian-numbers-83-of-electricity-cut-life-expectancy-drops-20-years.html (last accessed 15/04/16).

[3] Erika Soloman 11/05/2016: 'Syrian Currency's losing streak provokes anger with Assad regime', *Financial Times*, available on: http://www.ft.com/cms/s/0/369f583a-177a-11e6-b8d5-4c1fcdbe16 9f.html#axzz48Wlngh00 (last accessed 11/05/2016). The exchange rate changed to SP 214.3 to US $1 by March 2017 and by September 2017 it was SP 515.17 to US $1.

[4] *The Guardian*/Agencies 18/03/2018: 'Turkey claims Afrin city centre is under "total" control', *The Guardian*, https://www.theguardian.com/world/2018/mar/18/turkey-claims-afrin-city-centre-under-total-control-syria (last accessed 28/04/2018).

Syria from a Kurdistan Regional Government (KRG) official, the KRG announced in April 2016 that, with some exceptions, journalists would not be allowed to cross into Syria through the Fish Khabur border. As a consequence, in order to conduct the necessary fieldwork for this book, an alternative, and more risky, means of entering Syria had to be found.

Once inside Syria the security situation further complicated research. Although YPG-controlled areas benefited from greater security than many other regions, the risks of conducting research were still high. ISIS attacks, fighting between the Syrian government forces and the Kurds, and the US-backed military campaigns against ISIS in Manbij all impacted on freedom of movement and personal security. The nature of the project also required that research was conducted within PYD-led administration offices, militarized zones and areas that were targeted by ISIS and by the Syrian government. Inevitably, near misses and the proximity of threats – Syrian government arrests of foreign journalists, clashes between Syrian Army and Kurdish forces, ISIS suicide bombings, frontline confrontations and cyber-attacks – set limits on movement and forced the research to be cut short.[5] Constant monitoring and contact with people in the region was, however, maintained and facilitated the continuation of the research well beyond the fieldwork.

Security conditions and zones of control also set geographical limits on the stretch of the research. It was not possible to extend field research to Afrin due to its geographic isolation from the Kurdish areas of Kobani and Jazirah. Zones of ISIS, Syrian government and rebel control and the closure of the Turkish border with the area prevented travel to this region.[6] Research was also concentrated primarily in urban areas to facilitate access to the larger population and to limit exposure to risks. While travel and research within each canton required permission from the DAA's media offices, movement was generally unrestricted and unmonitored. Traveling between the Jazirah and Kobani cantons required permission due to the length of the journey, and travel to and from the frontlines required permission and escort by members of the YPG or Syrian Democratic

---

[5]   During a period of field research in Qamishli, clashes broke out between the Kurds and the Syrian government, 20–22 April 2016, and during the Manbij campaign clashes with government forces led to it bombing YPG buildings that had been a research site for this project. ISIS cells were also still active within the town and, on 21 May 2016, it targeted the Miami restaurant in the predominantly Christian neighbourhood, al-Wusta where research meetings had been set up (see Haci and Wilgenburg 22/05/2016: 'Islamic State carries out third attack on Christian district in Qamishlo', *ARA News*). On 27 July 2016, an ISIS VBIED detonated near the defence ministry, shortly after interviews with the Defence Minister. Over fifty-seven were killed.

[6]   Afrin was cut off from other areas of Kurdish control and the security situation in the area was, at the time of research, not conducive for fieldwork.

Forces (SDF). Any restrictions were compensated for to some degree through additional research conducted in the Kurdistan Region of Iraq as well as through telephone and electronic communications and continuous academic and open source research.

With the population and demography subject to continuous changes, assessing opinions about representation became complex and the findings subject to clarification. Interviews and surveys concentrated on the Syrian Kurdish population: How Kurdish identity was understood by them and its importance in relation to other sub-state, state level and pan-state loyalties and networks of representation. Much of the critical analysis in this book concentrates on the emergence and operation of the PYD-led administration (DAAs) in northern Syria and its claims to generate democratic and representative structures of self-governance. The subject of representation of non-Kurdish populations within DAA areas is, therefore, addressed within this book. These populations, however, were not the primary focus of research and surveys. Research was also focused on those inside Syria, but necessary research was also conducted among political leaders based in Erbil. The bulk of the analysis in this book is, therefore, based on opinions and data from Syrian Kurds remaining inside Syria and who lived under the PYD-led DAAs and what remained of the Syrian state government in these areas during this period.

Field research involved surveys and formal and informal interviews with representatives of Kurdish political parties, the PYD-led DAAs and with non-partisan Kurds from different socio-economic backgrounds. Interviews, questionnaires and surveys were designed to measure identification with state level and sub-state identities as well as to gauge the importance of various possible channels of representation available to Syrian Kurds. The bulk of the surveys were conducted with civilians randomly, from as wide a cross-section of society as possible and as equally as possible between the two regions. Surveys were conducted primarily within urban environments, as, owing to the security situation, complete freedom of movement was not possible. While it was on the whole unimpeded within these areas, conducting surveys was also complicated by general suspicions fuelled by the crisis in Syria, by tensions between Kurdish political groups and low-level monitoring by administration officials. Some unwillingness to participate in surveying was encountered and it has been necessary to consider this, as well as the general security and political environment in the regions, when analysing the data and opinions expressed within the surveys.

The ability to gain an overview representative of different sectors of Kurdish society was also affected by the migration of Kurds out of Syria. Migration had been caused by a number of factors, including the conflict with the Assad regime, ISIS, military conscription, economic uncertainty, and also by political motivations and friction with the PYD authorities. Within Syrian Kurdish society political and ideological tensions were high and informed dialogue about identity and representation. As a result opinions and conclusions differed greatly between different groups and a cross-section of all the various groups of Syrian Kurds had not always been possible. Migration affected the make-up of society and, consequently, the dataset available through field research.

When researching and writing this book, it was also necessary to address the fact that gaining a clear view of the situation inside Kurdish areas might not be possible within the timeframe set by the research itself. This was largely due to the security situation but was also a consequence of the nature of the political system in northern Syria itself and the social revolution on which it was premised. In the context of ongoing conflict in Syria, security needs played a decisive part in decision-making about political alliances and often outweighed or overlaid those of identity, especially the representation of a more personally or culturally defined sense of belonging. Displacement and military threats as well as deficits in availability of services, foods, medicines, weighed on daily life and existence impacting and influencing personal priorities and identity choices. Economic circumstances and access to resources and services can influence decisions about political allegiances and, therefore, affect understandings of and priorities related to identity and representation. While conducting this research within a period of massive change, disruption and uncertainty posed significant challenges and imposed restrictions on the research, this book provides a unique glimpse into the shifting dynamics of the struggle to attain long-sought-after rights within Syria. With the passage of time, it is hoped that it will also provide historical perspective on future events and governance structures that might emerge in Syria and within the Kurdish regions.

Clarifications and definitions

Identity

In this book identity has been assessed and contextualized through theoretical and empirical academic literature and through analysis of survey results and interviews. Surveys sought to gather data on personal identification with specific social and geographic criteria and also gauge whether this had changed over the course of the Syrian crisis. In looking at identity, this book examines peoples' conceptions of self-identity within their context. Identity is not a fixed or externally applied concept and its construction involves choice and influence, which may be predictable or quite idiosyncratic. Identity construction always involves some concept of the 'other' and, as allegiances and society changes over time and/or with dramatic events (such as the Syrian crisis), so understandings of identity also change. Similarly, identity is also not singular and the importance of various components of one's identity may ebb and flow with psychological change, personal circumstances and external influences. Consequently, research results must be contextualized by individual socio-economic profiling, where possible, by their respondents' historical and social roots, as well as by this extraordinary period of turmoil and flux. Uncertainty about the future of Syria and Kurdish self-rule itself complicates questions about how conceptualizations of identity might be framed among Syrian Kurds beyond the settlement of existing conflicts there.

This environment of unrest and armed conflict necessarily had an impact on respondents' decisions about an individual's or group's identity and the relative importance to be given by a researcher to the various aspects of belonging and the formation of collectives. While this has always been the case in such environments, the situation among the Kurds in Syria was further complicated by the fact that, since its establishment as a sovereign entity, the different ethnic and religious groups within its territory have not been equally represented. Quite the contrary. Thus, for many, choices about identity have been informed by the hostility of government institutions and forces to their ethnicity and nationalist aspirations.

Representation

Identity is intrinsically linked to ideas and channels of representation and this is the context in which it is examined here. The pursuit of representation and democratization among Kurds in Syria has been driven by state suppression of Kurdish ethnic identity and its restrictions on freedoms of expression. The sense of belonging to Kurdish ethnic and national identity and community created a platform for political mobilization at the local and state levels. In parallel to this, however, sub-state loyalties and identifications were also bolstered by the risks imposed on collective mobilization and identification by the central state. The denial of a state level and public platform for representation of interests and politics attached to Kurdish identity helped to prolong the longevity of traditional social networks and local channels of representation.[7] As political parties became a standard tool for political mobilization and representation during the 1950s, so Kurdish political parties began to replace and/or supplement traditional leaders. Operating outside the public sphere and denied participation in electoral processes and other state level representational systems, however, and with many leaders connected to notable families, Kurdish parties adopted the roles of traditional leaders and, in many ways, reinforced traditional power relations within Kurdish communities. Kurdish political parties have maintained a monopoly over representation among Kurds in Syria and, therefore, feature heavily in the analysis for this book.

Through surveys our research has attempted to gain insight into which channels of representation are popular and/or hold legitimacy within Kurdish society in Syria and identify aspirations for future representation. Due to the complex nature of the Syrian Kurdish society, these vary from official state representatives to family members to the complete rejection of formal channels of representation. It must also be noted that for many in northern Syria, particularly in rural areas, experience of and contact with official representatives was very limited, locating experiences of 'political' representation, or representation of their particular identity, within sub-state networks connected directly to that identity or identities.

Geographic terms

For ease of explanation, the term 'Kurdish areas' or 'northern Syria' is used to refer to the areas of northern Syria where Kurds are concentrated: that is, the Jazirah region (also referred to as Hasakah province), Kobani and Afrin regions. When referring to the administrative areas, canton is used as a suffix. Its use does not imply any politically motivated judgement on the ethnic or political character of the regions nor does it imply that these areas are homogenous ethnically. In March 2016 a federal entity came into discussion, the area of which was called the Democratic Federation of Northern Syria-Rojava, then the Democratic Federal System of Northern Syria, then, from December 2016, the Democratic Federation of Northern Syria. The federal structure was revised in September 2018 when, reflecting changes in alliances and in territorial control, a Self-Administration in Northern and Eastern Syria was declared. This book

---

[7] Harriet Allsopp 2014: *The Kurds of Syria: Political Parties and Identity in the Middle East*, I. B. Tauris, London, 143–4.

concentrates on the time period before this latter declaration and the territories in question included non-Kurdish majority areas between the three cantons that fell under YPG and SDF control. These areas were militarily contested by the Syrian government, by Syrian rebel groups, by ISIS and by Turkey and, as Turkish advances in northwest Syria proved, control over any ground was tenuous.

The democratic autonomous administrations (DAAs)

The governance structures in northern Syria have morphed and changed over the course of the crisis in Syria, even within the course of researching and writing this book. While the complex administrative structures and changes to them are given more explanation in Chapter 4, for ease of reference and explanation, the 'PYD-led administration' or 'Democratic Autonomous Administrations' (DAAs) or simply 'the Administration' are commonly used to refer to the general and canton governance structures. We use 'PYD-led' because this administration was developed in Syria by the PYD. While this political party has become just one in a myriad of organization involved in governing northern Syria, it was this party that spawned the democratic autonomy project there and maintained its development through the party and other affiliated organizations.

The area over which the PYD-led administration had control was also fluid and subject to substantial geographic change as well as changes to its name. The Administration itself was not fixed to any given territory suggesting its 'democratic autonomy' project was for all of Syria. The extent of its control was measured in terms of participation and alliances, and not on the basis of ethnic demography. Nevertheless, the core areas of its control and strength were Kurdish majority areas and the YPG-led Syrian Democratic Forces (the military forces connected to the PYD and the Administration) controlled identifiable territory and worked to expand that control and the democratic autonomy project through local councils, communes and other governance structures.

By making reference to 'the Administration' the authors and IIST do not imply any comment on the legitimacy of its control and acknowledged that its authority was not recognized or licensed by any formal agreement involving the sovereign Syrian state or any international powers. Its presence in the area and its ability to wield power and authority was, however, uncontested. While the authority has been referred to by many different names in the media, for ease of understanding and consistency this book refers to the body of organizations and institutions including the PYD, the YPG, TEV-DEM and its constituent parts and the various ministries of the cantons as the 'Administration.' When referring to any one of these organizations or institutions or their constituent parts they are referred to by their specific names.

Many other organizations – political, social and economic and military – have assumed roles of authority and decision-making within the northern regions and across Syria. In this book, commonly used names or acronyms are employed for ease of reference and clarity without conjecturing any judgement on their legitimacy or status. For example, reference to Rojava, the PYD-led administration, or to the democratic autonomy project, does not imply any inference about the legal status of the administration, its laws or ruling powers. Rather it is used as a direct way of identifying these institutions and governance structures. Likewise, reference to the Islamic State or ISIS is used as the common acronym for the organization, but its use does not imply any acceptance of its self-proclaimed status as a 'state' or that its rule is legitimate.

1

Identity and Representation I: Foundations of Identity Formation and Representation

In July 2012, the Democratic Union Party (PYD) and its military wing, the Peoples' Protection Units (YPG), stepped into the administrative and security gap left by the withdrawal of Syrian government staff and troops from Kurdish majority areas in northern Syria. The PYD's vision and its model of direct democracy then dominated local governance, security and civil organization in the predominantly Kurdish areas of northern Syria. It was a vision based on the teachings of imprisoned Kurdistan Workers Party (PKK) leader Abdullah Öcalan and guided by a broad revolutionary project involving a myriad of associated political, economic, civil and military organizations across the region.

The project in northern Syria was described by outside observers as 'a place where the seeds of the Arab Spring promised to blossom into utopia' ... 'one of few bright spots – albeit a very bright one – to emerge from the tragedy of the Syrian revolution', and 'a unique experiment that deserves to succeed.'[1] The autonomous government formed there claimed to provide the solution to problems of democratic representation of Syria's multi-ethnic pluralistic population. At the same time, for the Syrian Kurds, the project purported to offer an answer to questions of identity and representation that had shaped their history and their relationship with the central government, as well as with other groups in Syria. In a marked departure from Öcalan's earlier nationalist doctrines, which called for the creation of a Kurdish nation state, the 'nation' was defined in terms of democratic citizenship instead of by ethnicity and language. In the theoretical underpinnings of this experimental autonomy project in northern Syria, the revision of the concept of 'nation' was seen to release the model of representation from notions of cultural homogeneity and from intolerances associated with

---

[1] See Wes Enzinna 24/11/2015: 'A dream of secular utopia in ISIS' backyard', *New York Times*, (online) http://www.nytimes.com/2015/11/29/magazine/a-dream-of-utopia-in-hell.html?_r=0 (last accessed 19/05/2016).

'modern' conceptualizations of the nation and nation-state.[2] Northern Syria was presented as an area in which the seeds of democratic representation had taken root.

Although many other Kurdish political parties operated in Syria, it was the PYD that led the capture of territory from the Syrian authorities, from ISIS and from other rebel forces. It was the PYD that, through proxy organizations and institutions, gradually increased its control over governance and economic and social organization in the region. The party came to be described as the strongest Kurdish party in Syria, although before the start of the Syrian civil protests in March 2011, its capacity and influence in the country was not widespread. How and why was it that this particular party led the capture of territory from the Syrian government and came to develop far-reaching governance structures that captured the imagination of observers far removed from the realities of the Syrian conflict? And how representative were these governance structures of the society that it governed?

In this chapter we begin to address these questions through exploring the cognitive and political foundations that accommodated (or rejected) this radical governmental and social project. This is done through examining the demography on which these governance structures were built as well as by exploring what the questions of identity and representation among the Syrian Kurds looked like before the crisis in Syria and before the disruption of pre-existing governance and representative structures. A somewhat abstract and stylized account of the PYD governmental system is presented here with some contextual detail where necessary. (A more detailed analysis is deferred to Chapter 3.)

The demography of governance

The PYD democratic autonomy project was anchored firmly in the Kurdish majority areas of Syria, within Kurdish society and in their unique historical experience in Syria. The exact area under the control of the PYD-led administration, however, was not fixed and changed according to territorial gains and losses made by the YPG/YPJ and its allies against ISIS, the Syrian government, rebel forces and the Turkish army. Until March 2018 (when the

---

[2] Ahmet Hamdi Akkaya and Joost Jongerden 2012: 'Reassembling the political: The PKK and the project of radical democracy', *European Journal of Turkish Studies*, Vol. 14, available on http://ejts. revues.org/4615 (last accessed 18/05/2016).

Afrin region fell under Turkish/Free Syrian Army (FSA) control) the three autonomous cantons roughly coincided with the Kurdish majority areas of Afrin, Kobani and the Jazirah where Kurds had an historic presence along the northern borders of Syria.[3] The distribution of Kurds between these three regions[4] has been estimated as follows: Jazirah, in the northeast (an estimated 40 per cent of the Kurdish population), Kobani (10 per cent), and Afrin in the northwest (also known as the Kurd Dagh, 30 per cent).[5] This demography became the basis for the administrative division, by the PYD in 2012, of the Kurdish areas into three cantons. The distribution of the Kurdish population varied considerably within and across each of these three areas, with the exception of Afrin region where, pre-crisis, Arabs were believed to constitute only 2 per cent of the local population and inhabited the southern regions,[6] and Turkmen (estimated to be between 1.5 and 3 per cent of the total Syrian population) inhabited northern areas along the Turkish borders in the north and east.[7]

The Jazirah region (or Hasakah governorate) contained the greatest ethnic and religious diversity, although the distribution of ethnic groups across the region was not even. Kurds concentrated along the borders with Turkey and Iraq and formed majorities in the cities of Qamishli, Amude, Malikiyah, Qahtaniyah and Ma'abadah. In other cities, such as Hasakah, Arabs were a majority, but Kurdish majority areas existed within it. Assyrians, as the third largest ethnic group, had a majority in the upper Khabour river valley. In Kobani town and its vicinity Kurds were a majority. The town had a pre-2011 population of 45,000, and approximately one hundred villages in the surrounding sub-district. Kurdish

---

[3] There is not accurate data on number of Kurds in Syria, or elsewhere in the Middle East. The last Syrian censuses that included any reference to ethnic identity took place during the French Mandate (1923–46). Before Bashar al-Assad came to power in the year 2000, the Baath Party government denied that Syria had an indigenous Kurdish population. Even the infamous Hasakah Census of 1962, that stripped 120,000 Kurds of Syrian citizenship, did so on the grounds of residency rather than on that of ethnic identity. In September 2016 the PYD-led administration launched an initiative to conduct a census in areas under its control: like those that preceded it, the census form did not request information about ethnicity or religion. Consequently, existing data on the size of the Kurdish population in Syria is speculative. Many Kurdish sources would put the number at upward of three million, or 12–15 per cent of the Syrian population, even 25 per cent, while more conservative estimates put it at 1.5 million, or between 8 and 10 per cent. There was wide consensus, however, that Kurds constituted the second largest ethnic and linguistic group in Syria after Arabs.

[4] Kurds are also native to northern parts of Lataqiyah province, notably the Salma region. Ancient Kurdish enclaves also existed in Homs, Hama, Aleppo and Damascus alongside communities formed from more recent urban migrations from the north.

[5] Percentages of populations are drawn from Rasim Bozbuga 05/08/2014: 'Kurdish population in Syria', http://sahipkiran.org/2014/08/05/kurdish-population-in-syria/ (last accessed 30/03/2017).

[6] KurdWatch, n.d.: *Cities, KurdWatch*, http://www.kurdwatch.org/index.php?cid=183&z=en (last accessed 15/04/2016).

[7] Bozbuga, 'Kurdish population in Syria'.

sources estimated that 90 per cent of the total population was Kurdish.[8] Most
Kurds in this region were from the Barazi tribal confederation which included
the Alaaedin, Kitkan, Shiekhan, Shadedan and Pijan tribes.[9] The area between
Kobani and Afrin was also home to Arabs and Turkmen and the Kurdish
population there was more dispersed.

This demography and claims to territory in northern Syria, had long been
politicized. They were a core element of nationalist discourses: both about
the rights of Kurds to live in historic lands and be recognized as possessing a
distinct cultural and national identity and about the threat that Kurds posed to
the unity and territorial integrity of the Syrian state. Policies aimed at altering
the demography of the region in favour of Arabs, by moving Arabs into the
border areas, implemented by the nationalist government under French rule
in the 1920s and the Baath Party during the 1960s and 1970s, had contributed
to demographic change in the regions.[10] Against this, the Kurdish presence
in northern Syria also became, for many, a duty: a statement of existence and
presence against an existential threat.

The governance structures developed in northern Syria from 2012 sought to
build a truly representative system through which Kurds would be emancipated,
not only from a repressive central government but also from social norms
and practices that constrained the individual and maintained broad systems
of domination and exploitation. The PYD drew on resources and personnel
from a number of sources: from the *Koma Civakên Kurdistan* (the Union of
Communities in Kurdistan) – a Kurdish confederation of the PKK (Turkey), the
PYD (Syria), the Party of Free Life (Iran) and the Kurdistan Democratic Solution
Party (Iraq); from PKK bases in the Qandil Mountains; and from the earlier
quiet encroachment on local civil space within Syria. It mobilized large portions
of Kurdish society into this complex system of government and marginalized
other Kurdish nationalist political parties. The PYD formed an intricate system
of administrative units, civil and economic institutions, ministries and security
apparatus, all imbued with Abdullah Öcalan's ideological doctrine of democratic
autonomy (examined further in Chapters 2 and 3). Its rapid response to

---

[8] The 2004 census gives 192,513 as the sub-district's population.
[9] Bozbuga, 'Kurdish population in Syria'.
[10] Allsopp, *The Kurds of Syria*. Arabs were moved to the border areas and attempts were made to
     move Kurds into the Syrian interior. Demographic variations have also been caused by nomadic
     tribal movements in and out of the region, particularly by Arab tribes. Population figures were also
     affected by the denial of citizenship and associated rights to thousands of Kurds from the Jazirah
     as a result of the Hasakah population census conducted in the region in 1962, which led to the
     registration of thousands of Kurds as foreign migrants and left others completely unregistered.

opportunities, its engagement of youth, provision of security, aggressive mobilization and persuasive ideology of equality and rights all established the PYD as the dominant power in Kurdish areas and the strongest political party there. There was some opposition to this new political power in the region, as evidenced by early locally organized protests against the establishment of YPG checkpoints around Kurdish villages. Without the organizational capacity to sustain their momentum or armed forces for protection however, local acts of opposition melted away in the face of the PYD. Moreover, support for and cooperation with the PYD and the YPG gradually grew as it became the primary source of security, protection, services and employment in Kurdish regions.

The model of governance applied to Kurdish areas of Syria involved forming communes based on villages, neighbourhoods or districts. They were designed to put participants at the centre of decision-making about local issues, from: granting permission for residency; distribution of products and economic organization, to: conflict resolution in local disputes and judicial decision-making and justice. This model was applied in all areas which had been 'liberated' by the YPG, and participation in it was optional.[11] Media outlets that produced regular articles promoting the Administration reported that abstention was rare. Field research, however, showed that participation in the communes was not high, but also showed that it varied considerably between the regions according to the degree of saturation of the ideological doctrine into political, economic and social life. It also varied between social classes and geographic localities. Some accounts of the commune system suggested that material wealth offered choice about participation.[12] Certainly, because communes were linked to service provision, abstention could lead to exclusion from the distribution of goods and services and to difficulties in renting property or in working in areas run by communes. Participation had obvious benefits and communal organization, in one form or another, had become a common method of coping with the insecurities and consequences of war across Syria.

With a monopoly over the use of force and over public services, the PYD Administration gained state-like powers (albeit diluted between a myriad of

---

[11] IIST interviews with residents of Afrin (17/09/2016; 28/02/2017) suggested that residents were expected to participate in commune meetings, while in Jazirah the enforcement of participation appeared to be more relaxed. Many participants in IIST surveys mentioned that they had never been to a commune meeting.

[12] For example a wealthy shopkeeper expressed the opinion that the communes were a form of welfare system for the needy: see Zanyar Omrani 04/10/2015: 'Introduction to the political and social structures of democratic autonomy in Rojava', *Kurdish Question*, http://kurdishquestion.com/old article.php?aid=introduction-to-the-political-and-social-structures-of-democratic-autonomy-in-r ojava (last accessed 20/03/2017).

organizations) while it maintained a system of bottom-up, direct democracy and sustained a political and military struggle against those opposing it. Governance was divided between the three Kurdish regions in northern Syria: Afrin, Kobani and the Jazirah, described within the governance model as 'cantons'. The Administration maintained only limited relations with the Syrian government, which included a coexistence within Qamishli and Hasakah towns and in the Jazirah region more generally, as well as some economic relations. In Afrin, the Syrian government maintained a minimal presence in civil administration: processing applications for official documents and in the Sharia courts overseeing, among other things, marriages and divorce. The system came to be described by outside observers as Kurdish 'self-rule':[13] a term that recognized the Kurdish origins of the PYD itself and the particular demographic foundations of the governance system.

The PYD system of governance continued to alter and evolve in response to the changing configurations of territorial control in Syria. This brought with it the need to form tactical alliances with other non-Kurdish groups. The most significant expansions in its territory and changes to its political project were made in the context of the YPG fight against ISIS. A turning point for the PYD-led administration was the 'siege of Kobani' when, between 13 September 2014 and 15 March 2015, the so-called Islamic State laid siege to the Kurdish majority town of Kobani, which was almost lost to its army. The proximity of the town to the Turkish border allowed the media to follow closely the impending tragedy and garner Western support for embattled Kurdish fighters. Military intervention by the US-led anti-ISIS coalition and support from the Iraqi Kurdish Peshmerga helped tip the scales against ISIS and further legitimize the image of the Kurds as reliable Western allies. The battle marked a decisive shift in the role of the Kurds in the Syrian field and it changed outside perceptions of the PYD and the armed forces (YPG and YPJ) associated with it. US airstrikes against ISIS in Syria, initiated by the siege, began an enduring relationship of cooperation between the United States and the YPG and these Syrian Kurdish

---

[13] See, for example, Loqman Radpey 2016: 'Kurdish Regional Self-rule Administration in Syria: A new model of statehood and its status in International Law compared to the Kurdistan Regional Government (KRG) in Iraq', *Japanese Journal of Political Science*, Volume 17, Issue 3, September 2016, pp. 468–88, available on: https://www.cambridge.org/core/journals/japanese-journal-of-political-science/article/kurdish-regional-selfrule-administration-in-syria-a-new-model-of-stat ehood-and-its-status-in-international-law-compared-to-the-kurdistan-regional-government-kr g-in-iraq/E27336DA905763412D42038E476BBE61/core-reader (last accessed 06/06/2018); G. Sary, September 2016: 'Kurdish Self-governance in Syria: Survival and ambition', Chatham House Research Paper, London, available on: https://syria.chathamhouse.org/assets/documents/2016-09 -15-kurdish-self-governance-syria-sary.pdf (last accessed 06/06/2018).

forces became recipients of Western military assistance. For the Kurds, Kobani became a symbol of Kurdish strength and resistance and a source of political capital and legitimacy for the PYD.

The battle also initiated a territorial expansion of the democratic autonomy project and a diversification of the demography it encompassed. Amid the gains against ISIS in and around Kobani, Kurdish forces expanded their area of control, connected the cantons of Kobani and the Jazirah, and established a contiguous geographical territory extending eastwards from the Euphrates River to Malikiyah/Derik (the Tigris/Orontes River and the Iraqi border). West of the Euphrates, the area of Afrin in northwest Syria remained divided from other Kurdish controlled-areas – separated by contentious and strategic areas of territory approximately 60 kilometres wide, within which ISIS, FSA groups, Turkey, the YPG and allied forces vied for control.[14] Strong resistance from Ankara and Arab opposition groups to the establishment of a contiguous geographical area along Turkey's border dominated by the PYD complicated further the attempts of the Administration to accommodate the demographics of the region within its project.

Political and military alliances with Christian, Arab and Turkmen groups, located within and between majority Kurdish areas, provided the Administration with greater legitimacy, particularly within the context of the fight against ISIS. These alliances were complemented by the establishment of local administrative councils which could represent the diversity of ethnic and religious groups falling within the Administration's increasing territories and spheres of influence. Thus, territorial expansion and increased diversity within the Administration contributed to shifts in policy and encouraged military and political coalition-building within this region of Syria. Nonetheless, ethnic, tribal, religious, political beliefs and loyalties, as well as external alliances, continued to define population groups in northern Syria and had implications for identity and representation of the Kurds and the representativeness of the Administration, all of which are examined further in the course of this book. But, the demography of northern Syria (and changes to it) influenced ideas of representation among Syria's Kurds and of how it should be framed. It remained a contentious issue for organizations, groups and individuals seeking to maintain or claim channels of representation.

---

[14] Kurdish YPG forces were involved in the campaign to liberate these areas from ISIS in June 2016. See Wladimir van Wilgenburg 05/06/2016: 'On the frontlines in the bloody fight to take Manbij from ISIS', *The Daily Beast*, http://www.thedailybeast.com/articles/2016/06/05/on-the-front-line-in-the-bloody-fight-to-take-manbij-from-isis.html (last accessed 21/06/2016).

Demography remained a central component of Kurdish political and social organization that took on new meaning in post-2011 Syria. The wider conflict had transformed the demographics of the whole country. With this, the politics of Kurdish demography and its historic presence in Syria, on the one hand, was invigorated while, on the other hand, its political capital was diminished because more and more Kurds fled the country. In April 2018, 6.6 million people in Syria were estimated to be displaced internally and over 5.6 million had fled the country altogether.[15] Within Kurdish areas, Kobani was subject to most physical destruction, resulting from protracted conflict with ISIS in the area.[16] Estimates suggested that 70 per cent of Kobani town was destroyed in the fighting and the regional population of approximately 300,000 declined to 7–8000, with the majority having fled to Turkey and some to the Kurdistan Region of Iraq (KRI). Reconstruction was started soon after the defeat of ISIS and officials within the Administration estimated that the population had increased to 180,000 by October 2015.[17] Large-scale repopulation was, however, slowed by the lack of accommodation, poor infrastructure and medical facilities, as well as by funding shortages.[18]

After March 2011 several different waves and directions of migration occurred, which significantly altered the demography of Kurdish areas of Syria and which were caused by or influenced ideas about identity and threat. First, the reaction of the regime to the widespread civil protester and the escalation of violence around Damascus caused a reverse migration of Kurds who had moved to Damascus and other Syrian cities for economic reasons. The relative safety of the Kurdish north and the existence of family and land connections facilitated this 'return' migration. Second, insecurity also caused the migration of other ethnic and religious groups into Kurdish majority areas. It was estimated in 2016 that, in total, the Syrian Kurdish administration hosted over one million internally displaced persons (IDPs), but there were no accurate statistics through which to verify this.[19] The Afrin area became a point of refuge for Arabs from surrounding areas as well as from further afield.[20] Estimates from officials within the Afrin canton administration estimated that approximately 35,000 IDPs were

---

[15] UNHCR 18 April 2018: 'Syria emergency', http://www.unhcr.org/uk/syria-emergency.html (last accessed 08/05/2018).

[16] See drone footage of Kobani town published by the *Daily Mail*: Simon Tomlinson 05/05/2015: 'After the apocalypse', *Mail Online/Daily Mail*, http://www.dailymail.co.uk/news/article-3068937/Flying-apocalypse-Astonishing-drone-footage-reveals-sheer-scale-destruction-Syrian-town-Kobane-stormed-ISIS-pounded-months-coalition-air-strikes.html (last accessed 13/01/2017).

[17] IIST Interview: Idris Nassan, former vice minister of Foreign Affairs, 11/10/2015.

[18] Ibid.

[19] Society for Threatened Peoples (STP), June 2016.

[20] The Syrian government siege on Eastern Ghouta in 2018, and evacuations from this area relocated many rebels to Afrin, which was then under the control of Turkish supported FSA groups.

in the canton territory in May 2016.[21] This relative safety was eroded by the Turkish 'Operation Olive Branch', which resulted in the displacement of more than 137,000 people, mostly Kurds, from Afrin.[22] Although 150,000 civilians were believed to have remained in Afrin district, with 50,000 of those in the city itself,[23] fears among Syrian Kurds about politically motivated demographic changes instigated by Turkey and the FSA were further fuelled by the relocation of displaced persons from Eastern Ghouta and Qalamoun to Afrin in March and April 2018. In the Kurdish majority area of Serekani (Ras al-'Ayn), it was also reported that approximately 325 Iraqi refugees were accommodated in camps after they fled ISIS-held Mosul in January 2016.[24] Third, political incentives caused migrations of Kurds both into and out of Kurdish areas. The PYD project had drawn in Kurds, in particular, from Turkey and the PKK stronghold in the Qandil Mountains in Iraq. Many of the top-ranking members of the armed forces and administration were from Turkey and shared a commitment to implement Öcalan's visions of democratic autonomy in Syria. Similarly Kurdish activists from Turkey, Iran, Iraq and further afield, keen to become involved in the project or to defend Syrian Kurds, were believed to have entered Syria to join the administration or the ranks of the YPG. According to research conducted by the Atlantic Council, Kurds from Turkey accounted for 49.24 per cent of the YPG's self-reported casualties between January 2013 and January 2016.[25] The conflict in Syria was the primary driver for this wave and direction of migration and, one could presume that for most, it was a temporary relocation motivated by these specific circumstances or ideologies.

Contrariwise, a large number of Kurds critical of the PYD and, in particular, those activists and their families belonging political parties not recognizing the PYD-led administration, had left Syria for the KRI, to which their politics were more aligned, or to Turkey and Europe.[26] The majority of the registered 245,134

[21] Hisham Arafat 19/05/2016: 'Rojava's Afrin hosts 35000 Syrian Arab IDPs', *Kurdistan 24*, http://www.kurdistan24.net/en/news/9108bbe7-732a-4611-89e6-ab5181d6b821/Rojava-s-Afrin-hosts-35-000-Syrian-Arab-IDPs (last accessed 07/07/2017).

[22] UNOCHA 26/04/2018: 'Afrin displacement. Facts and figures', available on https://reliefweb.int/sites/reliefweb.int/files/resources/Afrin%20Fact%20and%20figures%2026%20April.pdf (last accessed 28/04/2018).

[23] Rudaw 25/04/2018: 'In Afrin, "demographic change is being carried out": Monitor', *Rudaw*, http://www.rudaw.net/english/middleeast/syria/250420181 (last accessed 28/04/2018).

[24] Hisham Arafat 05/02/2016: 'Rojava hosts 325 Iraqi refugees', *Kurdistan 24*, http://www.kurdistan24.net/en/news/884375f6-efe2-4fd0-9277-66338cec12db (last accessed 07/07/2017).

[25] Aaron Stein and Michelle Foley 26/01/2016: 'The YPG-PKK connection', *Atlantic Council*, http://www.atlanticcouncil.org/blogs/menasource/the-ypg-pkk-connection last accessed 13/01/2017)..

[26] Conversations with Kurds who had left the Afrin area suggested that the domination of the PYD over the administration of the areas contributed to their decisions to leave. IIST interviews September 2016.

Syrian refugee population in the KRI were Kurds from all three Kurdish areas of Syria.[27] Security concerns, poor economic conditions and the introduction of compulsory conscription were also prominent factors that influenced decisions to leave, regardless of political orientations.

As a consequence of these new governance structures and the accumulative effects of war and crisis, demography remained critical to ideas about the future representation of Kurds in Syria; to the historicity of claims to territory and to self-governance; and to understandings of lived experience.

Key influences on Kurdish identity formation

Much like the fractures in the Kurdish demography across northern Syria and the Middle East region, Kurdish identity has been described as deeply fragmented.[28] It is an abstract, subjective phenomenon that, among other things, can be racial, national, ethnic and/or local, based on language and/or shared culture and heritage or a synthesis of these. Restrictions on its expressions and a lack of state-sanctioned representative channels for it, rooted Kurdish identity in both traditional social structures and in modern conceptualization of belonging and representation. The division of Kurds across the four Middle Eastern states and a large diaspora has also given rise to varied experiences of identity formation and understandings of what being Kurdish means. Defined against a diversity of 'others' Kurdish identity has developed on contrasting trajectories but, at the same time, offers a transnational concept capable of surpassing and transcending its fragmentation. While the vast majority of Syrian Kurds identified themselves as Kurdish, where they placed this against the variety of other identities available to them, how they were synthesized or separated and how this affected their social and political behaviour varied significantly between groups and individuals and over time.

Shifting focus from demography on to identity and representation (to how the Syrian state and co-existing persuasive loyalties and 'others' feed into and/or compete with a Kurdish, or a specifically Syrian-Kurdish identity) allows nuanced understandings of identity and its effects on ideas about representation to be explored. Kurdish identity can be mapped according to key influences

---

[27] United Nations figures from 27 October 2015. UNHCR data portal: http://data.unhcr.org/syrianre fugees/region.php?country=103&id=65 (last accessed 20/05/2016).

[28] Abbas Vali 2006: 'The Kurds and their "others": Fragmented identity and fragmented politics', in Faleh A. Jabar and Hosham Dawod (eds), *The Kurds: Nationalism and Politics*, Saqi, London, 50.

upon it: first, that of Syrian state formation and of state institutions themselves. These have restricted and negatively shaped the construction of Syrian Kurdish identity but, at the same time, allowed it to become an accepted entity capable of representative process. Second sub-state loyalties and networks have enduring importance to personal identity and to social and political organization and are interwoven with ideas of Kurdishness. Local and traditional socio-economic relations, including the tribe/family, offer compelling and pervasive identities and provide alternative forms of representation and loyalty that do not involve ethnic assimilation. Third, nationhood is bound to ideas about identity and imagined communities that span state borders. On a more abstract level, a trans-state national identity and population, as well as religious and ideological beliefs, extends concepts of identity and loyalty beyond state borders. Fourth, the central role of Kurdish political parties in identity formation and cultural framing on all these levels produced an intricate synthesis of various aspects of Kurdish identity within national politics. The divisions between different interpretations of this concept also complicate definitions and add layers of ideological and methodological complexity to 'Kurdishness'. Finally, the effect of the crisis in Syria on understandings of identity is examined in a cursory manner. This is built upon over the course of the following chapters, but the crisis has ongoing effects which cannot be documented as yet.

Naturally, idiosyncratic factors like individual experience and relative social importance will have influences on priorities and identity construction. The dominant factors examined in this chapter, however, can be said to have universal influence and examination of them provides a general outline of the complexity and nuances of identity in Kurdish areas of Syria. As such, this chapter provides a basis for examining in later chapters the representativeness of the Administration and the many challenges that it faces, not only from external threats or 'others' but also from the constituent nature of Syrian Kurdish society itself.

State building and legitimacy

The Kurdish identity in Syria was influenced by a number of factors, but the major influence was the formation of the state of Syria which shaped the course of its development, its social and political meanings and provided the frame of reference for the various channels of representation available to Syrian Kurds. Before the French Mandate that defined the territory and sovereignty of Syria, Kurdish populations were segmented rather than characterized as a homogenous group. Kurdish society was largely tribal and agrarian, and identity was defined more in familial and local geographic terms than by belonging to an abstract ethnic, linguistic or national group.[29] Channels of representation formed around these socio-economic relations, semi-feudal organization and kin networks. Kurdish nationalism was but a nascent movement, developed in the late nineteenth century among the Kurdish intelligentsia in Istanbul and abroad, and its adoption by Kurdish society was not rapid.

The division of Kurds between Turkey, Iraq, Iran and Syria left them as a peripheral minority in all four states, not easily accommodated within new nation states and offered no guarantees of ethnic or national rights. 'Kurdishness' became inimical to attempts to centralize state authority and to the rhetoric of legitimacy adopted by the new nation-states. The subsequent exclusion of the Kurds from state representations in all of these states served to sharpen the sense of a distinct and unique Kurdish identity and to fuel the pursuit of a Kurdish nation state, or at least a recognition of the Kurdish identity within the existing ones.

The Turkish suppression of Kurdish revolts in the 1920s forced many harbingers of Kurdish nationalism into exile in Syria, where they organized politically and militarily.[30] The failures of these military driven campaigns to gain territory or rights from the Turkish state led Kurdish nationalist intelligentsia in Syria to prioritize a culturally driven campaign to protect Kurdish identity against the threat of the 'others'. Western-oriented conceptualizations of the nation were promoted, in which culture, education and civilization were associated with modernity, development, progress and, ultimately, statehood. This ethos had a profound influence on Kurdish political organization and identity and was enshrined in the nationalist mandate of the first Kurdish political parties formed in Syria in the 1950s. The pursuit of the Kurdish nationalist agenda was, however, restricted by international and regional developments inimical to it achieving its aims. Instability and competition in Syria following independence from colonial rule in 1946 was accompanied by the steady rise in a radical Arab nationalist ideology and symbolism and its use as a source of legitimacy and means of gaining political capital. Despite Syria's multi-ethnic and multi-confessional character, state building and policy connected Syrian identity directly and institutionally

---

[29] Jordi Tejel 2009: *Syria's Kurds: History, Politics and Society*, Routledge, London, 9.
[30] Many exiled Kurdish intellectuals, tribal and religious leaders organised within the Xoybun League (formed in 1927). Xoybun directed its political and military activities against the new Turkish government, and participated in the Ararat, or Agri Revolt of 1930. For more on Xoybun see Tejel, *Syria's Kurds*.

to the Arab nation and nationalism. Although ethnic identity remained a critical component of many coups that rocked Syria following independence, the use of Arab nationalism as a tool for gaining political legitimacy established it as a dominant regional ideology. This had several negative implications for the representation of Kurdish identity and interests in Syria.

Arabism drew individual states, leaders and prospective leaders to a wider trans-state entity and set of norms and objectives crowned by the dream of Arab unity. Various unification proposals were floated between 1945 and 1955. Then in 1958, at the height of Arab nationalist politics in the Middle East, the Syrian Republic (1930–1958) joined with Egypt and became part of the United Arab Republic (1958–1961). Within this union policies aimed at controlling Kurdish areas were developed. Independence from Egypt was won through a military coup in 1961 following which the Syrian Arab Republic was declared. From this point forward Arab nationalism became enshrined in all state institutions and laws and, to date, few of these have been subject to significant reform. Kurds became targets of discriminatory policies aimed at both weakening and forcibly assimilating an ethnically pariah population that was deemed inimical to the nation-state identity and potentially destabilizing and subversive.

The constitution of the Syrian Arab Republic (1973) attached sovereignty, territory and citizenship directly to the Arab ethnic identity:[31]

1. The Syrian Arab Republic is a democratic, popular, socialist, and sovereign state. No part of its territory can be ceded. Syria is a member of the Union of the Arab Republics.
2. The Syrian Arab region is a part of the Arab homeland.
3. The people in the Syrian Arab region are a part of the Arab nation. They work and struggle to achieve the Arab nation's comprehensive unity.[32]

The revised constitution of 2012 (a concession of Bashar al-Assad's government in response to the protest movement) as well as reaffirming the president's powers[33] reasserted (although somewhat more mildly) this connection.

---

[31] In Arab nationalist ideology an 'Arab' has generally been defined as someone who speaks Arabic as their mother tongue or whose primary language is Arabic. Most Kurds, (bar many Damascene Kurds who are more assimilated than the vast majority of Kurds) retain Kurdish as their mother tongue and it is the dominant language used within Kurdish communities. Syrian Kurds therefore fall out of 'Arab' as an identity group. David Romano 2006: *The Kurdish Nationalist Movement: Opportunity, Mobilisation and Identity*, Cambridge University Press, Cambridge, 187, n. 13.

[32] Constitution of the Syrian Arab Republic 1973, Chapter 1, Part 1, Article 1.

[33] For further analysis of the constitution, see, for example, Fares 08/05/2014.

The Syrian Arab Republic is a democratic state with full sovereignty, indivisible, and may not waive any part of its territory, and is part of the Arab homeland; the people of Syria are part of the Arab nation.[34]

Moreover, Syrian Nationality Law, enacted in 1969, directly and explicitly connected nationality and citizenship to the Arab identity.[35] The law defined a 'Syrian Arab' as 'any person who enjoys the nationality of the Syrian Arab Republic'.[36] These stipulations on the Syrian identity and territory affected all laws that followed it and, despite changes to the constitution, Syria's legal framework continued to exclude, implicitly but collectively, non-Arabs from equal representation, unless their ethnic or national identity was personally repudiated. The principles of equality and the protection of rights enshrined in the constitution, such as freedoms of speech, expression, the right to property and equality without discrimination on grounds of sex, origin, language, religion or creed, had ambiguous application to non-Arabs.[37] Similarly, the Penal Code guaranteed against abuses of authority, against physical and mental torture and obstruction of the law.[38] It protected freedoms of association, expression and assembly but forbade it on the grounds of race or sect. Paradoxically, these same clauses, designed to protect against discrimination, were regularly drawn upon to persecute Kurdish activists.[39]

Guarantees of basic freedoms and human rights and stipulations about democratic government set out in the constitution and penal code were never fully binding in Syria. A state of emergency was declared on 8 March 1963, predating the constitution and the penal code, and it remained in place until April 2011. The law, which became by proxy Syria's permanent legal framework during this time, extended to the president and to his deputies extraordinary powers, including powers to suppress opposition, restrict freedoms and confiscate property. The security and intelligence services were given exceptional powers of arrest, detention and torture. Lifting Emergency Law in 2011 did not reduce the

---

[34] Constitution of the Syrian Arab Republic 2012, Article 1. The 2012 constitution was less heavily Arabist than the previous one and contained references to Syria's cultural and social diversity. This one article, however, linked citizenship to Arab ethnicity and consequently denied equivalent representation to Kurds.

[35] *Syrian Nationality Law, Legislative Decree 276*, 24/11/1969.

[36] Article 1, f. *Syrian Nationality Law, Legislative Decree 276*, 24/11/1969.

[37] Constitution of the Syrian Arab Republic, 2012, Article 8.1; 8.4; 33.3.

[38] Article 19, 1998, 20–1.

[39] Examples of common charges against Kurdish activists include inciting racial or sectarian strife (article 307), seeking to annex part of Syrian territory and attach it to another state (Article 267) and seeking to weaken the national consciousness (285 and 286). Harriet Montgomery 2005: *The Kurds of Syria: An Existence Denied*, Europäisches Zentrum für Kurdische Studien, Berlin, 65; Allsopp, *The Kurds of Syria*, 102.

powers of the presidency or the security apparatus. The legal framework for the suppression of protest, opposition and organization remained within the penal code and other domestic laws and were reinforced by laws promulgated in the run up to its abolition. Presidential powers continued to overlap with military, judicial and legislative powers defined in the constitution.[40]

The Baath Party itself relied on the Arab identity and on nationalist rhetoric for legitimacy. With its seizure of power in 1963 and Hafiz al-Assad's internal party coup of 1970, Baath rule in Syria and the prominence of the al-Assad family itself were embedded within the institutions of state, including the constitution of 1973. Syrian domestic and foreign politics were dominated by the rhetoric of Arab nationalism, unity and confronting external threats. Kurdish identity was perceived increasingly as an obstacle to the construction of a Syrian identity, shaped progressively more by Arab nationalism.[41] Kurdish ambitions for equal representation were treated as a threat to national security, and the Kurdish areas as Syria's Achilles heel.[42] This perceived threat provided the rationale for many policies implemented from the 1960s onwards, such as the Arabization of Kurdish majority areas through artificial demographic change, replacing Kurdish geographical names with Arab ones, removal and denial of citizenship to thousands of Kurds in the Jazirah and extraordinary security measures affecting property ownership in several Kurdish inhabited areas.[43] All impacted negatively on Kurdish identity and physical presence. Public expression of the Kurdish identity was deemed subversive: it was politicized and criminalized and, as Kurdish ethno-nationalism grew, tensions between the central government and the Kurdish communities increased.[44]

---

[40] *Constitution of the Syrian Arab Republic* 2012: Articles 133 and 105.

[41] Tejel, *Syria's Kurds*, 13.

[42] Anti-Kurdish propaganda from the era linked Kurdish nationalism to Zionism and described the Kurds as separatists and traitors. In 1963 a book by the Baathist lieutenant, Muhammad Talab Hilal, outlined a twelve-point plan for dealing with the Kurds of the Jazirah, which included denial of citizenship; artificial demographic change through moving Arabs into Kurdish majority areas, denial of education and impoverishment of society. Allsopp, *The Kurds of Syria*, 21, 23–4; Ghadi Sari, September 2016: 'Kurdish Self-Governance in Syria: Survival and ambition', Chatham House Research Paper, Chatham House, London, https://www.chathamhouse.org/sites/files/chathamhouse/publications/research/2016-09-15-kurdish-self-governance-syria-sary_0.pdf (last accessed 29/09/2016).

[43] Decree 41 of 2008. See Allsopp, *The Kurds of Syria*, 26–7. For more detailed information, see Allsopp, *The Kurds of Syria* and Tejel, *Syria's Kurds*.

[44] To this end, during the 1970s–1990s Kurdish place names were changed to Arab alternatives. Businesses in the Jazirah were banned from using Kurdish letters in business names. Children given Kurdish names were expelled from schools and universities, or would not be registered as citizens, and bans on music were periodically enforced. Organizing as Kurds was explicitly criminalized within the penal code, (specifically Articles 267, 285, 286 and 307. See Allsopp, *The Kurds of Syria*, 102). Political parties formed from the 1950s onwards were declared illegal and those involved in them operated under the threat of arrest.

As a consequence of the attachment of citizenship to Arab identity, representation of Kurds on the state level only occurred when Kurdish politicians entered parliament as independent MPs, required to accept tacitly an Arab identity and the domination of the Baath Party. Even then, issues loosely relating to Kurds could only be addressed in terms of local government. Local *mukhtars* (mayors) of Kurdish ethnicity were employed in some areas and were able to mediate between state services and the local communities and to adjudicate in local disputes. In many cases, however, (particularly in the Jazirah and within local government, education and in oil production) state employees of Arab ethnicity were deliberately moved to work in Kurdish dominated areas.

Syrian law, coupled with pervasive policing and surveillance by the intelligence services, restricted the space for organization or association around an identity and for purposes not sanctioned by the state. Kurdish identity and interests in Syria were provided no official or public channels for representation or expression. As a result, both Kurdish cultural and political organization became clandestine and limited to the private sphere. Kurdish political party activity concentrated on Kurdish society itself and on support for the Kurdish movements in Iraq and Turkey, through which, it was hoped, a solution would also positively reflect on Syrian Kurds. Cultural framing and facilitating Kurdish cultural expression became a primary area of Kurdish party activity, as did intervention and mediation in local affairs and problems and teaching the Kurdish language. With this, however, public expression of Kurdish identity became taboo and subject to risks. Before March 2011, with the exception of the March 2004 unrest in Qamishli, public protest by Kurds were rare, small and regulated events and were normally met with arrests and forced dispersal by the security services.[45] A sphere of sub-state activity that avoided state intervention arose, albeit monopolized by Kurdish political parties and flanked and monitored by the state.

Negotiation of these restrictions on Kurdish identity became second nature to many seeking to avoid confrontation with authoritarian state apparatus. Kurdish identity, while precious, was primarily private. Syrian government officials, on rare occasions, met with leaders of Kurdish political parties. These discussions concentrated on the issue of the stateless Kurds of Hasakah region – an issue that the government was prepared to address as a technical problem connected to migration rather than as a political one specific to the Kurdish

---

[45] For examples of such protests, see Allsopp, *The Kurds of Syria*, 102–9.

population.[46] Similarly, on many issues relating to Kurdish interests and regions, state officials called on traditional tribal leaders to represent local communal interests. In doing so, the Syrian government attempted to support Kurdish tribal configurations against Kurdish political parties and bolster their power as representatives of social interest. As discussed further below, the majority of Kurdish tribes conceded representation on Kurdish national and political matters to political parties.

State denial of Kurdish ethnicity and representations of Kurdish identity in Syria had a dual effect of (a) internalizing it and preventing modernization of Kurdish regions and (b) politicizing and problematizing it so that its protection and representation became bound up in the very understandings of this identity. The state structure, however, also gave Syrian Kurds a strong sense of *Syrian* identity. Many Kurds candidly admitted that their sense of shared experience and identity with other Syrians was greater than that with Kurds of Iraq or Turkey. Social norms and practices and shared experience and education developed within the state context fostered a Syrian identity based on lived experience and with political discourses connected to universal rights, equality and the development of democracy rather than on an imagined community. This Syrian identity has not been without problems for the Kurds, not least because of its popular connection to Arab nationalism, and developments in pan-Kurdish politics and communications technologies since the 1990s also increased identification with pan-Kurdish nationalism. As a consequence, although Kurds across Kurdish areas participated in large numbers in the civil protests in Syria, joining the national slogans and calls for the fall of the regime, the domination of the Syrian opposition by Arab nationalist and Islamist groups contributed to the development of a distinct Kurdish response that stressed the recognition of Kurdish national identity and the right of Kurds to represent and protect their own communities and areas.

Tribal and local sub-state identities and channels of representation

Identification with local geographical areas and kinship networks remained a feature of Kurdish society, with pronounced 'cultural' divides between the three Kurdish regions of Syria. The role of the tribe, however, changed considerably after the centralization of political authority and Syrian independence. The demise of tribal authority among Kurds in Syria has been attributed to several

---

[46] Allsopp, *The Kurds of Syria*, 172.

factors that eroded traditional sources of political power, such as armed militias and land holdings that severed economic ties between landlords and peasants. Land reforms that began during the years of the United Arab Republic produced dramatic changes in the fortunes of notable families and were used by the state to reduce the powers of the Kurdish nationalist elite.[47] Tribal leaders and an elite connected to ownership of land and production continued to exist, but social mobility as well as the mechanization of agriculture promoted the development of professional classes and released former peasant classes from feudal ties to landlords. With the further division of land through inheritance, individual land holdings have become progressively smaller, increasing incentive to seek out or develop alternative economic activity. Insufficient employment opportunities in rural Kurdish areas, exacerbated by underinvestment and droughts, led to significant urban migration (within Kurdish areas as well as out of them)[48] and the further erosion of ties to traditional socio-economic relations. Kurdish working class men were drawn into industries such as construction and the service industry, as well as developing entrepreneurship. Traditional networks and loyalties, however, had enduring relevance to personal identity, although its importance and meaning varied between tribes and regions. Field research conducted in the Jazirah and in Kobani demonstrated considerably greater identification with family networks within the Kobani region compared to the Jazirah.[49] In the Afrin region existing research suggested that connections to traditional socio-economic relations were weaker still.[50] This discrepancy can be explained by several local factors: tribes in the region became sedentary earlier than those of either Kobani or the Jazirah; Afrin's geographical proximity to Aleppo's commercial centre diversified economic activity in the area; the historical presence of peasants' movements in the region dating back to the Arab

---

[47] For example, the family of nationalist tribal leader, Hasan Hajo Agha, was stripped of all land in Syria.

[48] For further detail on the effects of drought on the Syrian peninsular, see Massoud Ali 2010: *Years of Drought: A Report on the Effects of Years of Drought on the Syrian Peninsular, Heinrich-Böll-Stiftung - Middle East Office*, https://lb.boell.org/sites/default/files/uploads/2010/12/drought_in_syria_en.pdf (last accessed 14/10/2016).

[49] Some 49 per cent of participants in IIST surveys in Kobani selected 'family member' in answer to the question 'Who represents you?' This was the second most popular choice after 'political party', which was selected by 60 per cent of participants. In comparison, in the Jazirah region, 'family member' was selected by 26 per cent of participants. Similarly when asked 'What people/institutions/ organisations do you think have the capacity to represent you?' 'family member' was joint highest with 'local/municipal council', selected by 25 per cent of participants. In the Jazirah 'family member' was selected by 9 per cent.

[50] Pierre Rondot 1939: 'Les Kurdes de Syrie', *La France Mediterranee et Africaine*, Vol. II, No. 1 (Lib. Sirey, Paris), 88–126; Allsopp, *The Kurds of Syria*, 136.

revolt of 1920s;[51] the strength of the Syrian Communist Party in the 1950s[52] and of the PKK in the 1980s.

Many Kurds, even tribal leaders, denied the importance of traditional tribal relations to Kurdish politics and identity.[53] Yet, the majority of Kurds could identify their tribe[54] and retained some degree of social bond with others within these broad kinship communities. The tribe and kin relations remained important ways of organizing and understanding local society for those belonging to it as well as a means of identifying and categorizing individuals within it. Morals, norms and values associated with tribal structures and kin relations were similarly coveted by many within Kurdish society and they continued to play an important role in social relations as well as in understandings of personal, group and Kurdish identity. Tribal leaders themselves described their role as primarily social and publicly ceded representation on political matters to party representatives.[55]

The ability and willingness of traditional leaders to involve themselves in politics was limited. Research suggested, however, that power structures embedded in tribal relations continued to play a significant role in the formation and fracturing of Syrian Kurdish political parties.[56] Although Kurdish nationalism was developed under the tutelage of Kurdish urban intelligentsia, the cooperation and support of the traditional elite was necessary to popularize the doctrine and prevent political divisions developing between the tribal leadership and Kurdish intelligentsia. Traditional socio-economic relations were accommodated within Kurdish political organizations and tribal leaders seized Kurdish nationalism as political capital. Integration of this traditional elite into the political parties provided them with an alternative source of power at a time when the foundations of their authority were being eroded by land reforms and the centralization of state power. As a consequence, while Kurdish nationalism and political organization for Kurdish representation was a modern movement framed by Western conceptualizations of the nation-state and the discourse of inalienable rights, political parties also became vehicles for extending the power of traditional elites.[57]

---

[51] The *Muroud* was a peasants' movement active in the 1930s in the Afrin region. Allsopp, *The Kurds of Syria*, 62–5.

[52] See Allsopp, *The Kurds of Syria*, 137.

[53] Ibid.; IIST research.

[54] The majority of participants in IIST surveys included the name of their tribe when requested.

[55] Allsopp, *The Kurds of Syria*, 142.

[56] Ibid., 142–7.

[57] Ibid.; Vali, 'The Kurds and their "others"'.

Similarly, the close-knit nature of Kurdish society – an enduring feature of Kurdish life in many respects – allowed political parties to control information and views with ease, allowing parties to become embedded in society, control their environment and for party ideology and loyalty to be handed down through families, from one generation to the next. Kurdish political parties' programmes were kept relatively simple, concentrating on nationalist rhetoric and the discourse of rights. This allowed for wide acceptance across social divides existing within communities. Yet, decisions about representation and political affiliation were frequently made on the basis of family networks and relations. Accordingly, the meaning of tribal networks and their influence on Kurdish society was also transformed. Nuances and variations in the strength and role of tribal relations between Kurdish regions and communities were demonstrated by answers to the question: 'Who represents you?' Around 26 per cent of Kurds surveyed in both Kobani[58] and the Jazirah selected family and/or tribe. Results from Kobani, however, showed that in this area a significantly higher percentage believed that a family member would have the capacity to represent them.[59]

The connection of tribal identity and certain channels of representation to territorial and social networks also compounded physical, geographical divisions between Kurdish groups in Syria. Similarly, the division of the Syrian Kurdish population between three non-contiguous territorial regions prevented the homogenization of Kurdish identity across their communities. State control over communications technologies limited access to them until after the year 2000 when the internet and mobile telecommunications were made available to the public. Even then, state monitoring prevented their effective use by political parties as a tool for political mobilization across the Kurdish regions. The vast majority of party leaders hailed from the Jazirah and relied heavily on local and traditional social networks. There were few (1957) party leaders resident in the Afrin and Kobani regions, limiting the parties' appeal over geographical and social divisions. The reliance of party leaders on personal networks, in turn, meant that support for parties was often dictated by family allegiances and rivalries and that party leaders assumed permanent positions. Disagreements within a party's leadership would often lead to the formation of blocs within it

---

[58] Around 25/93 Kurds surveyed in Kobani selected 'family' or 'tribal chief'.
[59] When asked 'What people/institutions/organizations do you think have the capacity to represent your interests and identity?' 9 per cent from Jazirah and 25 per cent of those from Kobani selected 'family member'. The significant difference in results reflected the greater adherence to traditional social networks in Kobani.

and the fracturing of the party.[60] Conversely, family disputes were also known to lead to defections from political parties and alliances with rival parties.

In addition to these social and geographic fractures in Kurdish society, complex class dynamics affected the Syrian population and had unique consequences for the Kurds. Class and social stratifications in Syria were produced and maintained by the preservation of tribal, sectarian and ethnic divisions; the co-option of key actors, sectors of society and social groupings to the government; land reforms; corruption and coercion. Added to this, punitive exclusion of groups and individuals from benefits accruing from state employment, health care and even citizenship, created underclasses not linked to either social or labour relations. Within Kurdish society, an estimated 120,000 Kurds were denaturalized by the Syrian government as a result of the 1962 Hasakah census. These Kurds were registered individually as '*ajnabi al-Hasakah*' or 'a foreigner of Hasakah province', while those who were left unregistered were known collectively as the *maktumiin*. By 2011 their combined number was estimated by some to be more than 300,000.[61] A unique underclass of Kurds was formed that crossed formal class and tribal structures. Until the beginning of the civil protests in Syria in 2011, these Kurds were denied even the conditional rights to representation, services and property that other Kurds in Syria could claim as Syrian Arab citizens. While among this group organization as a sub-class group did occur in efforts to gain concessions from the state, research suggested that attachment to the Kurdish identity superseded a sense of identity defined by their underclass or legal status.[62] The connection of stratification to ethnic discrimination served to heighten connection to that identity rather than to diminish it. Despite the Kurdish political parties' adoption of the issue as a potent symbol of the government's repression of the Kurds, over time, the accumulating effects of this policy translated into real social divisions within Kurdish society, to the extent that the stateless were pariah in marriage consideration and subject to negative stereotyping.[63]

---

[60] Allsopp, *The Kurds of Syria*, 72–99.

[61] Due to changes in the law made in April 2012, which extended to Kurds registered as *Ajanib* (foreigners) the right to apply for citizenship, the number of stateless Kurds was believed to have dropped to 160,000 by the end of 2013. Thomas McGee, June 2016: 'Statelessness displaced: Update on Syria's stateless Kurds', *Institute on Statelessness and Inclusion, The Netherlands*, available on http://www.institutesi.org/WP2016_02.pdf, 1 (last accessed 20/06/2016).. For more information on stateless Kurds in Syria, see Allsopp, *The Kurds of Syria*, Chapter 6; McGee 'Statelessness displaced'; Maureen Lynch and Perveen Ali January 2006: 'Buried Alive', Refugees International, London, available on http://www.refworld.org/docid/47a6eba80.html (accessed 10/06/2016).

[62] Allsopp, *The Kurds of Syria*, 148–76.

[63] Ibid., 167.

In Kobani in particular, new generations, further removed from traditional structures and connected to modern class structures and information technologies tended to identify more with Kurdish national identity and a non-ethnic Syrian identity. By the mid-2000s, there was evidence that new business classes were beginning to encroach upon space previously occupied by Kurdish political parties: sponsorship of Kurdish cultural events and festivals by Kurdish businesses in the Jazirah was becoming a visible feature that reflected the parallel detachment of political parties from cultural framing of Kurdish identity.[64]

When the Arab Spring reached Syria, disaffection from existing representative structures led much of the Kurdish population, particularly the youth, to find common cause with the message of the civil protests. Their alienation from mainstream Syrian opposition groups, the growth of sectarian organization, and the neutrality adopted by Syrian Kurdish political parties, however, thwarted the coordination that had developed between the Kurdish and Arab opposition. As the conflict continued, beliefs in Kurdish unity and common goals among Syrian Kurds strengthened. At the same time, the PYD ideology and governance structures sought to replace traditional hierarchical social networks with horizontal ones through social revolution. The PYD, like the PKK, drew much support from among the working class, or 'marginalized men' and women, and from those negatively affected by the wider conflict and attracted by its rapid armed mobilization and revolutionary ideas about levelling social hierarchies.

Pan-state identity

Overlaying state, sub-state and local divisions and attributes to identity in northern Syria, the Kurds are also connected through pan-state or international identities. The most significant of these to the Kurds in Syria and their understandings of representation have been international class solidarity, which heavily influenced political party development and ideology; religious affiliation which has both connected the Kurds to other ethnic groups in Syria and beyond and reaffirmed Kurdish specificity; and a pan-Kurdish national identity and nationalist historiography which linked Kurds through imagined communities, shared experiences of suppression and of resistance to subjugation and occupation as well as through their cultural and linguistic attributes.

---

[64] Ibid., 133.

International class solidarity

Not all class divisions in Kurdish society are the result of state discrimination against Kurdish people and majority Kurdish areas. However, the strength of Kurdish identity and the discrimination applied to them collectively formed a narrative of Kurdish economic marginalization, inequality and discrimination in state employment. While data that might shed light on the degree of economic discrimination against Kurdish people and against the northern regions of Syria (the Jazirah in particular) is unavailable, the ethnic element to state policies regarding the Kurds and Kurdish areas weakened class identification or association of inequalities with local power structures. The penetration of national unions and other representative organizations by the state also diminished any representative capacity or advocacy that they might otherwise have had. Across Syria, economic marginalization and hardship was blamed on the Assad government and on the absence of democratic structures – the primary driving force of the civil pro-democracy protests of 2011, with which Kurdish youth, in particular, found common cause.

The Kurdish nationalist movement and its leaders were not drawn from proletarian social backgrounds. Rather, the ideology and rhetoric of class mobilization and opposition to dominant others resonated with Kurdish experience within the state and was re-framed within a nationalist discourse.[65] Marxism and the international class movement had a significant influence on Kurdish politics and identity, primarily in its association with resistance and pursuit of equality. The rhetoric of communism and class struggle was adapted and modified to suit Kurdish nationalists in Syria in the 1940s and 1950s. The Syrian Communist Party (SCP) itself was led by Khalid Bakdash, a Kurd from Damascus, and its ranks were occupied by a considerable Kurdish contingency. The SCP provided Kurdish nationalist politicians with valuable political experience. Fundamentally at odds with the Universalist rhetoric of communism and the SCP's conformity to the dominant Arabist politics of the region, Kurdish nationalists soon found that their goals and principles could not be achieved through this ideology. Nonetheless, the rhetoric and ideological leanings of the majority of the parties of 1957 were leftist and many were influenced heavily by Marxism.

The PKK was also formed as a Marxist-socialist organization, presenting itself as part of the international communist revolution. Yet, the PKK project

---

[65] Fred Halliday 2006: 'Can we write a modernist history of Kurdish nationalism?', in Faleh A. Jabar and Hosham Dawod (eds), *The Kurds: Nationalism and Politics*, Saqi, London, 17.

was clearly a nationalist one; its ideology was adapted to a specifically Kurdish agenda, defined against Turkish nationalism, with its own historiography, symbols and myths. Since its inception the PKK ideology and theoretical groundings have undergone significant changes, while maintaining a radical revolutionary agenda aimed at liberating the Kurds. In the 1980s the party came to depend for its internal cohesion and loyalty on a progressively more social revolution, based on the Soviet Communist Party's visions of the 'New Man', but set within the nationalist historiography of the Kurdish people.[66]

Although both the parties of 1957 and the PKK, and subsequently the PYD, borrowed heavily from communist and internationalist ideologies, issues of class and ideas of inequality and repression were framed firmly against the 'other' within their political discourses: that is, against Arab and Turkish nationalisms. While class dynamics also had local and state level resonance, the domination of channels of representation by traditional nationalist elites and by the state made organization around class identity or universal policy problematic.

Religion

A second pan-state identity frequently drawn upon in identity formation in the Middle East is religion. Today, the majority of Kurds in Syria are Sunni Muslim, having been converted to Islam in early Islamic conquests.[67] Until the demise of the Ottoman Empire in the nineteenth century, Islam's dominance as an overarching identity was barely contested. The rise of nationalism as a tool to defend and secure the interests of diverse ethnic groupings within the empire precipitated a dialectic process of identity formation between Islam and modern nationalism in which synthesis between the two identities was met.[68] Early Kurdish revolts that sought to establish some form of Kurdish state contained a high degree of leadership and participation by Sheikhs – notably, Sheikh Ubaydullah of Nehri and the Sheikh Said revolt of 1925. The threat of the secularist Kemalist state to the authority of Kurdish tribal leaders led to several revolts and to the exiling of their religious, tribal and nationalist leaders to Syria and further afield.

Sufism remained the most influential form of Islam among Syrian Kurds. The strength of religious belief within Syrian Kurdish communities varied

---

[66] Olivier Grojean 2014: 'The production of the new man within the PKK', *European Journal of Turkish Studies*, (online) available on http://ejts.revues.org/4825 (last accessed 14/09/2014), 4.

[67] Hakan Ozoglu 2007: 'Impact of Islam on Kurdish identity formation', in Muhammad Ahmed and Michael Gunter (eds), *The Evolution of Kurdish Nationalism*, Mazda Publishers, California, 20–1.

[68] Ozoglu, 'Impact of Islam on Kurdish identity formation', 29.

considerably, with many Kurds only nominally religious. While the Middle East, in general, witnessed a rise of Islamism from the 1970s, political organization on a religious basis has been rare among Syrian Kurds, unlike the Kurds in Turkey and Iraq. This rise in Islamism went hand in hand with the rise of Kurdish identity.[69] Islam came to be seen as an impediment to modern Kurdish nationalism, which, as discussed above, had been influenced heavily by Marxism. The radicalization of Islamic policy and its pairing with Arab nationalism in many political groupings further prevented the Islamization of Kurdish identity in Syria.

The practice and understanding of religion was shaped distinctly by the Kurdish nationalist movement. Many Sufi sheikhs had sought refuge in Syria following the Turkish state's abolition of mystical orders in 1925. Many of these exiles continued and coordinated their political and military struggles against the Turkish state through the Xoybun League, formed in Beirut in 1927. Some of these sheikhs promoted an apolitical interpretation of Islam and endorsed the use of Arabic, while others, close to Xoybun, emphasized Kurdish identity in their teachings.[70] Local Sufi *zawiyas* (lodges) autonomous in relation to the state, used the Kurdish language for instruction and ethnicized local history, to the extent that Sufism came to be seen as a form of 'true' and 'Kurdish Islam'.[71] In the Afrin region particularly, the relative absence of Kurdish political parties gave Sufi sheikhs increased authority and prestige. Their authority brought them into conflict with the PKK after it arrived in the region in 1980, but also precipitated the accommodation of cultural, religious and political symbolism within both movements. Sufi sheikhs played a significant role in the re-ethnicization of Kurdish identity during this time. After the unrest in Qamishli in 2004, some Kurdish sheikhs began to play a more public role in promoting Kurdish identity and challenging state policy. In June 2005, unrest broke out in Qamishli after the Kurdish sheikh, Muhammad Mashuq al-Khaznawi, was kidnapped and killed following a series of sermons and public speeches in which he defended Kurdish rights and criticized the government. His death was blamed on the Syrian government.

Yezidism is a pre-Islamic monotheistic religion originating in Lalesh, northern Iraq. Yezidi's are ethnically Kurdish, and the population is in decline, with numbers estimated between 70,000 and 500,000. The Yezidis are often

---

[69] Tejel, *Syria's Kurds*, 95.
[70] Ibid., 96.
[71] Ibid., 100.

described as an ethno-religious community and Yezidism as a Kurdish religion.[72] In Syria, the Yezidi population was estimated to be 10,000 in 1964.[73] No accurate data on their population currently exists, but migration of Yezidis out of Syria has occurred, as has migration into Syria from Jabal Sinjar following the rise of ISIS and the atrocities it committed against Yezidi communities in Iraq. In Syria, Yezidis were concentrated in two communities, one in the Afrin region and one in the Jazirah (Hasakah province). Yezidis commonly lived together in close communities, with certain villages being known locally to be 'Yezidi villages'. Within them religious practices, customs and dress are shared with communities as far away as Iraq or Armenia. Yezidism sets them apart from other Kurds.

Yezidis have been subject to religiously motivated attacks and often wrongly labelled as 'devil worshippers' and heretics and marginalized within Kurdish society. Today, many Kurdish nationalists grant special status to the Yezidi and Zoroastrian religions as ancient and 'authentic' Kurdish religions, even denouncing Islam as a religion of occupiers. Again, the role of the PKK in promoting the 'originality' of the Yezidi religion and its use as a symbolic resource elevated the identification of its practitioners with Kurdish ethnicity. This, however, has not always been the case, starkly demonstrating the fluidity of identity and symbioses that are formed through historical process. Indeed, Hakan Ozoglu noted that the Yezidi, along with other religious sects found among the Kurds (*Ahl-e Haqq* and even Alevi Kurds) were not recognized as part of the Kurdish community in the pre-modern Kurdish identity narrative – that is, between the seventeenth and twentieth centuries.[74] Even today, while the ethnic origin of Yezidis is commonly accepted to be Kurdish by most academics and historians, groups of Yezidi who deny Kurdish ethnicity do exist.

For many Kurds, and in Kurdish communities, religious practice is not noticeably or strictly adhered to or central to external projections of identity. Yet, when asked to describe their identity, 'Muslim' was selected by 116 out of 180 persons surveyed (64 per cent) and almost equally between Kobani

---

[72] Opposition to this categorization of Yezidis as ethnically Kurdish has been encountered in Armenia, where the Yezidi Union of Armenia asserts that Yezidi is an ethnic identity, and in Iraq, where KRG patronage has undermined the independence of Yezidi communities. See, for example, Deniz Serinci 28/05/2014: 'The Yezidis of Armenia face identity crisis over Kurdish ethnicity', *Rudaw*, http://rudaw.net/english/people-places/28052014 (last accessed 04/10/2016); Human Rights Watch 10/11/2009: 'On Vulnerable Ground: Violence against minority communities in Nineveh Province's disputed territories', available on https://www.hrw.org/report/2009/11/10/vulnerable-ground/viol ence-against-minority-communities-nineveh-provinces-disputed (last accessed 04/10/2016).

[73] Thomas Collelo, ed. 1987: *Syria: A Country Study*. Washington: GPO for the Library of Congress, available on http://countrystudies.us/syria/23.htm (last accessed 15/04/2016), 100–1.

[74] Ozoglu, 'Impact of Islam on Kurdish identity formation', 35, n. 24.

and the Jazirah.[75] Due to the intertwining and synthesis of Muslim identity with Kurdishness, strong attachment to religious identities does not translate frequently into political ideology or policy among Syrian Kurds. When asked to describe their political ideology, only 8/180 participants selected 'religious'.[76] This result supported observations that, within Kurdish communities, religion was a more personal and private form of identity that did not have significant influence on political opinions. Research in Syria during the crisis also suggested that many Kurds had lost faith in the Muslim identity: some saw Islam as a new threat because of the perpetration of atrocities by ISIS in the name of religion in Syria and Iraq and because of the Islamization of many of the armed Syrian opposition groups.[77] This view was especially prevalent in the town of Kobani. Others, however, identified the PYD, as well as ISIS, as threats to their religious beliefs because of the former's secular character and because of the ideological and moral content of their programme, sometimes at odds with personal faith.

Pan-state Kurdish identity

The unique historical development of Kurdish majority regions, their geographical character and their political history led Syrian Kurds to attach a heightened importance to pan-state Kurdish identity and rely heavily on the political parties of Iraq and Turkey. A primary reason for this was the relative weakness of Kurdish political leaders in Syria and the difficulties in gaining necessary political and nationalist capital. The infiltration of the Syrian government in Kurdish affairs and the involvement of other Kurdish parties in Syrian-Kurdish politics have all acted as obstacles to generating credible institutions and leaders capable of mass support.

Without prominent indigenous nationalist leaders Syrian Kurds have historically looked to either Iraq or Turkey for solutions to Kurdish issues in Syria. The armed Kurdish nationalist movements in Iraq and in Turkey took precedence over local politics and Syrian Kurds turned to Kurdish political

---

[75] In answer to the survey question 'How would you describe your identity?' 67 per cent of participants from Kobani region selected 'Muslim' compared to 61 per cent of participants from the Jazirah region. (Participants could choose up to five descriptions of identity from a list or write their own). Females generally were more inclined to choose 'Muslim' than male participants (73.5 per cent of females compared to 61 per cent of males).

[76] The selection of religion as a political ideology was extremely low compared to 165/180 who selected 'Kurdish' to describe their identity. This demonstrated the significant weakness of religion as a political tool among Kurds in Syria.

[77] Comments made by participants in IIST surveys suggest that ISIS was seen as a threat to their moderate interpretations of Islam and the morals held by Kurdish communities. Likewise, the perpetration of atrocities in the name of Islam by ISIS and its deliberate targeting of the PYD, established radical religious ideologies as existential threats to the Kurds.

and military leaders in Iraq and in Turkey for inspiration and leadership. As a consequence, loyalties to indigenous political parties remained weak and allegiances to Kurdish parties in Iraq and Turkey that possessed necessary political and historic capital, were common among Syrian Kurdish people and party institutions. These connections have both influenced the construction of identity among Kurds in Syria and shaped beliefs about the correct path for the pursuit of representation.

A fundamental division in Kurdish politics and ideology, between the PKK and the Kurdistan Democratic Party (KDP), had deep and enduring effects on expressions of Kurdish identity in Syria and contributed to social divisions. The strength of PKK presence and support in Afrin and Kobani during the 1980s–1990s and the concentration of leaders of the 1957 genealogy of parties in the Jazirah contributed to political divisions between the areas and stereotypes about population groups. After March 2011, tensions between the two political groups played out directly within Syria, with the PYD dominating local governance. The involvement of both the PKK and KDP in Syrian Kurdish affairs through proxies and direct intervention further polarized and complicated issues of personal identity and political affiliation. Ideas of 'Kurdishness' espoused by Syrian Kurdish parties, examined forthwith, became bound intrinsically to competing political agendas.

Politics and political identity

Kurds successfully maintained some forms of local civil society despite the authoritarian surveillance state built by the Assad dynasty. Traditional social networks and modern political organization overlapped with attempts to protect and promote Kurdish culture and education. In the 1950s political parties gained a monopoly over Kurdish political and cultural organization, particularly after the first Syrian Kurdish party was formed in 1957. The political mandates and capacities of the multiple Kurdish parties that grew from this one organization were, however, limited by the nature of the Syrian state and its geography. Whereas in Iraq, Turkey and Iran, armed resistance had arisen and led prominent traditional and modern leaders to gain power and legitimacy through armed struggle, in Syria armed resistance against the state never occurred. While Kurds in Syria faced discrimination during the French mandate over Syria and in the post-independence period, frequent military coups and short-lived governments and political unions prevented the centralization of power and local power relations remained strong. Formalized and sustained discrimination against the Kurds by the state was consolidated under the Baath Party and Assad family rule, which led to a steady increase in Kurdish political and cultural organization. Kurdish organization was continually monitored by the state: a fact that shaped the mandate and activities that these organizations could adopt while also avoiding repercussions from the government that would threaten their very existence. This feature of Kurdish political organization would have an enduring effect on the ability of these parties (of 1957) to adapt to changes caused by the start of the crisis in Syria.

Political parties, as institutions firmly connected to the Kurdish identity, attempted to synthesize and define different aspect of identity, in order to promote its homogeneity, as well as to gain political authority and legitimacy as representatives of Kurdish interests. They dominated sub-state organization and channels of representation among Syrian Kurds. As such, they have featured decisively in identity formation and reproduction among the Kurds and have been the institutions within which various aspects of Kurdish identity converge or diverge. Their dialogue and dialectic relations with state identity, sub-state identities and trans-state identities placed them at the heart of any discussion of Kurdish identity in Syria. Often subtle differences in projections of these overlapping identities distinguished and divided the parties from each other, while outwardly, their political projects and goals appeared remarkably similar.

The unique historical development of the Kurdish areas of Syria led a specifically Syrian Kurdish identity to form, shaped by international borders and the Kurds' relations to the central state authorities. It was also influenced by their relative proximity to and integration in large commercial cities and other sectors of Syrian society, as well as their role in support of the wider Kurdish national struggles. Kurdish political parties aided in forming this Syrian-Kurdish identity, by defining themselves as 'Syrian', or by attaching 'in Syria' to their party names. Thus, Syrian-Kurdish political parties became bridges between the local and more personal social structures influencing identity, (often based in tribal/kin relations) and an imagined pan-Kurdishness that extended beyond the borders of the state. Kurdish nationalism became a vehicle for overcoming the social and territorial fractures of Syrian Kurdish society; it provided a vision of the past and a goal for the future,[78] shaped through negotiating central state politics, local and traditional power relations and inter-party politics.

---

[78] Grojean, 'The production of the new man within the PKK', 3.

Kurdish political parties placed the Kurdish identity, its protection and reproduction at the centre of their raison d'etre. Accordingly, they assumed a central role in the lives of Syrian Kurds in framing their understanding of who they were. In fact, developing Kurdish culture and identity became a social project and a means of engaging political participation and encouraging support for the parties. The political party became the unchallenged vehicle for representation and expression of Kurdish identity in Syria, often co-opting weaker civil society movements that developed independently. Even as the parties lost their monopoly over information and cultural framing, as their direct cultural and social role diminished, generational divides deepened and incentives to support political parties weakened, they maintained their monopoly over organization.

Alternative conceptualizations of Kurdish identity did arise due to the influence of the PKK and from among the Kurdish youth groups. The imprisoned PKK leader, Abdullah Öcalan's philosophy promoted radical re-evaluation of the Kurdish psyche, (examined further in the following chapter) transmitted through civil organizations as well as political parties and through membership of them. Youth groups drew heavily from the experience and symbols of Kurdish political gains in Iraq, as well as from their unique Syrian Kurdish identity, and they utilized modern communications technologies to develop alternative networks of supporters. Lack of financial and organizational support meant that many originally non-partisan organizations were co-opted by larger political parties or faded into insignificance. Many of these organizations, however, rejected the domination of the political parties by what were considered to be traditional elites with a high degree of detachment from the concerns and interests of younger generations.

Although attempts were made to develop more policy-based political platforms, the two broad understandings and projections of Kurdish identity, developed by opposing political blocs corresponding with the ideological and political divisions between the KDP and the PKK, remained dominant. The two trajectories were embodied in, first, the parties of the 1957 genealogy (influenced by the KDP and the Patriotic Union of Kurdistan) and second, the PKK and its successor, the PYD, which became the dominant party in the northern Kurdish regions of Syria. In addition to this broad framework, political parties within Syria offered slight variations on these identities, and local social networks and conditions could induce loyalty to a particular party and adoption of particular understandings of Kurdish identity and personal roles in society. Comparison of these parties' policies and practices is provided in more detail in the following chapter.

The effects of the crisis on identity

The complex and multilayered nature of identity among Kurds in Syria has been shaped by the state institutions and laws; by traditional sub-state socio-economic relations and networks; by trans-state nationalisms and political entities, as well as by modern political parties and associations established to defend 'Kurdish' identity and specifically aimed at achieving its representation. But preliminary research conducted in Syria during the crisis indicated that a significant number (47 per cent of survey participants) recognized a change in their indices of identification as a direct result of the conflict in Syria.[79]

Causes for this change that were voiced by participants in surveys included the withdrawal of the state and the development of new ruling authorities and legal structures in northern Syria, the religious nature of ISIS's threat, the deepening of sectarian divides and the conflict in Syria. Many participants expressed change in a positive manner, connecting it to a realization of rights and identity: to liberation and to new understandings of their own individual value. Others connected it more to external threats and to a retreat to the safety of Kurdish identity: the experience of loss of home or family, or a loss in confidence resulting from the crisis in Syria. Significantly, 63 per cent of participants from Kobani, compared to just 35 per cent of those from the Jazirah region, claimed that their identity had changed since 2011. This disparity in results can be explained by the experience of the siege of Kobani by ISIS in 2014–2015, the destruction and refugee crisis it produced, the corresponding influence gained by the PYD and YPG there and by the greater identification with tribal/kin networks preceding the conflict. In general, the actual impact of these changes on understandings of personal identity appears to have led to greater sympathy with Kurdishness and with the local region. The combination of external threat, PYD seizure of resources and the dramatically increased capacity to mobilize independently of the state, in turn, increased the attractiveness and feasibility of public identification with the ethnic identity, previously defined as pariah by this state.

While at the time of writing, Kurdish ethnicity and cultural expression was no longer subject to repressive state policies or monitoring, other political freedoms remained challenged in northern Syria. The withdrawal of the Syrian government and establishment of the PYD self-administration created opportunity for the expression and representation of ethnic identity to emerge

---

[79]　94/180 participants.

in northern Syria, but popular opinion was split on the question of whether or not the PYD and its system were democratic.[80] Questions remained about whether institutionalizing freedoms to express ethnic identity were sufficient to satisfy demands for a democratic pluralistic government across Syria, and whether these gains in self-administration could be preserved in a future Syria. Although the Administration had enshrined ethnic representation and equality, it did so in a political vacuum beyond the reach of most governmental structures and institutions and within the context of insecurity and crisis. Syrian state laws discriminating against Kurdish ethnicity and denying representation of it remained in place as part of the apparatus governing the sovereign territory. The PYD-led administration, and the autonomy it had carved out of the turmoil in Syria, held no official status or recognition beyond northern Syria, and even there it was contested.

While further research on the exact consequences of the conflict on sub-state organization and identity was awaited, it was possible to infer from surveys, interviews and impressions from fieldwork in Kobani that tribal and familial relations had already been negatively affected. The migration of family members and dispersal of the tribe was a concern expressed by a significant proportion of surveys participants in Kobani. Here, 26 out of 93 participants, identified the family or tribe as an aspect of their identity that they considered threatened or underrepresented. The reasons given for this were twofold: first, the migration of family members due to the protracted conflict in the area caused physical division of families; second, the policies of the PYD projected an alternative Kurdish identity and installed a system of representation detached from traditional social relations. This concern both reflected the importance of the tribe to identity and representation and indicated the profundity of the changes to identity and representation that the conflict in this area had. Nonetheless, the general increase in identification with a Kurdish ethnicity in the modern social history of northern Syria had not replaced deeper local and micro-identities based on tribe and family, which many still linked to Kurdish heritage. This was true also within the KRI, where Kurdish nationalism, and increased adherence to it through the historical development of political autonomy, did not replace or significantly weaken familial or regional divides.

Above and beyond the various factors that feed into Kurdish identity in Syria – the state, sub-state and pan-state loyalties and political organizations

---

[80] As a guide, (many answers were nuanced with comments and clarifications) IIST survey results indicated that 77/180 or 42 per cent of participants characterized the Rojava Administration as not democratic, while 94/180 or 52 per cent would characterize it as democratic.

– a fundamental cause of the fracturing of Kurdish politics itself was found in conceptualizations of identity and how the Kurds should be represented in Syria. Mirroring the divide in political ideology between parties supporting the PYD-led administration and those supporting the Kurdish National Council of Syria (KNC), this difference in political rhetoric and ideology had also translated into social divisions among Syrian Kurds that bore geographical characteristics. The connection of sources of ideologies to the Kurdish regions of Iraq and Turkey and the extension of their influences across borders had caused broad ideological fissures to develop within the Kurdish movement in Syria that, in turn, translated into social divisions and tensions between local political groupings. The way that these fissures affected the representative channels established by the PYD is examined further in later chapters. Nonetheless, PYD rule in Syria and the freedom of expression and representation of Kurdishness guaranteed by it was a profound change from the Kurdish experience under the Baath rule. As noted at the beginning of this chapter, this fact had been seized upon by numerous outside observers who hailed the experimental project as revolutionary, democratic and progressive. Yet, judgements about the PYD's representativeness of Syrian Kurds must be nuanced within the context of the Syrian crisis. The monopoly over security and politics in the region and distribution of services guaranteed the administration participation resulting from basic needs and insecurities – shortages of food, medicine, need of services and utilities such as electricity, clean water and healthcare. Research suggested that many Kurds were yet to be convinced of the viability of the PYD project, raising questions about the representative functions of its communes, institutions and associations.

The Arab Spring and eruption of protests against the ruling Assad government in Syria in March 2011 provided a window of opportunity for Kurds to change their status in Syria and gain more equal representation. Differences in method and understanding of Kurdish identity across the main political groups, however, had marred attempts to establish a unified Kurdish voice within the political processes aimed at resolving the crisis. Despite this, on the ground, Kurdish political and military organization, led by the PYD, secured unprecedented gains in territory and control and established a form of direct democracy – a self-professed solution to Kurdish issues of representation and a model for the rest of Syria. The PYD administration had attempted to detach participation from ethnically defined concepts of identity, while simultaneously facilitating a social revolution of the Kurdish psyche.

The overwhelming identification with a Kurdish identity made the protection of ethnic rights and gaining a stake in local power relations/authority a priority, regardless of the orientation of the various political organizations seeking to represent the Kurds. While Kurdishness was a unifying identity accepted and adopted by the majority of Kurds, the precise definition of this and what it meant to different groups or individuals was subjective. As this chapter has shown, local, state and pan-state identities still held resonance among Syrian Kurds. The convergence and divergence of various identities and their adaption to local circumstances and to a common Kurdish identity was not uniform across Kurdish areas or people. Dialectical interactions of local identities and state and pan-state identities produced clashes as well ideological syntheses.[81] Within Kurdish society in Syria, a clash of ideologies of the two political blocs, in combination with the particular circumstances in Syria, had given rise to nuanced and less exclusive personal understandings. What could be interpreted as confusion in political ideologies among Syrian Kurds, was best interpreted as a prioritization of being 'Kurdish' over politically driven attempts to lead representation of the Kurds. For many, the importance of protection and representation were clearly recognized, as were the historic and present contributions of political parties and armed forces to protecting the Kurds and Kurdish areas. These formed part of personal understandings of Kurdishness at the time of writing, regardless of the political parties and ideologies they were attached to and which divided them. Alongside this, the commitment to democracy and a belief in existing systems of representation was common.

Despite the changes on the ground in Syria, political and ideological divisions remained within Kurdish politics, between sections of the Kurdish population and between Kurdish and other opposition groups. The stark divide between opposing political and methodological standpoints within Kurdish politics in Syria left many questions about the exact nature of Kurdish governance in Syria, the relationship of political organizations to the Kurdish population and its representativeness of those the administration sought to champion. A closer look at the political parties and the PYD-led administration in the succeeding chapters clarifies what distinguishes the two blocs from each other, as well as their contribution to both fragmenting and homogenizing Kurdish identity. It also allows for some speculation about the prospects for Kurdish self-rule in Syria and the position of Kurds within the unitary state of Syria.

---

[81] Ozoglu, 'Impact of Islam on Kurdish identity formation', 19.

2

Kurdish Political Parties:
A Comparison of Political Values

Representation of the Syrian Kurds has not been simply a matter of recognizing an ethnic identity or allowing representation on that basis. Nor have institutions claiming to be representative been based in or solely driven by that identity, as was shown in the previous chapter. Yet, within Syria, not only has the Kurdish identity been central to the political and civil organization of Kurds but their two blocs of political organizations also gained a unique role in, and monopoly over, channels for representing and framing identity. Whether popular or not, this domination makes Kurdish political parties central to any discussion of the political landscape in Syria and of its future.

This chapter focuses on examining, first, the parties of 1957 and the Kurdish National Council (KNC); second, the PYD bloc and, third, the policies and methods that distinguish and divide them. The self-generated narratives about these two blocs are strikingly different. They form the basis of internal divisions that have affected Kurdish politics in Syria since the 1980s and have gained further prominence during the Syrian crisis. Beginning with the 1957 genealogy of parties allows for the inclusion of historical description within this section. The longer historical presence in Syria of the first bloc allows an account of the substantial changes in Kurdish politics over time; a definition of the Kurdish political spectrum and the reasons for divisions within it. The PYD's rapid rise to power since 2011, on the other hand, demonstrates the importance of political pragmatism, resources and popular mobilization to governance. As well as outlining their distinct historical development, political platforms, ideologies and affiliated organizations, each section links back to the previous chapter to ascertain how these parties have performed their representative roles, how they have shaped Kurdish identity and what are the sources of their legitimacy. Concentrating on these two blocs, this chapter provides a cross-section of the political landscape at the time of writing. The fluidity of the situation in Syria and of the various political alignments makes future changes to party politics likely. The broad historical identity, role and functions of these parties, however, was unlikely to transform dramatically without a corresponding fundamental shift in social organization and identity construction.

Parties of 1957 and the KNC

The birth of the first Syrian Kurdish political party in 1957 began to popularize Kurdish national identity.[1] Its establishment was, at least partly, a response to the surge in Arab nationalism across the Middle East region and its incorporation into state rhetoric and policy by new political leaders seeking to legitimize new political structures. The identity pioneered by the 1957 genealogy of parties was grounded not only in a romantic attachment to the traditions of Kurdish society and a common cultural identity and language but also in a process of civilization and modernization understood as a means to preserve this identity and ensure its longevity and eligibility for statehood. As such, these parties worked to harness existing social orders and traditions to further 'modern' political objectives. This led to both a clash and a synthesis of the traditional and modern within Kurdish politics and identity. The parties accommodated tribal configurations and used pre-existing social networks as tools in their repertoire of contention while also projecting an 'authentic' view of Kurdish identity connected to 'modern' ambitions and capacities associated with statehood and self-governance. While the cultural and social traditions of semi-tribal organization were preserved and traditional social networks were woven intrinsically into nationalist projections of Kurdish identity, incorporation of these power relations also worked to maintain social divisions in Kurdish society and to limit the political actions available to these parties. These inherent strains between tradition and modernity sowed the seeds of future divisions within the party.[2]

The attachment of most prominent Kurdish political parties to pan-state Kurdish ethno-nationalism defined nationalism as a positive vehicle for gaining representation. All Kurdish political parties organized around claims of equal representation and around an attempt to protect the Kurdish identity from policies and ideologies aimed at suppressing and excluding it. But pragmatic

---

[1] A few small local political organizations had been developed prior to the founding of the Kurdistan Democratic Party-Syria in 1957. These either dissipated or were later absorbed by the KDP-S.

[2] Allsopp, *The Kurds of Syria*, 142–4.

choices, made to avoid accusations of separatism and subversion levied against them, induced the parties always to call for reform rather than for revolution and to avoid reference to 'Kurdistan'. By observing unwritten and fluid 'red lines' demarcating behaviours and rhetoric, the parties were tolerated by the Syrian government: but this tacit licence to operate had implications for both their political mandate and the cohesion of Kurdish society. Kurdish parties concentrated on private sphere and local cultural activities. Sponsorship of music and dance groups and of football teams became accepted practice for political parties and allowed them a degree of control over the cultural framing within Kurdish society. As the political parties fragmented, however, significant activities and cultural events, such as celebrations of Newroz, were also divided between spheres of party influence.[3]

The political spectrum and fragmentation

Many Kurdish political parties traced their origins to the first Syrian Kurdish political party established in 1957: the Kurdistan Democratic Party-Syria (KDP-S).[4] Their number was in constant flux as they divided or united in their leaderships' efforts to invigorate or fix the fractured Kurdish polity. On the eve of the outbreak of the Syrian civil protests in 2011, their number was, by some estimates, twenty. At the start of 2017, four of these parties had united to form one party (KDP-S), eleven were represented within the KNC (given later), five others had opted to cooperate within the PYD-led federal system and formed the Kurdish National Alliance in Syria (KNAS)[5] and one party (the Kurdish Democratic Progressive Party (*Pêşverû*) of Abdulhamid Haj Darwish) had declared independence of both these blocs. The divisions between these parties reflected decades-old fractures between those on the right, centre and left of their particular political spectrum.

Initial divisions within this genealogy of parties arose when the original party was targeted in 1960 by the UAR government and much of its leadership was arrested. The adaption of party principles and its programme to the dominant

---

[3] Ibid.
[4] There is some disagreement about the inclusion of the name 'Kurdistan' in the name of this party. Some activists involved in or close to the founding leadership say that the party was originally named the Kurdistan Democratic Party-Syria, while others say that this name was only employed for a short time after its founding.
[5] The parties that formed the Kurdish National Alliance in Syria were: Kurdish Democratic Unity Party in Syria (*al-Wahda*) of Sheikh Ali; Kurdish Democratic Party in Syria (*el-Partî*) of Nasruddin Ibrahim; The Syrian-Kurdish Democratic Reconciliation Party; the Kurdistan Left Party in Syria of Salih Gedo; Kurdish Reform Movement in Syria of Amjad Othman.

Arab nationalist powers was deemed, by some of the leadership, as a necessary compromise to ensure the survival of the party in a more hostile environment. Others disagreed, claiming that Kurdish identity and aims were fundamental and defining principles that could not be bargained. In 1965 the party split in two, and the new parties offered differing definitions of Kurdish identity in Syria that would become markers of the Syrian Kurdish political spectrum. The leadership divided between (a) the left: those who advocated a definition of the Kurds as a national group living in their historic land, which should be recognized as such in the constitution of Syria and granted national rights and (b) the right: those who would define them as an ethnic group seeking minority and cultural rights in Syria.[6] Choices about political party representation were also choices about identification as a sub-state ethnic minority in Syria or as a trans-state national group.[7] Parties defining Kurds as a minority group secured better relations with state officials and, with that, other benefits deriving from them, such as powers to mediate in issues that state officials might otherwise have been involved in.[8] As such, they were classified as more politically conservative.

A further layer of complexity was added to this initial split by the involvement in Syrian Kurdish politics of the main Iraqi Kurdish parties such as the Kurdistan Democratic Party (KDP) and the Patriotic Union of Kurdistan (PUK). Their patronage of particular Syrian Kurdish parties has coloured politics there ever since. The 1964 split in the KDP that led to the formation of the PUK in 1975 by the Ahmad-Talabani faction influenced the political mandates of the Syrian Kurdish parties. The left was influenced more by Barzani while the right (in particular *Pêşverû* led by Abdulhamid Haj Darwish) was influenced by the PUK. In 1970, the intervention of Mustafa Barzani in trying to bring the two sides back together led to the creation of a third, traditionalist, centre party, with close ties to the KDP Iraq. Further splits occurred within this party and in the left wing, as members of the leadership attempted to steer Kurdish national organization more towards the Marxist left-wing and to establish parties with greater independence from both the KDP and the PUK.

At the heart of subsequent divisions within the parties were questions of navigating the domination of the political environment in Syria by the Baath

---

[6]   This distinction between left and right was made in the new parties' names.

[7]   Several participants in surveys chose 'minority' (19/180) or 'majority' (24/180) to describe their identity.

[8]   With the rise in Kurdish nationalism in Syria through the 1990s and 2000s, the presumed relations of party leaders to the authorities became an increasing point of criticism from the youth and intellectuals and an indication for them that the parties were not representative of Kurdish interests. Allsopp, *The Kurds of Syria*.

Party. Kurdish political parties were illegal and organization around ethnic identity was criminalized in both the constitution and the penal code. The state's perceptions of the Kurds as threatening the unity and identity of the state and its imposition of strict limits on their political activities led to pragmatic decisions about policy and how they framed Kurdish identity and representation. As suggested above, party leaders who defined Kurds as a minority, rather than a national group cultivated closer and more open channels of communication with government officials. These relations were also a point of contention within the parties and a further cause of fractures.

Factions also resulted from the internalization of political competition within the parties. The absence of legal channels for negotiating Kurdish interests and demands or for electoral competition and representation, led to increased competition within each party's leadership. Party leadership was the highest point of authority within this sub-state political system causing parties to become personalized. The early incorporation of the traditional Kurdish leadership into the parties as a means of expanding their support bases allowed leaders to draw on existing social networks to bolster their power: the parties became sources of personal power and status. Differences that formed around local socio-economic factors led personalized blocs to emerge within parties, so that they fragmented easily. Interviews with political and traditional leaders also suggested that the Syrian government sought to create and exploit tensions within Kurdish society and within the parties in order to undermine their representational capacity and popularity.[9] Paradoxically, while the arrest of a political leader might award him and the party political capital and legitimacy, prolonged detention might render the party inoperable. On the other hand, his release might raise questions about his relations with the Syrian authorities.

Divisions originating within the first and founding party, compounded by local socio-economic structures and by the specific political environment in Syria over the years produced more than twenty factions. All possessed broadly similar political doctrines shaped around the peaceful pursuit of Kurdish rights and representation through promoting democracy and human rights in Syria as a whole. However, their very multiplicity diminished their representative capacities and precipitated their gradual detachment from Kurdish society. Having enjoyed significant roles in mediation and cultural framing in Kurdish society in the past, the parties' focus on managing the status quo in Syria and on building relations with the Arab opposition led to their gradual disengagement

---

[9] See also Allsopp, *The Kurds of Syria*, 90–1.

from this society and to a withdrawal of intellectuals and youth from the parties. When protests erupted in Syria in March 2011, divisions between them and their weak social bases hindered their capacity to lead the Kurdish response to the unrest.

The dominant parties of the 1957 genealogy

At the centre of the political spectrum was the KDP-S, affiliated to and supported by the KDP in Iraq. The party was formed in April 2014 through the merger of four other parties. On 15 December 2012 the Kurdish Democratic Party-Syria (*el-Partî*) of Dr Abdulhakim Bashar, along with the two Kurdish Freedom (*Azadî*) parties[10] and the Kurdistan Union Party[11] formed what was known as the Political Union. This short-lived alliance was later replaced with the actual merger of these parties and the founding of the KDP-S. The merger represented a decisive shift in the policy and rhetoric of the parties involved. The programme reflected popular calls for the removal of the Assad government; it was committed to federalism as a solution to Syria's problems of representation, and to working with the Syrian opposition. Including the word 'Kurdistan' in their party name increased its nationalist rhetoric and reflected the lifting of taboos on Kurdish expression that had burdened Kurdish politics before 2011. The KDP-S was considered to be one of the most prominent parties. Much of its popularity and strength was due its open connections to the KDP Iraq, which it inherited from the KDP-S (*el-Partî*) of Dr Abdulhakim Bashar and from which it gained ideological and financial support. Dr Abdulhakim Bashar held the chairmanship of the KNC from its establishment in 2011 until 2014, when Si'ud Mala assumed the leadership of the party.

The Kurdish Union Party (*Partiya Yekîtiya Kurd li Sûriyê*, or simply *Yekîtî*) was the main party positioned on the left of the political spectrum. *Yekîtî* maintained greater independence from the Iraqi Kurdish political parties, although financial requirements and the need for external support necessitated some relation with the KDP and the PUK. The party programme, however was not attached to those in Iraq and the party took a relatively more active role within Kurdish society,

---

[10] *Partiya Azadî ya Kurdî li Sûriyê* (the Kurdish Freedom Party in Syria) had split in 2011 between the leadership of Mustafa Jumaa and Mustafa Oso. Both parties maintained the name and political programme.

[11] The inclusion of the word 'Kurdistan' in this party name came about in 2009 and was the result of a split within the *Partiya Yekîtîya Kurdi li Sûriyê* party. A faction of the European branch of the party split off after proposals to change the party name to include the word Kurdistan and to include autonomy in its political demands were rejected in the party conference. The majority of its leadership were in exile, which allowed the party to avoid regime suppression for use of the word Kurdistan. Allsopp, *The Kurds of Syria*, 94.

particularly organizing demonstrations and protests both against the Baath Party (which it spearheaded after 2000) and against the PYD after 2011. *Yekîtî* leaders remained in Syria throughout the crisis and became active in protesting what they believe to be PYD abuses of power. The party also supported federalism as a solution to the crisis in Syria and to problems of Kurdish representation. Ibrahim Biro, *Yekîtî* party secretary from 2013, held the chairmanship of the KNC coalition from July 2015. The leadership of the *Yekîtî* party rotated within the members of the politburo, allowing the party to claim greater internal democracy than many other Kurdish political parties.

The main party on the right of the political spectrum was *Pêşverû*, which defined the Kurds as a minority in Syria and avoided referencing them as a national group. This moderate political platform, as well as Darwish's personal status in Kurdish society, enabled the party to develop channels of negotiation with local Syrian authorities. *Pêşverû* maintained strong relations with the PUK in Iraq and its political programme reflected that relationship. It also suffered significantly less internal fracturing than other Kurdish parties in Syria and had been under the same leader since its formation in 1965.[12] *Pêşverû* was a founding party of the KNC in 2011 and remained in the organization until 2 July 2015 when it opted to operate independently of both the KNC and the PYD bloc. Its inclusion in the KNC and consequent agreement to describe Syrian Kurds as a national group and to support federalism marked a shift in its policy towards the centre of the Kurdish political spectrum. Its suspension of its membership of the KNC, however, reflected a belief that the Syrian National Coalition (SNC) had betrayed the Kurds and that a solution to Kurdish issues in Syria was more realistic through negotiation with the government than with the SNC.[13]

Outside the 1957 genealogy one party played a significant role and mustered notable popular support. The Kurdish Future Movement (*Şepêla Pêsrojê ya Kurdî li Sûriyê*) founded by Mashaal Tammo in 2005, took an active part in leading the Kurdish street response to the Syrian protests movement and was involved in the founding of the Syrian National Council in 2011. Tammo became the only Kurdish executive on the council but withdrew support after the final declaration of the founding conference failed to recognize the Kurds in Syria. In contrast to other Kurdish parties, the Future Movement did not define the Kurdish issue as

---

[12] The notable split in this party was the formation of the Kurdish Reform Movement led by Faysal Yusuf. Later Amjad Othman split from this party and formed a second party of the same name (the Kurdish Reform Movement in Syria).

[13] See, for example, Madar al-Youm 03/01/2017: 'Abdulhamid Darwish shifts: Regime is better than the Coalition', *Syrian Observer*, http://syrianobserver.com/EN/News/32153/Abdulhamid_Darwish_S hifts_Regime_Better_Than_Coalition (last accessed 18/12/2018).

a regional one but sought full participation of Kurds in Syrian affairs through proportional representation. Tammo was assassinated in his home in Qamishli in October 2011. Following this, on 6 July 2012 the party divided as a result of a leadership contest between Jangadir Muhammad and Rezan Sheikhmus. The Future Movement did not join the KNC until June 2015. The party was vocal against the PYD, blaming them for the assassination of their leader, although many sources suggested that the Syrian intelligence services were to blame. The Sheikhmus wing of the party elected Siamand Hajo as its chairman at the party congress of 17–19 October 2014; it was agreed that it would operate clandestinely in Syria and establish a military wing to protect Kurdish civilians in the regions.[14]

The KNC

The KNC was formed in Qamishli on 26–27 October 2011, by ten Kurdish political parties in addition to independent activists, youth and women's organizations, human rights advocates and professionals. Before March 2011, the 1957 genealogy of parties had formed various political alliances aimed at uniting the political movement and the Kurdish voice, but which broadly reflected the divisions within the political spectrum. In response to the unrest in Syria, the KNC united parties from across the spectrum and sought to represent Syrian Kurds amid the scramble for political positioning that ensued. The number and nature of the parties within the coalition have changed over time, due to parties leaving, splitting or merging and due to the incorporation of new parties. In early 2017 the following parties constituted the KNC:

1. The Kurdish Union Party in Syria (*Yekîtî*) – (chairman: Ibrahim Biro)
2. The Kurdistan Democratic Party-Syria (PDKS) – (chairman: Si'ud Mala)
3. The Kurdish Reform Movement-Syria – (chairman: Faisal Yusuf)
4. The Kurdish Democratic Equality Party in Syria – (chairman: Ni'mat Dawud)
5. The Kurdish Democratic Patriotic Party in Syria – (chairman: Tahir Sa'dun Sifuk)
6. The Kurdish Democratic Party in Syria (*el-Partî*) – (chair: vacant)
7. The Kurdish Democratic Union Party in Syria (Democratic *Yekîtî*) – (chairman: Hajar 'Ali)
8. The Kurdistan Democratic Union Party – (chairman: Kamiran Haj 'Abdu)

---

[14] KurdWatch 30/10/2014: 'Future movement founds military wing', http://www.kurdwatch.org/?aid=3260 (last accessed 11/01/2017).

9. The Kurdish Democratic Left Party in Syria – (chairman: Shalal Gado)
10. The Kurdistan Left Party-Syria – (chairman: Mahmud Mala)
11. The Kurdish Future Movement in Syria – (chairman: Siamand Hajo)
12. The Kurdish Future Movement in Syria – (head of the communication office: Narin Matini)
13. Syrian Yezidi Assembly – (chairwoman: Mizgin Yusuf)
14. Avant-garde Party Kurdistan-Syria – (chairman: Ismail Hesaf) [15]

KNC policy and internal divisions

The KNC united on a rationale of representing the Kurdish people and interests in Syria and providing a unified voice with which to enter relationships with and negotiate with other Syrian groupings. The scramble for external political support tied many emerging Syrian opposition groupings to Turkey, while Islamist agendas had undermined broad alliances based on a pan-Syrian pro-democracy platform. Within these opposition alliances, Kurdish voices were marginalized or completely absent and the issue of recognizing the Kurdish identity became a seemingly unbridgeable obstacle to cooperation. Kurdish political groups boycotted the SNC as well as the National Coordination Body for Democratic Change (NCB) choosing to represent the Kurdish national identity against what it saw as Arabist and Islamist agendas. Similarly, the KNC position was distinct from that of the PYD and reflected failed attempts to cooperate within the first few months of civil protests against the government. Long-standing rifts between the parties of the 1957 genealogy and the PKK/PYD as well as fundamental differences in ideology and policy on Kurdish identity, rights and representation (examined further below) marred attempts to cooperate and pitted the two blocs against each other.

The establishment of the KNC, however, united the 1957 parties on a number of critical points, including describing the Kurdish people as indigenous to their historic land and demanding constitutional recognition of the Kurds as a national group. The KNC capitalized on opportunities to increase Kurdish demands as the power of central government weakened and as the PYD self-government was institutionalized. Individual parties within the KNC began to call for a federal solution to Syria's failures in representing the Kurds and denial of their rights. Finally, in the Fifth Conference of the KNC on 1 June 2015, its political programme was amended to include federalism, and Ibrahim

[15] List correct to 09/07/2018. For changes check the KNC Geneva website: http://knc-geneva.org.

Biro (secretary of the *Yekîtî* Party) was elected chair of the KNC, replacing Tahir Safouk (of the Kurdish Democratic Patriotic Party in Syria). After taking office as chairman, Ibrahim Biro stated that 'a federal system is the only guarantee for the rights of all sectarian, religious and national components of Syria. After all this killing and destruction, Syria cannot be a central state like the previous eras'.[16] Nevertheless, the KNC did not recognize the system of government and administration developed by the PYD in northern Syria and, despite the KNC's official support of a federal solution, it condemned the Administration's declaration of federalism in March 2016. The KNC described the declaration as unilateral and void of the necessary debate and political processes involving all elements of the Syrian opposition.[17]

The KNC's attempts to consolidate its role as a legitimate representative of the Kurds was hindered by fractures within it. Significant splits within the KNC occurred in 2014 and, in December of that year, three parties – Syrian-Kurdish Democratic Reconciliation (*Rêkeftin*), the Kurdish Democratic Union Party (*al-Wahda*) and Nusradin Ibrahim's KDP-S (*el-Partî*) – were expelled from the KNC due to their decisions to cooperate with the PYD administration. Breakaway factions of two of these parties, formed subsequently, re-joined the KNC in June 2015, as did splinters of Muhammad Musa's Kurdish Left Party in Syria (led by Muhmud Mula) and Salih Gedo's Kurdish Democratic Left Party in Syria, which had been expelled in February 2014.[18] Adding to the complexity of these divisions and alliances, three of the four parties that were expelled from the KNC, as well as Amjad Othman's Kurdish Reform Movement in Syria, formed the KNAS on 14 February 2016.[19] The KNAS supported the Federation of Northern Syria announced in March 2016, and the continuation of peace and provision of services in the northern regions. Mustafa Mashayikh, spokesman

---

[16] Massoud Hamed 17/09/2015: 'Kurdish National Council: We must remove the top of the pyramid in Syria', *Al Monitor*, http://www.al-monitor.com/pulse: /originals/2015/09/kurdish-official-biro-oppo sition-syria-regime.html (last accessed 26/06/2016).

[17] Wilgenburg 19/03/2016: 'Kurdish National Council in Syria condemns federalism declaration by Kurdish rival', *ARA News*, http://aranews.net/2016/03/kurdish-national-council-syria-condemn s-federalism-declaration-kurdish-rival/ (last accessed 20/01/2017).

[18] The two splinter parties were Kurdistan Democratic Union Party in Syria under the leadership of Kamiran Haj 'Abdu and a faction of *el-Partî*. KurdWatch 01/06/2015: 'Kurdish National Council accepts new members', *KurdWatch*, http://www.kurdwatch.org/?aid=3448&z=en (last accessed 26/06/2016).

[19] The Kurdish National Alliance in Syria (KNAS) included Sheikh Ali's Kurdish Democratic Unity Party in Syria (*al-Wahda*), Nasruddin Ibrahim's Kurdish Democratic Party in Syria (*el-Partî*), the Syrian-Kurdish Democratic Reconciliation (*Rêkeftin*), Salih Gedo's Kurdistan Left Party in Syria and Amjad Othman's Kurdish Reform Movement in Syria.

for the KNAS, said that its main objective was 'to stress the necessity of unifying the Kurdish ranks in the face of the current challenges'.[20]

Divisions within the KNC also negatively affected its ability to establish a clear and strong Kurdish representation and to rally popular support. By 2017, arguably, its political platform appeared stronger as a result of the formal separation of the various blocs within it. For example, interviews suggest that the adoption of the military group, the *Rojava Peshmerga* (see *Military organizations* section below), by the KNC was blocked by some parties within it, notably the Syrian Kurdish Democratic Party of Jamal Sheikh Baqi. The decision of those parties to leave the KNC in favour of cooperation with the PYD administration in 2014 allowed for the military group to be formally linked to the KNC during the congress of 2015.[21] The Progressive Party's (Abdulhamid Haj Darwish) suspension of its KNC membership in July 2015 similarly lessened internal disagreements within the council and allowed for more decisive policy formation, witnessed in the conference of 2015. Fractures based on historic policy choices, on patronage networks extending to the KRI and on local personal loyalties and rivalries, had prevented the KNC from forming clear and stable political alliances capable of positioning the parties against and within other opposition groupings. Internal disagreement remained visible within the organization, first, concerning the position of the KNC within the SNC and, second, around relations with the PYD-led administration. The number of expulsions from the KNC and splits within parties due to these relations in 2014 demonstrated the deep divisions within Kurdish politics itself. The failures of the SNC to adequately address Kurdish issues remained an active fault line within the KNC.[22]

Military organizations

The parties of 1957 never took up arms against the Syrian state. There are several reasons for this besides political policy and decision-making. First, early political organization was dominated by Kurdish exiles from Turkey and was

---

[20] Ahmed Shiwesh 14/02/2016: 'Syrian Kurds form new Political Alliance', *ARA News*, http://aranews.net/2016/02/syrian-kurds-form-new-political-alliance-call-for-federalism-as-solution-to-ongoing-civil-war/ (last accessed 20/01/2017).

[21] IIST interview: Saadon F. Sino, 11/03/2016, Erbil.

[22] IIST interview: Zara Saleh (*Yekîtî* party politburo member and UK rep. (September 2016). The Yezidi Council also left the KNC and the SNC after protests that Arabism and Islamism within the SNC had not been addressed and that the Yezidis had not been recognized as a religious minority in Syria. Paul Antonopoulus 19/09/2016: 'Ezidi National Council resigns from Turkey-based Syrian National Council', *al Masdar News*, https://www.almasdarnews.com/article/ezidi-national-council-resign-from-turkey-based-syrian-national-council/ (last accessed 08/11/2016).

focused on the Turkish state. Military organization for the Ararat Revolt of 1930 involved both Kurdish exiles and Kurds from within Syria and was coordinated by the Xoybun League[23] and its branches within Turkey. The failure of this revolt led to an abandonment of military tactics in favour of using intellectual and cultural development as a means of protecting the Kurdish identity. Organized nationalist politics did not focus on or target the central Syrian state until after Syrian independence and the rise of popular Arab nationalism in the 1950s. Second, the armed resistance by the KDP in Iraq and by the PKK in Turkey drew significant support from Syrian Kurds. Many joined the Peshmerga or actively supported the party by other means, particularly during the 1960s–1970s, while, during its time in Syria in the 1980s and 1990s, the PKK drew taxes from the local population and thousands of Kurds joined its guerrilla groups. Third, the geography of Syrian Kurdish areas was not favourable for the type of non-state unconventional armed resistance that the mountains of northern Iraq and south-east Turkey sustained. The foothills and steppes of the northern borders and the non-contiguous demographic spread of Kurdish populations left them more exposed and vulnerable to the state and to local sectarian hostilities than those in Iraq, Turkey or Iran, where armed organization has been enduring features of Kurdish political movements.

After March 2011 the 1957 parties did not seek to take up arms in an organized manner. They maintained instead a commitment to peaceful diplomatic resolution of the Kurdish issue in Syria, which was confirmed by the KNC mandate. Nevertheless, between 2012 and 2013 several individual parties formed small armed units to protect local offices and civilians.[24] These had faced restrictions and members had been arrested by the Assad government (particularly in the Jazirah) as well as by armed organizations connected to the PYD.[25] According to local sources, which included the *Yekîtî* leader Ibrahim Biro, conscription to both the Syrian Army and to the PYD's forces induced many young men, not ideologically inclined to support either of these, to leave Syria and to join the *Rojava Peshmerga* in the KRI.[26]

---

[23] The Xoybun League was formed in 1927 in Beirut. Xoybun was a secular nationalist organization which united Kurdish tribes and intellectuals around the desire to unite the Kurdish movement and to unify political efforts to liberate the Kurds. At this point in history, Turkey was the main 'enemy' of the Kurds and the organization directed the struggle against Turkey to achieve the liberation of Kurds from 'Turkish claws'. Muhammad Mullah Ahmed 2000: *Jama'iahat Khoybun wa al-'Alaqat al-Kurdiyah Armaniyah*, KAWA, Bonn, 37–8.

[24] The *Yekîtî* party, for example, seized one building in the city of Amude from the Baath Party and later formed its own militia in November 2012. KurdWatch 30/11/12: 'Amude: Yekiti forms armed battalion', *KurdWatch*, http://kurdwatch.org/?aid=2703&z=en (last accessed 05/01/2017).

[25] IIST interviews: Majdal Dalil, *Yekîtî*, Qamishli, 01/03/2016.

[26] IIST interview: Ibrahim Biro, Erbil, 13/03/2016.

In July 2015 the KNC announced its official affiliation with the *Rojava Peshmerga* – a group estimated to be between 2,000 and 6,000 Syrian Kurds, many of whom had defected from the Syrian Army and re-grouped and received additional training in the KRI. The *Rojava Peshmerga* cooperated with the Kurdistan Regional Government (KRG) Peshmerga against ISIS, but only within the KRI. Negotiations with the PYD to allow the *Rojava Peshmerga* into Syria had failed to produce agreement, with each side placing responsibility on the other for their continued exclusion from Syria. The PYD asserted that the individuals within the *Rojava Peshmerga* should be absorbed within the YPG to avoid the coexistence of potentially conflictual partisan military formations within Syria. In comparison, the KNC viewed the YPG as a partisan and ideologically driven military group within which the *Rojava Peshmerga* should not be absorbed. In June 2014, the KNC rejected a suggestion made by SNC president, Anas Abdah, during a visit to Erbil, that the Syrian Peshmerga join the FSA forces in confrontations against ISIS in and around Azaz. Such a move would have increased chances of military confrontation with YPG forces. Similarly, the KNC rejected the idea of joining the Syrian Democratic Forces (SDF) citing concerns about possible relations between the SDF and the Assad regime.[27] Political and ideological differences and tangled military alliances constituted significant barriers to cooperation between the two blocs, and all parties agreed on the need for a comprehensive official agreement over the terms for the return of these forces to Syria in a manner that would not ignite internecine conflict.

KNC alliances and affiliations within Syria

On 27 August 2013 the KNC signed an agreement to join the SNC.[28] The KNC position within the SNC was not straightforward and there remained fundamental differences between visions for the future of Syria. The issue of decentralization and methods of decision-making became central to rifts between the two coalitions.[29] The SNC promoted administrative decentralization

[27] Wilgenburg 14/06/2016: 'Rojava's Peshmerga forces refuse to join Azaz battle to avoid confrontation with fellow Kurdish troops', *ARA News*, (online) available on http://aranews.net/2016/06/rojavas-peshmerga-forces-refuse-to-join-azaz-battle-to-avoid-confrontation-with-fellow-kurdish-troops/ (last accessed 15/11/2016).

[28] The agreement was approved by the KNC and the SNC on the 6 and 14 September 2013 respectively. Ibrahim Hameidi 28/08/2013: 'Syria's Kurds formally join opposition coalition', *Al-Monitor*, http://www.al-monitor.com/pulse/politics/2013/08/syria-kurds-join-national-coalition.html (last accessed 15/05/2017).

[29] See also the proposal for a Kurdistan region of Syria, published by *Yekiti Media* 06/01/2017: 'Mawqʻa Rudaw yanshr dustur Kurdistan suriya alathi iqtaraHihi al-majlis al-watani al-Kurdi', *Yekiti Media*, http://ara.yekiti-media.org/ال-سوريا-كردستان-دستور-ينشر-رودواو-موقع/ (last accessed 16/06/2017).

only and rejected the idea of both political decentralization and a federal Kurdish area. Fears of Kurdish separatism, fuelled by the Assad government and the dominance of Arab nationalism over the Syrian identity, remained significant obstacles to cooperation. Despite this, KNC leaders had been encouraged by Western powers, not willing to support political sectarianism in Syria, to join the mainstream opposition group. The SNC's failure to address adequately Kurdish issues within its programmes and hostilities towards Kurdish ambitions expressed by some individuals and groups within it fed distrust among the Kurdish population of the coalition. The decision to join the SNC also opened rifts within the KNC. Some members viewed joining the SNC as a 'political loss' for the Kurds, while others considered it the only means to guarantee Kurdish rights in a post-Assad Syria.[30]

The agreement between the SNC and the KNC confirmed a joint commitment to the constitutional recognition of the Kurdish peoples' national identity, the recognition of the Kurdish national rights within the framework of Syrian unity and to the cancellation of and compensation against any discriminatory policies and decrees. It was also agreed that the name of the Syrian Arab Republic would be changed to the Syrian Republic. Eleven members of the KNC were included in the SNC's 114-member general commission and three KNC members were included within the nineteen-member political commission. The representation of the KNC in the SNC provided it a place at the negotiating table in Geneva and extended it greater international legitimacy and some international support. In February 2016 the KNC opened an office in Geneva with the purpose of 'strengthening the role of the Kurdish delegation to the High Negotiations Committee during the next round of Geneva talks; of developing relations between the KNC and the diplomatic missions as well as of emphasizing the vision of KNC in the Western media'.[31] Although KNC's place within the SNC was criticized by many Kurdish activists and the agreement was not viewed as sufficient to meet Kurdish demands for representation, its representative role beyond Kurdish areas was enhanced and extended through international recognition of the SNC as the legitimate Syrian opposition grouping.[32]

---

[30] ARA News 08/09/2013: 'Kurdish National Council to join SNC', *ARA News*, available on: http://ara news.net/2013/09/kurdish-national-council-joins-the-syrian-coalition/ (last accessed 28/06/2016).

[31] Rudaw 28/02/2016: 'Syrian Kurdish Council opens Geneva office to "contribute to peace"', *Rudaw*, http://rudaw.net/english/middleeast/syria/28022016 (last accessed 30/06/2016).

[32] Harriet Allsopp July 2016: 'Are the old Syrian Kurdish Parties relevant anymore?', *LSE Blog*, http:// blogs.lse.ac.uk/mec/2016/08/30/are-the-old-syrian-kurdish-parties-relevant-anymore/ (last accessed 15/05/2017). The alliance between the US-led coalition and the YPG against ISIS which resulted in military recognition of the YPG, and indirectly, the PYD, however, further weakened the position of the KNC.

The main point of contention between the KNC and the SNC was the extent of decentralization which, in the document, was defined as administrative decentralization only. The terms of the document were, however, left open to review and the KNC delegation put a reservation on the phrase 'adoption of a decentralized administrative system'. Nevertheless, failure to achieve substantial commitments to the devolution of political decision-making to Kurdish representatives and the boost in legitimacy gained by the PYD through the military alliance between the US-led coalition and the YPG against ISIS further tarnished the position of the KNC within the SNC.

The PYD

The PYD was built on the back of the PKK. The PKK presence in Syria developed after Abdullah Öcalan took refuge there in 1980 and it remained strong until Öcalan was expelled from Syria in 1998 following a rapprochement between Ankara and Damascus. The PKK presence was greatest and most influential in the regions of Afrin and Kobani where its successor, the PYD also gained a 'natural' legitimacy when it was established in Syria in 2003. Ayse Efendi, co-chair of the Kobani's People's Assembly said 'They have been educated by Mr. Öcalan. Most people have seen him and eaten with him. The people of Kobani admired Öcalan.'[33] In comparison, the PYD was much weaker in the Hasakah province because of its geographical distance from former PKK strongholds and because of its contiguous territory and social and historical links with the KRI and the leadership of the 1957 genealogy of parties. The PKK had a significant impact on Kurdish identity, however. The promotion of Kurdish cultural identity through music and song, clothes, popular culture, social organization at the grass-roots level was used as a tool for engaging the population in the party's struggle and ideology. Crucially, the PKK's armed resistance within Turkey and its establishment of training grounds within Syria and Lebanon facilitated recruitment. The PKK deeply infiltrated political and social organization among Syrian Kurds and large numbers joined its armed units.[34]

---

[33] IIST interview: Ayse Efendi, Kobani, 17/06/2017.
[34] Estimates suggested that up to 10,000 Syrian Kurds were killed in Turkey fighting with the PKK. David McDowall 2000: *A Modern History of the Kurds*, I.B. Tauris, London, 479; Allsopp, *The Kurds of Syria*, 40.

The PYD was co-chaired by Salih Muslim and Aysa Abdulla between 2012 and 2017[35] and from September 2017, by Shahoz Hassan and Aysha Hisso.[36] During the Syrian crisis it became the dominant political force in Kurdish areas of Syria. The party operated within the umbrella structure of the *Koma Civakên Kurdistan*, the Kurdistan Communities Union (KCK), which was formed by the PKK in 2003–2005 to link affiliated armed and political organizations across Kurdish areas of Turkey, Iran, Iraq and Syria. The highest legislative body of the KCK was *Kongra-Gel* (the People's Congress), which served as the representative body for its constituent members (the PKK, the Party of Free Life, Iraq's Kurdistan Democratic Solution Party, and the PYD, as well as other civil and military organizations). The PYD's pre-2015 internal code stated that *Kongra-Gel* was the supreme legislative authority of the Kurdish people and Abdullah Öcalan the leader of the party.[37] Amendments to the internal code removed these clauses leaving only a recognition of Öcalan as the ideological inspiration for the party and the governing coalition (Movement for a Democratic Society (TEV-DEM)) as the democratic and communal organization that represents the party in Rojava.[38]

Like its affiliates in other countries, the PYD adopted a pyramidal structure and described itself as a democratic and populist party. Directions and instructions were top-down, whereas report submission was bottom-up. A process of evaluation, submitting suggestions, criticism and self-criticism was described as a fundamental pillar of the party that was intended to solve internal party problems and continuously correct and renovate the party's path.[39] This model of continuous bottom-up evaluation was also applied to individuals within society and to the political process within the wider administrative system, examined further in Chapter 4.

The objectives of the party concentrated on the development of democratic self-administration and the extension of the system to all Syria. During the crisis in Syria the PYD initiated the formation of a myriad of administrative organizations and institutions among different sectors of society and

---

[35] Salih Muslim chaired the PYD from 2010 but the co-chair system was introduced in 2012 to guarantee gender equality.

[36] Hisham Arafat 30/09/2017: 'Syrian Kurdish PYD elects new co-chairs in Rojava', *Kurdistan 24*, http://www.kurdistan24.net/en/video/4861d542-8761-4ea6-a90a-38d6eb8233ed (last accessed 29/04/2018).

[37] Internal Code of the PYD, pre-2015. See also Ragip Soylu 19/02/2016: 'Archives, testimonies confirm PYD/YPG's organic link with PKK terror organization', *Daily Sabah*, (online) http://www.dailysabah.com/war-on-terror/2016/02/20/archives-testimonies-confirm-pydypgs-organic-link-with-pkk-terror-organization (last accessed 10/11/2016).

[38] PYD 'Rules of Procedure of the Democratic Union Party (PYD)' (Internal Code) 2015, Section 2.

[39] PYD 'Rules of Procedure of the Democratic Union Party (PYD)' Section 10.

geographical areas, all bound by a commitment to the 'democratic autonomy' project. Consequently, unravelling the PYD from the administrative system and various political, civil and armed organizations is not straightforward. External observers and Kurds alike often referenced the PYD when referring to the Administration in more general terms. While it remained important to distinguish between the various elements of the political, social and economic system in northern Syria, all operated within the same framework and were defined by the project implemented by the PYD: the party itself provided a direct link to the KCK and to Abdullah Öcalan.

The PYD aimed to support Kurdish liberation struggles in all parts of Kurdistan, 'in order to achieve and consolidate Kurdish national unity, based upon the principle of democratic communal confederalism without compromising political borders'.[40] During the turmoil created by the start of the civil unrest in Syria, the PYD began to implement a project of 'democratic autonomy' within Kurdish majority areas of Syria. The project involved the practical application of Öcalan's theories and the promotion of democratic confederalism, which were inspired by the theoretical work of American anarchist and libertarian socialist, Murray Bookchin (1921–2006). Bookchin argued that hierarchical relationships, not capital, were our original sin and that ecological problems that we faced were the result of these relations of domination. These hierarchical relationships, he argued, were supported by the nation state. He advocated a more municipally based form of democracy: 'libertarian municipalism' based on Hellenic models of direct democracy through which injustices could be addressed and revolutionary movements could avoid the trap of reproducing the inequalities they set out to defeat.

Abdullah Öcalan's prison writings and communications advocated setting up municipal assemblies, which together would form a confederation of assemblies, extending across Kurdish areas in Turkey, Syria, Iraq and Iran and be united by common values – political, religious and cultural pluralism, self-defence and protection of the environment.[41] The model allowed the PKK to advance the establishment of a hybrid structure of communities, within and across states, and to avoid having to 'take' state power itself. Its application in Syria, particularly after the Kobani siege, was driven by a response to trans-state Kurdish issues: building a democratic decentralized form of governance within Syria that could also be adopted by other communities, within and beyond Syria's borders, through

---

40 Ibid., Section 1.D.
41 Ibid., Section 1.D. Wes Enzinna 24/11/2015: 'A dream of secular utopia in ISIS' backyard'.

non-state organizational structures and direct democratic dialogue. This model was seen both as a solution to regional Kurdish issues through application in other states and as a solution to issues of democratic representation in Syria as a whole.

The PYD was central to the myriad of social, political, economic organizations and security apparatus that developed as part of this system from July 2012. In the same manner that the PYD was organizationally separate from the PKK but organically linked to it within the KCK, through TEV-DEM, it was also inextricably connected to the administration and security of Kurdish areas of Syria but maintained formal separation. The PYD itself was the initial driving force in Syria behind the expansion of control over Kurdish areas, the formation of the YPG/J and other security forces, as well as the formation and positioning of TEV-DEM as the driving force of the 'social revolution' and its administration. Countless institutions, organizationally independent of the PYD, retained a connection to the party and to the KCK network through individuals within them and through attachment to the ideological doctrine and revolutionary social project they pursued. Over the years in which the Administration developed, the names and roles of various organizations within it changed and morphed to accommodate and adapt to the changing political and security environment and to seize opportunities for expansion. During this time, the public involvement of the PYD in decision-making itself diminished and, in its place TEV-DEM, the institutions of state and local communes assumed primary decision-making roles. The 'social revolution' itself was given the appearance of gaining its own momentum by the apparent withdrawal of the PYD to the back-stage. The PYD, however, remained the driving force behind this movement and all that had developed had evolved (and morphed) from it. Over time the momentum of the project had increased, and territorial and political gains were made and institutionalized as the PYD adapted to new opportunities and the ever-changing environment of the crisis in Syria.

Armed forces

Armed organization by the PYD and its proxies was based on the principle of a legitimate and 'natural' right to self-defence. According to some sources the arming of the PYD began as early as 2004 following the crackdown on Kurdish protesters in Qamishli.[42] Certainly, documents produced by Abdullah Öcalan

---

[42] Danny Gold 31/10/2012: 'Meet the YPG, the Kurdish militia that doesn't want help from anyone', *VICE News*, http://www.vice.com/read/meet-the-ypg (last accessed 15/07/2016); Michael Knapp, Anja Flach and Ercan Ayboga 2016: *Revolution in Rojava*, Pluto Press, London, 133.

in 2007 on the subject of Syrian Kurds encouraged the establishment of self-defence groups and resulted in the group starting to organize itself covertly in Kurdish cities and training fighters.[43] The start of the popular protest movement in Syria in 2011 gave rise to an intensification of armed organization in the form of the YPG which was instrumental in seizing control of territory from the Syrian government in July 2012. The YPG was officially announced in 2012 and, as the ranks of this organization swelled, it was restructured by former PKK activists and commanders into a quasi-state security force. This transformation was directed by veteran PKK commander Xebat Derik, and in early 2013 the official YPG founding conference was held. By early 2017 the YPG was estimated to number approximately 50,000[44] and was the largest armed force in northern Syria.

With the intensification of armed conflict in Kurdish regions, a law for compulsory military service was adopted in July 2014 by the local administration in the Jazirah, which led to the creation of the Self-Defence Units (*Hêzên Erka Xweparastine*) within which military service would be spent. This law was applied to the cantons of Afrin, in April 2015, and Kobani, in June 2016.[45] This force existed alongside the YPG and individuals could opt to join it at any time but were usually employed as a defence force or a holding force in liberated areas rather than joining frontline combat.[46]

Although the YPG was developed by the PYD and the PKK, numerous attempts were made to assert the political independence of the armed force. After the Erbil agreement of 2012 between the KNC and the PYD (see below) the YPG fell under the joint command structures of the Supreme Kurdish Council.[47] On 18 September 2012, however, it announced itself organizationally autonomous of any political party, including the PYD. From October 2015 it operated under

---

[43] The Organizational Charter of the Kurdish Community in Western Kurdistan KCK-Rojava 2007, called for a 'direct democracy' and self-rule system based on Öcalan's Democratic Confederalist ideology.

[44] See, for example, Global Security 19/08/2016: 'Kurdish peoples' protection units YPG', *Global Security*, (online) http://www.globalsecurity.org/military/world/para/ypg.htm (last accessed 11/01/2017).

[45] Some interviewees reported that conscripts in Afrin were being drafted directly into the YPG (IIST interviews 28/02/2017; 17/09/2016). Afrin Canton 19/05/2015: 'Law of self-defence is taking place in Afrin canton with global unique advantages', *Canton Afrin*, http://cantonafrin.com/en/news/view/1050.law-of-self--defense--is-taking-place-in-afrin-canton-with-global-unique-advantages.html (last accessed 16/06/2017); Democratic Self-Administration Executive Council for the Kobani Canton Committee of Defense and Self-Protection 02/06/2016.

[46] Knapp, Flach and Ayboga, *Revolution in Rojava*, 140.

[47] YPG: 'Rules of Procedure', 2013, available in Appendix II of HRW 2014: *Under Kurdish Rule: Abuses in PYD-run Enclaves of Syria*, https://www.hrw.org/report/2014/06/19/under-kurdish-rule/abuses-pyd-run-enclaves-syria (last accessed 01/02/2017). Available also in Arabic on https://www.hrw.org/sites/default/files/reports/syria0614ar_kurds_ForUpload.pdf (last accessed 01/02/2017).

the SDF umbrella and cooperated closely with the US-led coalition in the Kobani and the Jazirah regions.[48] Some analysts, however, claimed that many YPG units were commanded by PKK veterans (of Syrian or Turkish origins) which provided a 'skeletal' structure for the YPG, 'fleshed-out' by local recruits.[49] The YPG–PKK–HPG (*Hêzên Parastina Gel*, or Peoples Defence Units, attached to the PKK) overlap, therefore, was indirect but clearly present.

The YPG was described by the Kurdish Project as 'a democratic socialist organization in which Officers are elected by troops and equality regardless of gender, religion and ethnicity is guaranteed'.[50] The members of the YPG had to undergo continuous training including re-education and ideological indoctrination. The official YPG website described the YPG as 'the Democratic Nation's protection force and not related to any political party'.[51] Its political independence, however, was undermined by its commitment to Öcalan's project expressed through its rhetoric and use of the concept of the 'democratic nation'. The YPG international website also described the YPG as 'more than a military force. It is a revolutionary organization that protects the transformation towards the ethico-political society against its external and internal enemies in accordance with the principles of democratic confederalism'.[52] Hence, the YPG had a clear political and social function in the revolutionary process guiding the administration and the democratic autonomy project.

The YPG became the dominant military force in northern Syria and forged strategic alliances with politically sympathetic or strategically aligned groups there. The most prominent and enduring of these was the SDF established in October 2015. Alliances formed on the military front naturally overlapped with political ones. The SDF, an alliance of armed forces, including Arab, Syriac and Kurdish forces, was formed on the basis of the mutual benefits of removing ISIS from the area. The SDF claimed to be fighting for a democratic secular federal Syria and, in December 2016, was named as the official defence force of the

---

[48] In the Afrin canton and the Kurdish neighbourhoods of Aleppo, where the YPG and the SDF developed significantly different alliances, the YPG received no support from the US-led anti-ISIS coalition.

[49] Jenkins 19/04/2016: 'The PKK and the PYD, comrades in arms rivals in politics?' *The Turkey Analyst* (online), Central Asia-Caucasus Institute & Silk Road Studies Program Joint Center, https://www.turkeyanalyst.org/publications/turkey-analyst-articles/item/535-the-pkk-and-the-pyd-comrades-in-arms-rivals-in-politics?html (last accessed 20/01/2017).

[50] The Kurdish Project is an online portal aimed at raising awareness about the Kurdish people. The Kurdish Project, n.d.: 'YPG: Peoples Protection Units', http://thekurdishproject.org/history-and-culture/kurdish-nationalism/peoples-protection-units-ypg/ (last accessed 30/06/2017).

[51] YPG: 'About the Peoples Protection Units (YPG)', available on YPG website, https://www.ypgrojava.org/About-Us (last accessed 07/07/2017).

[52] YPG International, n.d.: 'Support YPG in Rojava', available on https://ypginternational.blackblogs.org/ (last accessed 15/05/2017).

Democratic Federal System of Northern Syria.[53] The Arab forces within the SDF ranged from local tribal groups to armed battalions also allied to the FSA and to the SNC. The SDF, while dominated by Kurdish forces, was also a means of enabling other non-Kurdish forces to take control of liberated areas where Kurds did not form majorities, and of preventing the development of resentment to Kurdish rule within these communities. The formal separation of the YPG from the PYD and the diversification of military groupings through the SDF also enabled these forces to maintain US military assistance in the fight against ISIS, despite Ankara's objections.

PYD alliances and affiliations within Syria

The political map of the northern regions of Syria came to be dominated by the PYD and by the network of organizations and institutions connected to it through TEV-DEM and operating within the administration of Federal Northern Syria – Rojava. Many political parties and organizations which cooperated with the Rojava Administration, such as *al-Salam al-Dimoqrati*, were unheard of before the PYD took control over Kurdish areas of Syria, reflecting the fractured nature of social and political organization in the governance void in this country.

In order to gain and protect territory and support, the PYD and the YPG brokered strategic alliances with diverse, even conflicting, political and military groups. Adding to the complexity of these relations, dealings with certain groupings differed according to local strategic objectives. On the local level for example, in the Jazirah region, the Syriac Christian communities were divided in their alliances. The Syriac Union Party had a long-standing connection to the PKK and it cooperated with the PYD. Its military force, the Syriac Military Council, became part of the SDF, and the Sutoro police, part of the Asayish. It believed that the ideological project of Öcalan could provide a solution to problems Syriacs faced in Syria.[54] To make things more complex, there were also Christian militias, such as the Gozarto Protection Force (GPF) and a second faction, the Sootoro, that were part of the pro-government National Defence Forces (NDF). People in the region often explained differences in political allegiances within groups as a product of external interference. Siham Yousef

---

[53] Before the publication of this constitution the mandate of the SDF was linked to the Rojava administration and to the social revolution.

[54] Carl Drott 25/05/2015: 'The Revolutionaries of Bethnahrin', *Warscapes*, http://www.warscapes.com/reportage/revolutionaries-bethnahrin (last accessed 18/12/2018).

Kyo, the co-head of the foreign relations commission of the Administration in the Jazirah, said:

> At the beginning this Sootoro belonged to the canton administration and worked all together, but the Syrian regime created a dispute within the Syriac community, to attack each other, as it did with the Kurds. ... In reality, the regime split us in two parts.[55]

Administration officials regularly accused the KNC and KDP of cooperation with Ankara and explained resistance to the DAA's rule in these terms.[56] Similarly, KNC supporters and other Syrian opposition factions accused the PYD of maintaining relations with the Assad government. The PYD stressed that it followed a 'third way':

> We are not with the opposition or the regime. We follow the third way, we believe in the democratic nation [project]. This is a new idea.[57]

No obvious formal agreement existed between the two sides but, in general, a pact of non-aggression appeared to have been to the strategic advantage of both. A precedent of unofficial cooperation between the Syrian government and the PKK existed in Syria between 1980 and 1998 in which the PKK leader, Abdullah Öcalan was provided refuge in Syria and PKK training camps were set up in Lebanon and Syria. Driven by domestic issues and relations with Turkey rather than support for the PKK, the move also placated Syria's own Kurds.[58] Some accounts, especially from those who opposed the PYD, suggested in 2011 that the collapse of Syrian-Turkish relations that had led to the expulsion of the PKK from Syria in 1998 and Öcalan's subsequent arrest in 1999 rekindled Bashar al-Assad's relations with the PKK.[59] In an interview with the British daily newspaper, *The Sunday Times*, on 6 December 2015 Bashar al-Assad publicly stated that the government had provided the 'Kurds' with arms and that they had cooperated in fighting terrorism.[60] Salih Muslim and other PYD

---

[55] IIST interview: Siham Yousef Kyo, 12/02/2016.

[56] See, for example, ARA News 10/01/2017: 'Barzani backed Syrian Kurdish party denies secret talks with PYD', *ARA News*, http://aranews.net/2017/01/barzani-backed-syrian-kurdish-party-denies-secret-talks-with-pyd/ (last accessed 18/01/2017).

[57] IIST interview: Sihanok Dibo, PYD presidential advisor, Qamishli, 02/05/2016.

[58] Christopher Phillips 2011:'*Turkey and Syria*', in Turkey's Global Strategy, LSE IDEAS, LSE, London, available on http://www.lse.ac.uk/IDEAS/publications/reports/pdf/SR007/syria.pdf (last accessed 06/05/2017), 35.

[59] Soner Cagaptay 05/04/2012: 'Syria and Turkey: The PKK dimension', *The Washington Institute*, http://www.washingtoninstitute.org/policy-analysis/view/syria-and-turkey-the-pkk-dimension (last accessed 06/05/2017).

[60] Transcript of interview available on: SANA (Syrian Arab News Agency) 06/12/2015: 'President al-Assad: Britain and France have neither the will nor the vision on how to defeat terrorism', *SANA* http://sana.sy/en/?p=63558 (last accessed 16/06/2017).

officials, however, denied any direct relationship to the regime. The regime, nevertheless, had for the most part, refrained from confronting the PYD, favouring its neutrality in the conflicts between Syrian opposition rebels and the government.

In comparison to the parties of 1957, which were shaped through reference to state discrimination experienced by Kurds in Syria, the PYD internal code instead concentrated on its ideological and political visions of democratic society. The PYD did not define its political position through reference to that of the Syrian government or any other political actor, but by a holistic radical revolutionary agenda. Nevertheless, statements and rhetoric used by PYD officials, as well as by officials within TEV-DEM and other administrative institutions, expressed opposition to the Baath government and referred repeatedly to the persecution that their own supporters faced under the Assad government.[61] For their part, Syrian officials never made statements in support of the PYD or the DAAs and opposed any form of federalism in northern Syria.

Militarily, coincidences of interest between the YPG and the Syrian Army and mutual benefits of cooperation were more identifiable in some instances. The YPG and the Syrian Arab Army and NDF were reported to have worked together against ISIS in Hasakah and discussed terms of collaboration on several occasions in 2015.[62] In 2016, the YPG was also accused of assisting the Syrian Army and Russia against Syrian rebel strongholds in Aleppo. While the YPG and DAA officials denied formal relations, there were instances of YPG cooperation with both the Syrian government and rebel groups in contact areas where control was contested or tensions had arisen. For example, in Aleppo, an agreement was reached with the FSA in November 2012;[63] and then in December 2015, with the Fatah Aleppo operations room.[64] These agreements were made with either the Syrian government or the Syrian rebels depending on which faction was stronger and on local circumstances.

---

[61] Knapp, Flach and Ayboga, *Revolution in Rojava*, 47–51.
[62] See, for example, KurdWatch 15/10/2015: 'Damascus: PYD negotiates with Assad and the Russian military', *KurdWatch*, http://www.kurdwatch.org/?e3631 (last accessed 30/06/2015); Al Jazeera 04/08/2015: 'Syrian Kurds set terms for partnership with Assad', http://www.aljazeera.com/news/2015/08/syrian-kurds-sets-terms-assad-partnership-150803191234786.html (last accessed 30/06/2016).
[63] KurdWatch 15/11/2012: 'Afrin: PYD concludes an agreement with the Free Syrian Army', *Kurdwatch*, http://kurdwatch.org/?aid=2687&z=en (last accessed 17/03/2017).
[64] Syrian Observatory for Human Rights 19/12/2015: 'Sheikh Maqsood neighborhood is witnessing an agreement between YPG and Fath Aleppo operations room', *SOHR*, http://www.syriahr.com/en/?p=40690 (last accessed 18/06/2017).

Clashes between YPG and the Syrian Army had been sparked, primarily, by local skirmishes and opportunities to expand control (such as in Qamishli on 22 April 2016), or had focused on strategic assets (such as oil field and facilities in Hasakha province). Between January and March 2013, YPG fighters expelled and isolated unsupported Syrian Army battalions from the area. Clashes on the contact line between the Syrian government and the Kurds in Qamishli in April 2016[65] escalated and led to the expulsion of government forces from the Allaya prison and some gains in territory for the YPG. Likewise, skirmishes between the NDF and the YPG in Hasakah city in August of the same year led to a week of intense clashes in which the Syrian government employed air strikes against Kurdish forces for the first time. The conflict was ended by a Russian mediated truce on 23 August, leaving the city almost entirely under Kurdish control.[66] Other strategic assets in the regions remained in government hands and decisions not to challenge the modus vivendi in certain areas had been taken by DAA officials: the YPG, for example, refrained from taking the Qamishli airport:

> We won't take the regime down by doing this. Why would we control it and let our city be bombed from the air. … We will not risk our cities because some parties say 'kick out the regime'. (Aldar Xelil, co-head of TEV-DEM)[67]

As a result of the PYD's neutrality, the Syrian Kurds were successfully spared direct confrontation by the Syrian air force and the worst effects of the civil war. The presence of groups loyal to the Assad government within the DAA regions and the government's continuation of public services to the areas provided it with a foothold in the region. Critics continued to raise questions about perceived ambiguities in the PYD position, while Kurdish DAA officials suggested they would collaborate with anyone, either the Syrian government or the Syrian opposition, to achieve their objectives: 'Anyone who [is] ready to work for democracy, who accepts the diversity within Syrian people [society], we are of course ready to coordinate with them, I told you some examples, with the opposition but also with the regime', Idris Nassan, the co-head of foreign

---

[65] Wladimir van Wilgenburg 21/05/2016: 'Kurdish "capital" erupts in battle between Assad militias and Kurds', *Middle East Eye*, http://www.middleeasteye.net/news/kurds-syria-confront-syrian-reg ime-their-unofficial-capital-880343545 (last accessed 04/04/2017).

[66] Wladimir van Wilgenburg 24/08/2016: 'Hasakah: Truce reached between Syrian regime, Kurds after Russian mediation', *ARA News*, http://aranews.net/2016/08/hasakah-truce-reached-syrian-regi me-kurds-russian-mediation/ (last accessed 04/04/2017).

[67] ISST interview: Aldar Xelil, Executive Committee Member of the Democratic Movement Society (TEV-DEM) in Syria, Amude, 02/05/2016.

relations in Kobani, told Al Jazeera news in August 2015.[68] This pragmatic approach to other parties and interests in Syria was typical of the PYD and could also be observed in local political and military alliances around Aleppo within the SDF and within its predecessor, the joint FSA-YPG operations command of Euphrates Volcano, established in September 2014 to fight ISIS.

Within the wider Syrian opposition, the PYD was a member of the NCB between 2011 and January 2016, when it was led by Haytham Manna. The NCB had support from Russia and was largely tolerated by the Assad government during the crisis in Syria.[69] Haytham Manna resigned from the NCB in in early 2015, when he set up the *Qamh* organization and also co-chaired the Syrian Democratic Council (formed on 10 December 2015 in Malikiya,) which was said to be the political wing of the SDF. Manaa, in March 2016, resigned from the council, condemning the DAA's announcement of federalism.[70] This isolated the PYD and DAA further from the Damascus-based mainstream opposition groupings and limited the reach of its alliances within Syria to local ones.

In a bid to widen the local support base for the democratic autonomy project and to gain local and international legitimacy, institutions within the administrative network were often rebranded and reformed to accommodate local diversity and Western interests and concerns. The system itself had evolved from governance of local cantons to a transitional self-administration to a much wider federal entity. With that, the rhetoric employed by the PYD-led administration also changed and security operations were carried out in the name of the YPG, the Euphrates Volcano and the SDF. The YPG/J remained the dominant force within these alliances and was instrumental in organizing and establishing the governing councils in areas that the SDF liberated from ISIS, such as Manbij. Reports suggest that, while the liberation of the region was welcomed, there was a marked distrust of the PYD and the governing institutions installed there.[71]

[68] Al Jazeera, 'Syrian Kurds set terms for partnership with Assad'; Zaradesht Khalil 09/08/2014: 'YPG spokesperson: Our cooperation with Syrian regime is logical under current conditions', *ARA News*, http://aranews.net/2014/08/ypg-spokesman-cooperation-syrian-regime-logical-current-conditi ons/ (last accessed 30/06/2016).
[69] Aron Lund 03/03/2015: 'We need to end this dirty war: An interview with Haytham Manna', *Diwan* Carnegie Middle East Center, https://carnegie-mec.org/diwan/59237 (last accessed 18/12/2018).
[70] See, for example, ARA News 21/03/2016: 'Arab ally of Kurds turns his back on federalism', http://ara news.net/2016/03/arab-ally-kurds-turns-back-federalism/ (last accessed 15/05/2017).
[71] Tom Perry 22/06/2016: 'Conflict among U.S. allies in northern Syria clouds war on Islamic State', *Reuters*, http://www.reuters.com/article/us-mideast-crisis-syria-north-insight-idUSKCN0Z8238 (last accessed 01/06/2017).

Cooperation and disagreement between the PYD and KNC

The PYD and the KNC signed three power-sharing agreements which were mediated by the KDP Iraq. The Erbil Agreement (11 June 2012) set in motion the formation of the Supreme Kurdish Committee (SKC) to coordinate political and diplomatic work and develop a unified political objective. Additional joint committees were to be formed to coordinate practical work and protection. On 1 July a supplementary agreement outlining the functions of the SKC was signed and a committee formed of five representatives of each side was established on 9–10 July. Within days, the PYD stepped in to fill the governance vacuum left by the withdrawal of the Syrian government's administrative and security forces and it declared nine towns and the Ashrafiyah and Sheikh Maqsud neighbourhoods of Aleppo liberated. These unilateral actions taken by the PYD caused tensions between the KNC and the PYD to escalate and the Erbil agreement to derail. The two sides were brought together once again in late September 2012. The Erbil II agreement was an attempt to iron out differences between the two parties and to focus on reconciliation, power-sharing, joint administration and security within the SKC. By the end of 2013 the SKC was completely obsolete.

A further attempt to reach a lasting power-sharing agreement was made in Duhok on 22 October 2014. The Duhok Agreement was mediated by Massoud Barzani and reached in the midst of the ISIS siege on Kobani. Representatives of the PYD and KNC parties agreed to set up a thirty-member power-sharing council to run the Kurdish cantons in Syria and to form a joint military force. The main PYD and KNC elements would have twelve seats each. Simultaneously, the decision was made by the KRG to send Peshmerga forces to Kobani to assist the besieged YPG retake the town. The agreement was interpreted by many as symbolic of the Kurds uniting in the face of a common enemy. Differences between local political parties, however, were not bridged and power sharing failed.

Each side blamed the other for the failure of these agreements. The KNC cited unilateral decision-making by the PYD as a cause for its withdrawal from the SKC on 8 December 2013. The decisions to form local administrations based on the principles of democratic autonomy and to divide Kurdish areas into three cantons were pursued without participation of other major Kurdish political parties and the KNC. PYD representatives, however, stressed that the KNC parties had been asked to participate but had refused to respect the council system, leading to their exclusion from it. Security also became an obstacle preventing cooperation. The KNC's requests that the *Rojava Peshmerga*, located in the KRI, return to Syria were denied by the PYD. Instead the PYD suggested that the members of the *Rojava Peshmerga* join, as individuals, the ranks of the YPG, in order to prevent the existence of potentially hostile military blocs. Despite these three agreements, cooperation between the PYD and the KNC proved untenable. To understand why this was so and what this meant for wider questions of representation for Kurds in Syria a closer examination of the differences between the two blocs follows.

A comparison of political values

The KNC parties lagged behind the PYD in the formulation of policies and gaols that responded to the crisis in Syria. Historical limitations on their ability to seek power or mobilize society left the parties of the 1957 genealogy with underdeveloped and untested policies, which they were slow to reform after March 2011. In comparison, the PYD's social project and opportunistic occupation of political, social and economic voids in northern Syria necessitated the development and continuous adaptation of that party's policy and procedures. On the one side, the KNC and constituent parties were left to catch up on developing and defining clearly their position on a number of pertinent policy questions. On the other, pinning down PYD policy became complicated by the frequent changes to it, to the administrative structures and to the relations between constituent organizations. Nonetheless, significant differences in policy and method could be identified and described; in particular, the different approaches to 'democracy' and the role of the individual, national and ethnic rights, women's rights and, finally, what these meant for their visions of future representation in Syria and policy application.

Democracy and the individual

Both the PYD and the KNC parties declared a central commitment to 'democracy'. Definitions of democracy, however, are not always straightforward and models of democracy differ significantly. Ideals of democracy are commonly associated with fair representation of the 'people' or 'the ruled'. But the basic concept of a model of a government in which people rule is problematized by differing definitions of 'the people' and the exact meanings of 'rule' and 'rule by'.

Such an exercise demonstrates the scope of possible variances in meaning – for example, positions on the accountability of rulers, the contractual obligations of those ruled and the role of non-participants. The models of democracy envisaged by different political groups within what was broadly defined as the Syrian opposition were widely different. For the Syrian state itself, the definition of the 'people' as Arab denied representation to people of Kurdish ethnicity generating inequalities in representation as well as in development, culture and opportunity. As a consequence, Kurdish party understandings of democracy became grounded in the pursuit of ethnic representation and equality in all areas. Indeed, central to that thought was the idea that the Kurdish issue and the equal representation of ethnic groups was fundamental to achieving representative democracy in Syria and in the Middle East.

Within the Kurdish political field itself, the extension of representation to the Kurds and other marginalized groups became fundamental to their politics, regardless of the broad political cleavages that distinguished the two blocs within Syria. Many of their desired outcomes, in terms of representation, were similar. Both the PYD and the KNC shared the vision of reducing arbitrary power of the state over Kurdish issues and its intrusive powers in society. They shared the desire to meet political, economic and social conditions for the development of the people and the regions as a basis for producing democracy, equality and freedom. Their models of democracy, however, and prescriptions on how it should be pursued were defined in markedly different terms.

The KNC's political goals and platform were shaped around the achievement of democracy and equality through decentralization, Kurdish self-determination and an attempt to define legitimate power in relation to Kurdish issues. The parties of the 1957 genealogy use concepts of democracy commonly associated with a Western political system of participatory elective democracy. 'Democracy' itself was not problematized nor were further stipulations made about its definition within the discourse of these parties. Self-determination and political decentralization, however, were seen as key to its realization. Democracy as a model of government was based on representative democracy and the election of officials to represent the interest of citizens within the framework of the rule of law. It was understood to define political and economic boundaries over which rights of (Kurdish) individuals could not be negated and it went hand in hand with political pluralism, fair electoral processes, human rights, justice and equality which were central tenants of these parties' policies and those of the KNC. Self-determination and political decentralization were defined as the means to achieve a fair distribution of power[72] that would allow decisions about regional matters to be taken within the Kurdish communities. The KNC went one step further than most individual political parties by declaring federalism to be their preferred model for government in Syria and 'an essential corner stone for a just, democratic, and united Syria'.[73] It positioned itself as a democratic force in opposition to the Assad government and to the PYD-led administration, which it described as repressive and as a dictatorship.[74]

The PYD definition of democracy was given greater attention and clarification through its connection to the ideology and theories of Abdullah Öcalan. According to Öcalan, democracy in the Middle East could not be achieved within the nation state system; hence, the promotion of the alternative social paradigm of a nation of peoples united by participation in local self-administration. The model of democracy was one based on direct participation of citizens in decision-making on public affairs through communes and local councils: a grass-roots direct democracy. The citizen and the development of his/her identity played an integral part in the functioning of democracy itself. In contrast to the parties of 1957, the PYD projected an identity based on Abdullah Öcalan theories and the PKK version of the 'New Man'. The activist was expected to dedicate him/herself completely to the party and in doing so break from a flawed understanding his/her past existence and transform through social revolution to become a liberated new man.[75] Öcalan adapted Kurdish nationalism and Marxism to support his party's mechanisms for preventing subversion within them. Education, training and supervision centred on notions of humanism, individual emancipation, liberated personality and self-criticism: the Kurds within the party were being liberated from enslavement and alienation both by Turkey and by traditional social structures.[76] Öcalan projected an ideal of the transhistorical or 'pure' and 'authentic' Kurdish identity, which had been distorted by enslavement and persecution, alienation and inequality.[77] Thus, in Syria, the expression of an 'authentic' Kurdish identity was intrinsically bound up with the PYD-led political project and 'social revolution' in that country and beyond it. In comparison to

---

[72] Political programme: Partiya Yekîtî ya Kurd li Sûriyê Article IV.2.
[73] KNC 05/07/2016: 'Position of the Kurdish National Council on Political Decentralization, Federalism and Local Governance'. http://knc-geneva.org/wp-content/uploads/2016/07/KNC-Federalism-and-Decentralisation.pdf (last accessed 11/07/2017).
[74] KNC 18/11/2016: 'Amude – Along the lines of Stalinism: PYD security forces shut down another radio and raid Yekiti office', available on http://knc-geneva.org/?p=795&lang=en (last accessed 29/11/2016).
[75] Grojean, 'The production of the new man within the PKK'.
[76] Ibid., 4.
[77] de Jong 18/03/2016: 'The new-old PKK', *Jacobin*, https://www.jacobinmag.com/2016/03/pkk-ocalan-kurdistan-isis-murray-bookchin/ (last accessed 10/10/2016).

the educational doctrines of the 1957 genealogy of parties, which promoted the development of the Kurdish intellect through culture, learning and 'civilization', in Öcalan's theories intellect was gained through loyalty and self-criticism rather than through formal education.[78]

For the PYD, the practice of democracy occurred as individuals come together within a local commune. Within the commune, local matters, disputes and problems should be discussed and, where possible, resolved without resort to higher state authorities or courts. At the centre of that organization was the individual which through education, training and indoctrination was liberated, transformed and who emerged entirely dedicated to the system. While the commune could accommodate non-partisan individuals, the commune system should be implicitly accepted as a means of representation and decision-making. This social revolution envisaged within Öcalan's theories and the practical implementation of democratic autonomy in northern Syria allowed the PYD to rapidly expand its popular base without relying on, or being hindered by, pre-existing power based networks, as other Kurdish parties had been. The adulation of the person and theories of Abdullah Öcalan released the political movement from the traditional power structures that underlay Kurdish society and Kurdish politics more generally.

This system of direct democracy through councils is examined further in the following chapter in which its application in practice is also assessed. At the time of writing, the application and development of the PYD model was ongoing and fluid. In comparison to the KNC policy, which was based on reforms, democratization and the decentralization of existing structures of power and governance, the exact revolutionary processes through which individuals would be 'liberated' from hierarchical bonds and through which the PYD vision of 'democracy' could be achieved was not elaborated on.

National and ethnic rights

The KNC parties associated the repression of Kurdish ethnic identity by the state with an existential threat and attributed to the Kurds legitimate rights to national self-determination which were bound intrinsically to building a representative democracy in Syria. In the tradition of the 1957 genealogy of parties, the party's role in society was described as one of building Kurdish

---

[78] Grojean, 'The production of the new man within the PKK', 9.

consciousness and self-reliance through civil society.[79] The *al-Wahda* Party of Sheikh Ali, focused its political programme on the constitutional recognition of the Kurdish nation in Syria, lifting oppression from it and granting legitimate rights to Kurds, all within the framework of the unity of the state.[80] The parties of the 1957 genealogy had not changed their political programmes significantly during their lifetime, reflecting the controlled and static political environment that they developed and operated in, as well reflecting their need to survive it. This began to shift as the Syrian crisis continued. Parties began to move beyond their developmental legacy and their observance of taboos, which had married them to an unfavourable modus vivendi with the government. By January 2017, three parties had chosen to include the word 'Kurdistan' in their party names.[81]

Although the PKK, during the 1980s, supported the idea of liberation through the establishment of a Kurdish nation state and the capturing or overthrow of state power in Turkey, Abdullah Öcalan's arrest in 1999 led to a decisive paradigm shift in its ideology and understanding of how Kurdish liberation could be achieved. Öcalan cast off Kurdish ethno-nationalism as the driving force of the PKK/PYD political agenda, focusing rather on the theoretical construction of a 'democratic nation' and cooperative 'communities', democratic autonomy and its practical application in Kurdistan through a confederation within sovereign entities.[82] It was understood as a continuous and long-term social and institutional project or 'revolution' investing economic, social and political sovereignty in all parts of society.[83] Accordingly, the PYD also rejected organization around the concept of national or ethnic rights or a territory defined by ethnic identity, opting instead for the promotion of universal rights and democratic autonomy within which Kurdish or other identities would be represented through communal organizations.

The political programme was changed in 2015 to reflect this departure from framing Kurdish identity in nationalist terms and the need to de-ethnicize the political project in northern Syria and locate it within the social structures of the region. The PYD programme still referred to the Kurds as an ethnic group, but this was framed within the primary context of the democratic autonomy project.

---

[79] Political programme: Partiya Yekîtî ya Kurd li Sûriyê 2009.

[80] Party programme: *al-Wahda*, n.d.

[81] *al-Wahda* of Kamiran Haj Abdu, which split from the original party in 2015, renamed this faction as the Democratic Union Party of Kurdistan. Other parties using the word Kurdistan were the Kurdistan Union Party which adopted the name in 2005 and the Kurdistan Democratic Party-Syria formed in 2014.

[82] Abdullah Öcalan 2009: *War and Peace in Kurdistan*, International Initiative Edition in Cooperation with Mesopotamian Publishers, Neuss, 32.

[83] Öcalan, *War and Peace in Kurdistan*.

Officials within the Administration, however, continued to use Kurdishness and ideas of distinct Kurdish rights as legitimate rallying calls. Outside observers and many of its supporters continued to define the PYD and its governance structures as 'Kurdish' and much of their popular support and legitimacy rested on this identity.[84] Notably, the 2013 Rules of Procedure governing the YPG included significantly more references to the Kurdish identity than the PYD party programme, such as the 'Kurdish people', 'Western Kurdistan' and 'free Kurdistan'.[85] The official YPG website also described the YPG as the security forces of a 'free Rojava' and 'democratic Syria'.[86] Nevertheless, in the governance void left by the retreat of the state from northern Syria, the PYD-led self-administration had bypassed policies, laws and practices of the Baath government that discriminated against Kurds and had replaced them with its own authority and institutions. Promoting Kurdish language and identity became central components of the practical political and social landscape projected and developed by the Administration that enabled it to gain popular legitimacy. While the Kurds, as an ethnically defined group, were central to the success of the PYD project and to its claims to legitimacy, the project in Syria stretched far beyond any ethno-political landscape to the extent that, within the political rhetoric of the Administration, reference to the Kurds, Kurdish identity or Kurdistan was limited. Instead the Administration projected its own symbols and identity based on the democratic moral society and the sacrifice of martyrs for that cause.

Women's rights

The issue of women's rights and representation was an area in which the PYD and its Administration heavily enforced regulation and encouraged social change. Gender issues became central to the PYD policy and revolutionary project after the start of the Syrian crisis and the rapid expansion of the PYD democratic autonomy project. From 2012, every position within the Administration had to be co-chaired by a man and a woman. In every council a ratio of 40 per cent women had to be filled. Women's associations existed within every commune and at every level of the system. Laws were enacted to redress inequalities

[84] IIST surveys showed that many people were satisfied with the Rojava administration because it was Kurdish and officials spoke Kurdish.
[85] The words 'Kurdish people', 'Western Kurdistan' and 'free Kurdistan' (see Arabic version Article 3) and simply 'Kurdistan' can be found in Articles 1,3,5,7,16, of the PYD Rules of Procedure, 2013 (HRW 2014: Appendix II).
[86] See the YPG homepage: https://www.ypgrojava.org/arabic (last accessed 01/02/2017).

entrenched in Syrian state laws and domestic violence against women was treated very seriously. Institutions aimed at protecting women from domestic violence and mediating in relationships were established and the numbers of women using them suggested that normative changes had begun to occur.

While women's rights in Syria were never formally protected or enhanced under state law, Kurdish women often experienced more liberal cultural norms held by Kurdish communities generally and promoted by political parties. In many communities the practice of wearing headscarves was not commonly observed, segregation was minimal and participation of women in traditionally male-dominated activities was in many cases less restricted than in other areas of Syria.[87] In more heavily religious or traditional communities, adherence to social norms such as wearing headscarves publicly was more common. This still largely depended on family and individual beliefs and customs. Women continued to face stigma surrounding public roles and traversing traditionally male-dominated territories remained challenging for them.

Women always had a presence in the Kurdish political movement in Syria, which ebbed and flowed in accordance with the wider social environment in the country. The political programmes of all other Kurdish political parties as well as the KNC included stipulations about women's rights. For example, Article II.9 of the Kurdish *Yekîtî* party programme described a community policy of

> supporting women in their quest for education at all levels, and the right to work and freedom of opinion, and the participation alongside men in the national democratic struggle, so that to achieve their equality with men, and to reject the mentality of underestimating their role and capabilities.

And on the national level, of

> realizing the principle of equality between men and women, and ensure the rights of all, in line with the principles of the secular state and the laws of the international community in this regard, it must also respect and protect the rights of children and to ensure their full sponsorship.[88]

Again, there was little elaboration on broad statements of belief in equality and, in practice, the traditional leadership of the KNC parties was dominated by men, while the PYD and TEV-DEM had significantly more female leaders as a result of their legislations.

---

[87] The position of women and commonality of covering hair and observing segregation varied considerably between areas.
[88] Party programme: Partiya Yekîtî ya Kurd li Sûriyê 2009, Article V.10.

In examining the PYD position on women's rights and emancipation it is necessary to return again to Abdullah Öcalan's theories. Here, women are intrinsic to universal emancipation and, consequently, to the social revolution envisaged by it:

> Without gender equality, no demand for freedom and equality can be meaningful. In fact, freedom and equality cannot be realised without the achievement of gender equality. The most permanent and comprehensive component of democratisation is woman's freedom.[89]

Women's rights became central to revolution – 'The role the working class have once played, must now be taken over by the sisterhood of women'[90] – and central to the liberation of men.

With the retreat of the state from northern Syria the PYD gained the opportunity and capacity to institutionalize women's equality. The process and the focus on women were seized upon by media around the world. In practice, organization and policy differed between cantons and different social needs.[91] For example, in Afrin, where tribal structures were weak and women's roles in society were less restricted, attention was given to facilitating the integration of refugee populations to this society and preventing violence against women.[92] In Kobani, greater importance was placed on preventing sexual violence against women and allowing 'a positive social climate to emerge'.[93] Surveys conducted in Syria in 2016 showed that women's rights was one of the primary developments associated with the PYD-led administration.[94] Women participating in the administration and in the YPG were, in general, positive about their experience and conveyed a sense of 'liberation' from attitudes associated with traditional society.[95] The women's organization, Yekîtiya Star, operated within communes to offer political education focused on the agenda of the revolution and the council system.[96] The stress on education and empowerment of women stimulated changes in attitude and in participation by women themselves as

---

[89] Abdullah Öcalan 2013: *Liberating Life: Women's Revolution*, International Initiative Edition in Cooperation with Mesopotamian Publishers, Neuss, 52.

[90] Öcalan, *Liberating Life: Women's Revolution*.

[91] Knapp, Flach and Ayboga, *Revolution in Rojava*, 67–9.

[92] Ibid., 68.

[93] Ilham Ahmed cited by Knapp, Flach and Ayboga, *Revolution in Rojava*, 68.

[94] When asked to choose what participants associated with 'Rojava', 'women's rights' was selected by 98/180 participants, ranking second after security.

[95] See for example, Glen Johnson 29/10/2013: 'Meet the Kurdish Female freedom fighters of Syria', *Vice*, (online) https://www.vice.com/en_us/article/meet-the-kurdish-female-freedom-fighters-of-syria (accessed 13/01/2017).

[96] Knapp, Flach and Ayboga, *Revolution in Rojava*, 64–5.

well as by men. While women had clearly benefited from this focus on gender, surveys and conversations with Syrian Kurdish women indicated that some felt uncomfortable with the ideologizing of women's rights, the implicit associations of liberation with militarization and the method of implementation of equalities, while some men considered these a practical threat to traditional customs and identity.

Dissected, the category of 'women' itself is controversial in Abdullah Öcalan's theories. According to Öcalan, women were biologically more compassionate and empathic than men, had more 'emotional intelligence' and were closer to nature than men as a result of their biological role and association of women with motherhood.[97]

> Woman's authority is not based on surplus product; on the contrary, it stems from fertility and productivity, and strengthens social existence. Strongly influenced by emotional intelligence, she is tightly bound to communal existence.[98]

> The natural consequence of their differing physiques is that woman's emotional intelligence is much stronger than man's is. Emotional intelligence is connected to life; it is the intelligence that governs empathy and sympathy. Even when woman's analytic intelligence develops, her emotional intelligence gives her the talent to live a balanced life, to be devoted to life, not to be destructive.[99]

> Woman's link with life is more comprehensive than man's and this has ensured the development of her emotional intelligence. Therefore, aesthetics, in the sense of making life more beautiful, is an existential matter for woman. Ethically, woman is far more responsible than man. Thus, woman's behaviour with regard to morality and political society will be more realistic and responsible than man's. She is thus well suited to analyse, determine and decide on the good and bad aspects of education, the importance of life and peace, the malice and horror of war, and measures of appropriateness and justice.[100]

While women's right to legal equality and equality in participation had been enforced in the PYD regions, Öcalan's view of women can be seen as essentialist. Öcalan spoke of 'emotional intelligence of woman that created wonders, that was humane and committed to nature and life',[101] and collapsed biological functions into generalized social characteristics. For many within social constructionism

---

[97] de Jong, 'The new-old PKK'.
[98] Öcalan, *Liberating Life: Women's Revolution*, 26.
[99] Ibid., 50–1.
[100] Ibid., 56.
[101] Ibid., 22.

and feminist theory essentialism is critiqued as having a negative effect on women's liberation and gender equality. The participation of women in Rojava's security services in particular, and the creation of the women's defence unit, the YPJ, had certainly done much to challenge and break down more traditional social understandings of women's roles. And in practice, the active participation of women in all aspects of social, political, military and economic life had empowered some women and challenged the patriarchal norms of Kurdish society. However, Öcalan's essentialist understanding of women and the connection of women's associations and organizations to ideologically driven institutions and system of government remained problematic.

The future of Syria

On questions of what rights and forms of representation should be available, Kurdish political parties supported the same basic stipulations that promoted a pluralistic and democratic state, with decentralized structures that protected the interests of different groups. As a result of the conflict in Syria, both the PYD and the KNC parties called for a federal solution to problems of representation in Syria and saw it as the only viable means of guaranteeing Kurdish rights and representation as well as the unity of the Syrian state.[102] Decentralized government and the devolution of decision-making to local councils was also a popular choice according to survey data collected in Syria. Both political blocs were committed to the territorial integrity of the Syrian state but asserted the importance of recognizing the multicultural and multi-ethnic character of the Syrian people.

Fundamental difference between the PYD and the KNC models occurred in their associations of identity with territory. The KNC supported the idea of a geographical federal region akin to the Federal Kurdistan Region of Iraq, defined territorially by Kurdish ethno-national historiography and carrying the name 'Kurdistan', while also including other national, ethnic and religious groups.[103] The hybrid structure and system of federalism proposed by the PYD and Administration was significantly different to the KRI model preferred by the KNC parties. In the words the PYD co-chair Salih Muslim:

> We think of a democratic nation or democratic state, they [the KNC] are still looking for a nation-state, which is different. We accept pluralism for living

---

[102] IIST interview: Kamiran Haj Abdo (KDP-S) by Skype, 10/03/2016.
[103] IIST interview: Majdal Dalil, Yekiti, Qamishli, 01/03/2016.

together with Arabs and other components [ethnic groups]. They are calling for a nation-state for the Kurdish people. They cannot accept Arabs and other minorities.[104]

The PYD defined the boundaries of its federal entity through participation. In line with the de-ethnicization of the PKK project and of the Administration in northern Syria, TEV-DEM rejected the establishment of a federal system based on Kurdish identity or on a specific geographical territory associated with 'Kurdistan,' envisaging a system in which different areas could govern themselves but also form part of a single federal council. Salih Muslim stated: 'The federalism we talk about is not a geographical line. Maybe tomorrow it's going to be expanded to Raqqa, and other places. … Maybe even the people of Daraa will join.'[105] This de-ethnicization of the administrative system and broadening of political alliances occurred in parallel with increased international and regional involvement in Syria. The adaption of the administration to the evolving situation in Syria involved securing alliances and the participation of the diverse groups in northern Syria.

The KNC, like the wider Syrian opposition and the Assad government, denounced the PYD declaration of federalism for northern Syria in March 2016. Despite also supporting federalism as a solution, the KNC described the announcement as damaging and unilateral, stressing that federalism should result from process on a Syrian national level and in 'complete compliance with international resolutions, led by United Nations Resolution 2254, which calls for resolving the Syrian crisis politically according to the outcomes of Geneva I and its connected resolutions'. The KNC stressed the need to negotiate the terms of federalism within the wider Syrian context and in parallel to 'a constitution defining standards that cannot be subject to challenge (e.g. the equality between men and women), the division of powers, and fair electoral laws'.[106]

Despite the non-ethnic character of the Democratic Federal Northern Syria, the model was not accepted by all in the region. A coalition of Arab and Turkmen tribes rejected the proposed constitutions of the PYD and the KNC and instead asserted the need for a single constitution guaranteeing rights and liberties

---

[104] IIST interview: Salih Muslim, Kobani, 26/05/2016.
[105] Wladimir van Wilgenburg 17/03/2016: 'This is a new Syria, not a new Kurdistan', *Middle East Eye*, http://www.middleeasteye.net/news/analysis-kurds-syria-rojava-1925945786 (last accessed 19/10/2016).
[106] KNC Geneva, 'Position of the Kurdish National Council on Political Decentralisation, Federalism and Local Governance', available on http://knc-geneva.org/wp-content/uploads/2016/07/KNC-Fe deralism-and-Decentralisation.pdf (last accessed 18/12/2018).

prepared by representative Syrian people following the fall of the government.[107]
Arab groups, including the main opposition's High Negotiating Committee, the
Turkish-backed *Liwa Ahfad Salaheddin* and the Christian Guardians of Khabour,
maintained that the PYD administration was akin to the division of Syria and
rejected any move that promoted sectarian divisions.[108] More importantly, the
Syrian government and Bashar al-Assad himself rejected the federal system,
describing Democratic Federal Northern Syria as something temporary and not
permissible by law:

> The constitution doesn't allow for it to happen, and amending the constitution
> needs a referendum, and the popular state is not amenable to that trend, even
> among the Kurds themselves. The largest section of the Kurds do not support
> this. (Bashar al-Assad, December 2016)[109]

Internally, within Kurdish society, significant variations in the degree that the
PYD ideology was adopted, even among those who were declared to be PYD
supporters, were observable. Many Kurds supported the outward method and
principles of the party without wholesale abandonment to it or transformation
of their identity, viewing the party more as a vehicle for political representation,
transformation of external environment, social mobilization or power sharing.
Research data from fieldwork in Syria in 2016 demonstrated often stark
variations in the degree of internalization of the PYD ideology and identity
frameworks with many individuals expressing sympathies with the PYD as well
as the KNC, or with the YPG as well as the Peshmerga. It was not uncommon
for traditional leaders to support the PKK or the PYD, despite their theoretical
rejection of traditional socio-economic relations. Other research also suggested
that for many their financial support for the PKK, and cooperation with it
before 1998, was due to its domination of sub-state organization and channels of
representation and mediation, rather than due to personal belief in its political
agenda or theories.

This selective form of affiliation with the party was demonstrated clearly by
the PYD alliance formation outside the ethnically defined parameters of Kurdish

---

[107] Baladi News 04/08/2016: 'A coalition of Arab and Turkmen clans refuses the constitution of the
Kurdish National Council', *Baladi News*, http://baladi-news.com/en/news/details/8874/A_Coalition
_of_Arab_and_Turkmen_Clans_Refuses_the_Constitution_of_the_Kurdish_National_Council
(last accessed 20/10/2016).

[108] See Leith Fadel 08/06/2015: 'Official Statement from the Khabour Assyrian Council of Guardians',
al-Masdar News, http://www.almasdarnews.com/article/official-statement-from-the-khabour-ass
yrian-council-of-guardians/ (last accessed 11/01/2017).

[109] Cited in ARA News 09/12/2016: 'Assad says Kurdish federal zone in Syria "temporary"', http://ara
news.net/2016/12/assad-says-kurdish-federal-zone-in-syria-temporary/ (last accessed 15/05/2017).

society. The PYD and YPG alliances with non-Kurdish political and military groups within the northern regions of Syria demonstrated the Administration's attempts to secure allies as its fight against ISIS spread into more ethnically mixed areas. It was also an attempt to garner wider support for 'democratic confederalism' as a model for political and social organization in northern Syria. While the practical and strategic nature of these relationships was apparent, the ideological content of these alliances was often questionable. Many Arab tribes formed alliances with the PYD in order to gain an advantage in pre-existing, often long-term, tensions with rival tribal groupings, for example, the Shammar of the Jazirah region.[110] While tribal organization was described as a form of enslavement in Öcalan's theories, the tribes and tribal relations in northern Syria were used to extend the political authority of the PYD both within the Kurdish society and in non-Kurdish majority areas of Syria since 2014. The PYD administration itself was careful to allow self-administration by other groups in order to prevent disillusionment with the system and structure of government, but the ideological underpinnings and Kurdish origins of the governance system threatened its sustainability in non-Kurdish areas. This subject is returned to in succeeding chapters. Needless to say, the issue of identity and the connection of the administration with an ideological social project presented complications for the long-term survival of the Administration in northern Syria.

In the following chapter the implementation of the PYD models of democracy is examined in greater detail. Here, the value in comparison of political practice between the PYD and the KNC blocs is limited. The assumption of state-like powers by the PYD and connected institutions and associations within the governance vacuum left by the withdrawal of the state from Kurdish areas enabled these organizations to operate freely and practice politics according to their objectives. In comparison, the KNC reluctance to legitimize what they considered to be a one-party rule by participating within the administrative system left most of the KNC parties unregistered and, therefore, illegal under the PYD law. As a consequence they faced restrictions and their activities, policies and practices were shaped accordingly. Locally, the KNC parties repositioned in opposition to the PYD, while on the wider Syrian field they maintained their role as negotiators of Kurdish rights to equal and fair representation as a distinct national group within the internationally recognized Syrian opposition group

---

[110] See, for example, Wilgenburg 13/12/2013: 'Kurdish strategy towards ethnically-mixed areas in the Syrian conflict', *Terrorism Monitor*, Vol. 11, Issue 23, The Jamestown Foundation, USA, http://www .jamestown.org/programs/tm/single/?tx_ttnews%5Btt_news%5D=41754&cHash=bbedc896f6 cefadf8d7284fe2c7fe764#.V-PTVY-cHmI (last accessed 22/09/2016).

(the SNC). Shared beliefs that certain rights were 'legitimate' or 'natural' and could only be achieved through the decentralization of power to local areas and populations were overshadowed by seemingly unbridgeable fissures between the KNC and the PYD. What fundamentally divided these two blocs were their methods, understandings of identity and representation and the social conditions necessary to develop democracy; one firmly rooted in the social structures and territory that helped many people locate and define Kurdish national identity, the other revolutionary, seeking to replace existing local social structures and create a parallel democratic structure of governance.

Differences in political alignments within and outside the Kurdish field also underpinned divisions between the PYD and the KNC and played pivotal roles in the events unfolding in Syria. Neither the PYD nor the parties of the KNC, individually or as blocs, were capable of securing gains made in northern Syria without the external support of other Kurdish political parties or Western military aid. At the time of writing, the balance of power and resources in the region was heavily in favour of the PYD and its administration. The investment of foreign powers in fighting ISIS in northern Syria was successfully exploited to build and strengthen the legitimacy of the ruling powers there. In comparison, the KNC drew its resources and legitimacy less successfully, given the priorities of international coalitions, from within the wider opposition against the Assad government. These parallel trajectories, unbalanced by the priorities of foreign powers, are looked at in more detail in Chapter 5 on regional and international relations.

Their differing political and methodological approaches towards the Syrian protest movement set the two blocs further apart. The PYD (and related organizations) took advantage of the political vacuum caused by the Syrian crisis and the conflict with ISIS to entrench its position in northern Syria through well-organized military mobilization in July 2012. In comparison, the parties of the 1957 genealogy had struggled to position themselves within the crisis environment and to gain or assert power equivalent to the PYD. Their history of management of the status quo hindered their ability to adapt to the changes that occurred while the PYD's flexible and opportunistic approach facilitated its encroachment in ever-increasing areas of civil and political life. Whereas the 1957 parties worked with existing social structures and networks within Kurdish society, the PYD's revolutionary ideology sought to replace them and was, therefore, unhindered by socio-economic divisions and local conditions that informed and supported the 1957 parties and the fractures within this bloc. This factor, combined with resources and capacity to mobilize that its connection to the PKK gave it, expedited a rapid growth in the PYD's organizational capacity and facilitated its hegemonic expansion across the political, social and economic fields. The KNC's position in opposition to the PYD, while a persistent feature of post-2011 Syria, was marred by internal divisions between political parties themselves, as well as by the socio-economic divisions that characterized Kurdish society.

3

PYD-led Governance Structures:
From DAAs to Federalism

The practical implementation and form of the 'self-rule' project has changed several times in the course of the conflict in Syria – a fact that complicates description of its morphing governance structures. Different administrative structures and titles have applied to different stages, organizations and institutions within a relatively short historical period. The system which, in this book, is commonly referred to as the DAAs – and was declared in January 2014 – has been referred to by the PYD as the 'Interim Transitional Administration' (in 2013) and as the Democratic Self-Rule Administration-Rojava.[1] The areas under its governance have been called 'Western Kurdistan', 'the Autonomous Regions',[2] 'Rojava', Federal Northern Syria, the democratic confederalist autonomous areas of northern Syria; and in late 2015, the Federation of Northern Syria-Rojava and, from December 2016, the Democratic Federation of Northern Syria. In September 2018 the form of governance reverted to self-administration when a Self-Administration in Northern and Eastern Syria was formed to include SDF controlled areas around Raqqah, Manbij and Deir al-Zour. These changes in names and organization reflected various attempts to alter the external appearance of the Administration, de-ethnicize it, widen its appeal and meet pressures and satisfy concerns that inevitably arose from forming alliances, securing external support and building legitimacy. Consequently, these variations on the system and its institutions have overlapped, co-existed or dissipated.[3] Changes to names and

---

[1] Foreign Relations body of Democratic Self-rule Administration-Rojava, n.d. 2014: 'The Democratic Self-Rule Administration's Response to the Report of Human Rights Watch Organization', published by *Human Rights Watch*, https://www.hrw.org/sites/default/files/related_material/The%20Democratic%20SelfRule%20Administration%E2%80%99s%20Response%20to%20the%20Report%20of%20Human%20Rights%20Watch%20Organization.pdf (last accessed 04/04/2017)..

[2] The Charter of the Social Contract 29/01/2014, (available in HRW June 2014: 'Under Kurdish Rule', Appendix I, p. 54, https://www.hrw.org/sites/default/files/reports/syria0614_kurds_ForUpload.pdf (last accessed 20/08/2017).

[3] For example, the DAA is described as being part of the Federal System of Northern Syria/Rojava in Knapp, Flach and Ayboga, *Revolution in Rojava*, 92.

structures of governance were internal processes, not subject to public scrutiny or explanation. Added to this, difficulties arising from translations of names from Kurdish and Arabic to English led different analysts and commentators to employ different names. This inevitably increased confusion about the system and made unravelling the administrative structures more problematic. Public information online and published in the few books on the subject continued to refer to organizations such as the Peoples Council of Western Kurdistan (PCWK) as a leading organization in the governance of the areas,[4] while officials within the administration claimed that it did not exist anymore.[5]

The continuing crisis in Syria, proxy wars and tangled international relations promised to maintain this volatility, induce further changes and present future challenges. In what follows, a window to the Administration and its development through the course of the Syrian crisis is opened. Following this, the main institutions of government, its representative channels, the economy, education, media and security are examined, demonstrating and delineating the extent of its authority and penetration of society. The third section looks specifically at the move towards federalism, its driving forces and the obstacles to its realization. Through this, the PYD-led administration and its narrative on identity and representation are given the clarity necessary for understanding popular reactions to its governance structures and its potential for representation of diverse identities present in northern Syria.

The development of 'democratic autonomy': From the PYD to a federal region in under five years

The governance system in northern Syria began to grow after March 2011 from seeds distributed by the PYD. The PYD first adopted the 'democratic autonomy' project in 2007.[6] Under Baath Party rule implementation of its doctrine was limited to isolated local social projects which gained very little attention and did not challenge the pre-existing sub-state social structures directly. The weakening of central governance structures after March 2011 provided opportunity to seize greater autonomy and the PYD began expanding its civil organizations and forming armed groups on the local levels. This expansion and coordination

---

[4] For example Knapp, Flach and Ayboga, *Revolution in Rojava*.
[5] IIST email correspondence: Sinem Mohammed, EU representative of Rojava administrations, 10/10/2016.
[6] Foreign Relations body of Democratic Self-rule Administration-Rojava, n.d. 2014.

of it within the framework of the democratic autonomy project led to the establishment of an umbrella organization, TEV-DEM, in 2011. TEV-DEM also included civil organizations such as the women's movement Yekîtiya Star, youth and student organizations, cultural foundations, collectives, and other political parties, and went on to become one of the most important bodies coordinating the communes and council systems.

The PYD and its armed groups gradually asserted control, establishing armed checkpoints, first in the Afrin region, extending later to Kobani and, in June 2012, to Qamishli and other parts of Hasakah province.[7] Checkpoints were erected, initially, in parallel to Syrian government security services and structures.[8] The spread of the YPG checkpoints stirred tensions between the KNC and the PYD and many KNC activists and others resisting their establishment were arrested by PYD security personnel.[9] The PYD military dominance and assertion of local authority through armed forces gathered pace as the civil unrest in Syria militarized in early 2012. The PYD established courts and prisons in Afrin[10] and prevented other Kurdish parties from setting up their own small armed units.[11] In July 2012, as Syrian government personnel began its withdrawal from large parts of northern Syria and its army was redeployed against opposition rebels in the Damascus-Aleppo corridor, the PYD stepped into the governance void and took over key services and practical administrative duties. The Kurdish identity of the PYD and its military forces allowed the organization to extend its influence in a manner unparalleled in Syria.

The PYD's extension of power in northern Syria was facilitated by its active mobilization, increased popular identification with the organization, as well as by its efforts to prevent inter-Kurdish fighting. There were still attempts to challenge the PYD's growing authority: localized acts of community resistance occurred, small Kurdish factions tried to set up their own militias affiliated to

---

[7] KurdWatch 12/06/2012: 'Al-Qamishli: Further demonstrations—for the first time, the PYD constructs check points in alQamishli', *KurdWatch*, http://www.kurdwatch.org/index.php?aid=2555&z=en (last accessed 15/05/2017).

[8] Allsopp, *The Kurds of Syria*, 208.

[9] Ibid., 211–12; KurdWatch 02/06/2012: 'Afrin: Free Syrian Army attacks PYD and regime', http://www.kurdwatch.org/index.php?aid=2547&z=en (last accessed 15/05/2017); KurdWatch 11/06/2012(a): 'Afrin: Participants in a meeting of the Kurdish National Council kidnapped by the PYD', *KurdWatch*, http://www.kurdwatch.org/index.php?aid=2554&z=en&cure=245 (last accessed 15/05/2017); KurdWatch 11/06/2012(b): 'Afrin: PYD forces the construction of a checkpoint by kidnapping activists', *KurdWatch*, http://www.kurdwatch.org/index.php?aid=2552&z=en (last accessed 15/05/2017); KurdWatch 21/12/2012: 'Al-Qamishli: Armed attack on PYDcheckpoint', *KurdWatch*, http://www.kurdwatch.org/index.php?aid=2587&z=en (last accessed 15/05/2017).

[10] KurdWatch 11/06/2012(c): 'Afrin: PYD establishes courts', *KurdWatch*, http://www.kurdwatch.org/index.php?aid=2553&z=en (last accessed 15/05/2017).

[11] See, for example, Wilgenburg 21/02/2013: 'Border arrests reveal disunity, conflict among Syrian Kurds', *Al Monitor*, http://www.al-monitor.com/pulse/originals/2013/05/pyd-arrests-syrian-kurds.html (last accessed 05/04/2016).

the FSA[12] and other Kurdish political parties attempted to form armed militias.[13] Most of them were overcome, however, or disbanded by the PYD-linked security organizations.[14] Moreover, there was little appetite for an intra-Kurdish conflict. Despite opposition to the PYD power grab, the weakness of coordinated political organization and of armed mobilization by other Kurdish parties left the PYD largely unchecked and it became the primary mobilizing organization among the Syrian Kurds. External mediation in inter-Kurdish conflict by Masoud Barzani concentrated on negotiated power-sharing. The July 2012 Erbil agreement and the subsequent formation of the SKC to jointly administer these Kurdish areas failed to overcome the deep-rooted differences and inequalities in resources and in organizational and decision-making capacities between the PYD and the KNC. Any attempts to balance disparities in power finally ended in November 2013 when the PYD declared the establishment of a new decentralized administrative system and the KNC officially withdrew from the SKC.[15]

The decentralization of the system was a response to the non-contiguity of Kurdish majority areas and to the practical difficulties of administering centrally. The division was based on a Swiss canton model but rooted in the democratic autonomy ideology. Direct democracy would be developed through the application of the system. Each canton would have its own administration, legislative assembly and preparation and monitoring committee; it would strive for self-sufficiency. The precise details of the lead up to the declaration of an Interim Administration in November 2013 and the decision to divide the area into three cantons are unclear. Different sources give different accounts of the time, the various organizations consulted and those present in the meetings.[16] It appeared that these decisions were planned months in advance, during the period of SKC rule,[17] but did not involve the KNC.

---

[12] The Meshaal Temmo Brigade and the Salah al-Din Ayoubi Brigade, formed in 2012 in Ras al-Ayn and Afrin respectively, were two examples of local Kurdish FSA affiliated armed groups.

[13] The *Azadi* (Freedom) Party, *Yekiti* Party and KDP-S all established small armed groups. Most of the KNC party militias were disbanded by force. The *Yekiti* militia took over some buildings in Amude when the Syrian regime withdrew. Most defectors from the Syrian Army joined the Rojava Peshmerga in the KRI, not the FSA.

[14] Allsopp, *The Kurds of Syria*, 210.

[15] Wilgenburg 30/12/2013: 'Syrian Kurds agree to disagree', *Al-Monitor*, http://www.al-monitor.com/pulse/originals/2013/12/syria-kurds-geneva-opposition-delegation-peace.html (last accessed 10/03/2017).

[16] For example, Knapp, Flach and Ayboga, *Revolution in Rojava*; Foreign Relations body of Democratic Self-rule Administration-Rojava, n.d. 2014; KNK Belgium.

[17] Knapp, Flach and Ayboga, *Revolution in Rojava*, 110–12; KNK May 2014: 'Canton based democratic autonomy of Rojava (Western Kurdistan – Northern Syria)', *Peace in Kurdistan Campaign*, https://peaceinkurdistancampaign.files.wordpress.com/2011/11/rojava-info-may-2014.pdf (last accessed 05/05/2017).

The declaration forming the Constitutive General Council of the Joint Interim Administration and the decision to divide administration between three cantons was made between 12 and 15 November 2013. According to the PYD, forty-seven civil society organizations and eleven political parties, alongside Arab and Christian organizations, took part in the decision to create the transitional administration.[18] Most of those named had close connections to the PYD itself or were allied to it and many were unheard of before the start of the Syrian civil unrest.[19] On 15 November 2013 a body of sixty canton representatives was established and charged with forming a committee to draft a joint interim constitution, a 'committee on the comprehensive social convention' and a committee for the electoral system.[20] The formal administrative division and autonomy declarations of the Afrin, Kobani and the Jazirah cantons were announced on 21, 27 and 29 January 2014 respectively.[21]

On 29 January 2014 a social contract was also published (the Charter of the Social Contract,) which committed the administration to the development of DAAs and the development of 'the democratic society'.[22] It set out the administrative structures and was committed to ethnic, linguistic and religious pluralism, equality, democracy and local self-government. The charter also opened membership of the canton system that it governed to all towns, cities or villages in Syria that acceded to it[23] making participation voluntary outside the YPG-controlled areas. The PYD was criticized by the KNC, as well as by

[18] Foreign Relations body of Democratic Self-rule Administration-Rojava, n.d. 2014.

[19] Another source states that the conference was attended by eighty-six delegates, and included Kurdish, Arab and Christian representatives. According to the Kurdish National Congress (KNK Belgium) the political parties and organizations in attendance were: Syriac Union Party, Syriac Youth Union, Syriac Cultural Association, Syriac Women's Union, Syriac Academics Union, National Coordination Committee, Syrian National Bloc, Arabic National Commission, Communist Labor Party, Kurdish Leftist Party, Kurdistan Democratic Party, Kurdish Democratic Left Party, Kurdish National Democratic Gathering in Syria, Kurdish Peace Democratic Party, Kurdistan Liberal Union, Kurdish Syrian Democratic Party, The Star Union of Kurdish Woman, Syrian Women's Initiative, Human Rights Activists of Western Kurdistan, Civil Peace Committee, Democratic Union Party (PYD), Shoresh Organization of Women, Management of the Diplomatic Relations of Western Kurdistan, People's Council of Western Kurdistan, Kurdistan Democratic Party in Syria, Organization of the State for the Society and Citizenship, Sarah Organization for the Elimination of Violence against Women, Syria's Future Youth Gathering, Communist Party of Kurdistan, Movement of Democratic Society, Supreme Kurdish Council, Center of the Strategic Studies, Kurdish Students Confederation, Revolutionary Youth Movement and the Young Woman Revolutionary Movement. KNK May 2014: 'Canton Based Democratic Autonomy of Rojava', 10.

[20] KNK Belgium, May 2014: 'Canton based democratic autonomy of Rojava', 10–11.

[21] Kurdistan National Congress (KNK) 07/03/2014 'Briefly history of Syria and Rojava', *KNK*, http://www.kongrakurdistan.net/en/briefly-history-of-syria-and-rojava/ (last accessed 05/05/2017).

[22] Preamble, Social Contract 29/01/2014.

[23] Social Contract, Article 7. How this would occur in practice and the boundaries of such administration were unclear. Although defined by territory, there was no reference in the charter to the territory of the Administration or how it would be defined or managed, other than through participation. This raised questions about jurisdiction of state versus DAA laws, among other issues.

other Syrian opposition groups backed by Turkey, for what was understood to be a unilateral declaration of autonomy, and the administration was accused of cooperating with the Syrian government. The KNC refused to legitimize the canton system by operating within it and expelled parties that opted to cooperate with it. Ahmed Sulaiman, a representative of *Pêşverû*, which had worked with the PYD in 2013 but rejected the charter, explained that 'political decision-making is controlled by TEV-DEM: we cannot join it'.[24] In response, the PYD refuted accusations that it was acting in an authoritarian manner, claiming such allegations were propaganda by Ankara and the KDP.[25] It denied being the 'single authority in Rojava', saying that, although it had drafted the social contract, it had been open to public and professional review and amendments and that the KNC had also been consulted.[26]

The PYD and TEV-DEM claimed that the democratic autonomy project and canton structure offered 'a combination of centralization and decentralization', through which Syria's diverse peoples 'become part of a democratic family in a comprehensively democratic society ... able to ensure the existence of these communities'.[27] Diverse ethnic and religious groups were incorporated within the system through a myriad of institutions, political parties and communal organizations possessing varying degrees of autonomy and governed by the DAAs and interim administration. The principles of equality, participation and pluralism were central to its rhetoric and the council system that it established in Kurdish majority areas, examined further below, was the structure through which these principles could be fashioned through social revolution.

Power structures and constituent parts

Local DAA governance

The egalitarian rhetoric and governance structures of the DAAs attracted attention to the growth of grass-roots mobilization, participation and direct democracy in northern Syria and to the institutionalization of women's rights,

---

[24] Interview: Ahmed Sulaiman, leading member of Progressive Party, Qamishli, 06/05/2016. The Progressive Party stopped working with the PYD in June 2013.

[25] See, for example, Wilgenburg 07/02/2014: 'Relations among Syrian Kurdish parties hit new low', *al-Monitor*, (online) http://www.al-monitor.com/pulse/originals/2014/02/kurdish-party-relations-in-syria-reach-new-lows.html (last accessed 24/03/2017).

[26] Foreign Relations body of Democratic Self-Rule Administration-Rojava, n.d. 2014.

[27] TEV-DEM 16/02/2016.

minority representation and Kurdish language education. All were broadly positive outcomes of Kurdish self-governance, examined further below and in the following chapter. To focus exclusively on these aspects of the DAA government, however, would be to overlook parallel power relations and struggles that overlaid and imbued positive developments towards representation of ethnicity and gender. The governance system, as it existed, could not be untangled from the PYD and its radical philosophy. It incorporated multiple organizations and identities, but decentralization and local autonomy was managed and coordinated by central institutions and organizations that bridged the canton administrations, most prominent among them, the PYD and TEV-DEM – two inextricable organizations. The social revolution aspired to in Abdullah Öcalan's philosophy was incomplete, and driving the reorganization of society was a hierarchy of enlightenment, which positioned 'liberated' individuals in positions of authority within all governance structures, particularly those that coordinated and managed the DAAs.

The PYD, its ideology and relation to the KCK were discussed in the preceding chapter. Within Syria, the PYD led the movement for democratic autonomy. It was the source from which numerous other organizations and movements – civil, political, economic and military – sprung or emerged, or developed 'independently' while employing the same ideology or purpose. Yet, the democratic autonomy project and its philosophical purpose were shared with the PKK and the parallel structures of the KCK. While the PYD had autonomy to pursue and develop governance structures in Syria, it remained accountable within a wider structure and project.

Among organizations involved in public governance and managing the 'social revolution' within Syria, TEV-DEM became the most significant. Its exact role remained clouded by the complexities of the administration, its alliances and expansive networks and organizational structures. Added to this, official publications and commentaries by external observers focused largely on reportage and on grass-roots organization and decision-making rather than on hidden power relations and agency. TEV-DEM was described as both a 'movement' and as a 'coalition' governing the democratic confederal autonomous areas of northern Syria. It had its own executive body: the PYD was one of political organizations within it, along with Yekîtiya Star, the Syriac Union Party and some other previously unheard of political parties such as the Syrian Kurds' Democratic Peace Party of Telal Mihamed and the Kurdistan Liberal Union Party of Ferhad Telo. TEV-DEM both preceded and replaced the SKC which, itself, replaced the PCWK. The dominant organization within all these bodies remained the PYD. In practice, for many, the distinction between the PYD and TEV-DEM remained vague.[28] TEV-DEM in Syria became comparable to the KCK for the system that spans the borders between Kurdish majority areas in Turkey, Iraq, Iran and Syria. Like the KCK, it spawned from the political party itself. While TEV-DEM was not directly connected to the KCK, they were linked through the membership of the PYD and YPG. The DAAs and the proposed federal region in northern Syria were also connected, through the PYD, to a wider 'democratic confederation' encompassing similar structures in all of Turkey, Iraq and Iran.

TEV-DEM was also described as the driver of the social revolution in northern Syria, and as the 'civilian institution of the government' which 'coordinates the communes and council systems'.[29] The implication being that it had a social role and character. The connection of the social revolution to what, at least at present, appeared to be a vanguard authority and a radical political agenda embodied in the PYD (TEV-DEM's founding member), however, implied that its role was intrinsically bound up with the political agenda embodied by the PYD.

TEV-DEM's organization and structure encompassed and connected all the administrative regions and it was represented in the Syrian Democratic Council, (SDC) – the executive body of the Federal Northern Syria. TEV-DEM appointed ministers to the executive council, which acted as a joint coordination committee overseeing the implementation of policies developed by the Federal Assembly or the SDC. The SDC was the political wing of the SDF and was active in forming administrative councils and governing in non-Kurdish majority areas liberated by the SDF, such as those in Manbij and Raqqah. Furthermore, TEV-DEM members played a role in forming civilian councils in Arab towns such as Manbij, Tal Abyad, and Raqqah. Although some distinction between the governance of the Kurdish majority cantons and of the intermediate areas could be made (a subject returned to following further description of the canton administrations), they were connected and managed through TEV-DEM. In March 2018, a new party, the Syria Future Party, was established to further distance the political

[28] Robert Lowe, August 2016: 'Rojava at 4: Examining the experiment in western Kurdistan: Workshop proceedings', LSE, available on http://eprints.lse.ac.uk/67515/1/Rojavaat4.pdf (last accessed 23/03/2017).

[29] Eliza Egret and Tom Anderson 2016: *Struggles for Autonomy in Kurdistan and Corporate Complicity in the Representation of Social movements in Rojava and Bakur.* Corporate Watch, (Online) available on https://corporatewatch.org/sites/default/files/Struggles%20for%20autonomy%20in%20 Kurdistan.pdf and https://cooperativeeconomy.info/a-conversation-with-tev-dems-bedran-gia-kurd/ (last accessed 05/05/2017), 62.

system (at least in public) from PYD and TEV-DEM, although Turkish officials immediately described the party as the 'PYD by another name'.[30]

Under this system of local self-government the local district and neighbourhood councils and, at the base, the communes formed the institutions of direct democracy. The administration of each canton had a legislative assembly, an executive council, supreme constitutional courts, municipal and provincial councils and a high commission of elections. 'The legislative council is the parliament of the canton and who represent the people with 101 members from all cities, components [ethnic groups], both genders, parties and civil society organizations', said a member of the Diwan council of the legislative branch.[31] 'We make decisions to issue laws and decrees just to organize the social life in general instead of the regime according to the general public benefit', she said. According to the social contract, the people of the autonomous regions could 'freely elect their representatives and representative bodies, and may pursue their rights insofar as it does not contravene the articles of the Charter'.[32] Each canton would also send elected representatives to the general legislative council and co-presidents to TEV-DEM, which sat between the executive bodies and canton administrations and supported and coordinated between them. In this capacity TEV-DEM acted as the central or coordinating governing body. Commissions of women, defence, economics, politics, civil society, free society, justice and ideology existed on all levels of the DAA administration and overlapped with those in TEV-DEM. At the time of writing, municipal elections had been held in the Jazirah and Afrin cantons. Commune elections had been held on 22 September 2017 and municipal and canton elections (to elect town, district and canton council members and determine the local governments) on 1 December 2017. The third round of elections, for the Peoples' Congress and Peoples' Parliament of the Democratic Federation of Northern Syria Congress, had been scheduled for 19 January 2018, but was postponed indefinitely.[33] These three elections were held in the Cizîrê (Jazirah), Euphrates and Afrin 'areas' (a term replacing that of 'canton'

---

[30] Sputnik 17/04/2018: 'New Syria's Future Party Not a Kurdish Front, Not Created by US – SFP Head', *Sputnik*, https://sputniknews.com/middleeast/201804171063630023-syria-future-front-pyd-us/ (last accessed 07/05/2018).

[31] IIST interview: Perwin Mohammed Amin, legislative council member, deputy of the co-president, 19/04/2016.

[32] The Charter of the Social Contract, 29/01/2014, Article 8.

[33] ANF News 05/01/2018: 'Northern Syrian Democratic Federation elections postponed', *ANF News*, https://anfenglish.com/news/northern-syrian-democratic-federation-elections-postponed-24031

under the federal system).[34] Despite these elections, the influence of TEV-DEM, the PYD and their allies over governance remained strong.

The legislative councils of each canton were led by a prime minister and two deputies. In 2014 the prime ministers of each canton were listed as belonging to the PYD, as were their two deputies in Afrin and Kobani Cantons. Only in the Jazirah were the deputies drawn from other political backgrounds: one from the Syriac Union Party, ideologically linked to the PKK, and one from the Democratic Socialist Arab Baath Party, which was also a member of the NCB and the Syrian Democratic Council.[35] Ministers were reported to be selected from within the local populations. The executive council of each canton was divided into twenty-two executive council bodies,[36] likened to ministries. In 2016, their number was reduced to sixteen[37] following the development of the federal system.

Decentralized administration and differing needs and circumstances between the three cantons meant that differences in governance and institutions developed between them. Cooperation between the Kobani and the Jazirah cantons was increased in June 2015, when Tal Abyad was captured from ISIS and the two cantons were connected territorially. Nevertheless, the two

---

[34] Mustafa Mamay 30/11/2018: 'Elections in Northern Syria in 5 questions', *ANF News*, https://anfenglish.com/rojava/elections-in-northern-syria-in-5-questions-23426

[35] See, for example, Karlos Zurutuza 28/10/2014: 'Democracy in "radical" in northern Syria', *IPS News*, http://www.ipsnews.net/2014/10/democracy-is-radical-in-northern-syria/ (last accessed 24/03/2017).

[36] For example, the Jazirah canton included the following ministries: Interior Minister; Regional Commissions, Councils and Planning; Finance; Labour and Social Security; Education; Agriculture; Health; Trade and Economy; Martyrs' Families; Culture; Transportation; Youth and Sport; Environment and Tourism; Religious Affairs; Women and Family Affairs; Human Rights; Industry and Commerce; Information and Communication; Justice; and Electricity, Industry and Natural Resources.

[37] The executive council bodies were: (1) Municipalities and Environment Authority (consisting of the following directorates: General Directorate of Environment, Directorate General of Supply (and its branch: the Office of Internal Trade and Consumer Protection), Directorate General of Transport and Communications, the General Directorate of Municipalities, which supervises the work of all Municipalities in the province, and the Directorate General of Drinking Water and Sanitation); (2) Foreign Relations Authority; (3) The defense body; (4)The internal body; (5) Martyrs Affairs Authority; (6) Women's body; (7) Culture and Art Authority (connected to the Directorate General of Arts and Theaters, Directorate General of Literature, Publications and Exhibitions); (8) Tourism and Antiquities Protection Authority; (9) Education Authority; (10) The Economic Commission (consisting of the following directorates: General Directorate of Plant Production, Directorate General of Animal Production, Directorate General of Irrigation and Water Resources, Directorate General of Feed, General Directorate of Badia Island Development, Directorate General of Seed Breeding and Directorate General of Industry and Commerce, External); (11) The Authority of Finance, including the General Administration of Banks and the Directorate General of Customs; (12) Labor and Social Affairs Commission; (13) Health Authority; (14) Energy Authority, (including the following directorates: General Directorate of Electricity, General Directorate of Oil, Gas and Mineral Resources and General Directorate of Communications); (15) Youth Authority; and (16) Justice Commission.

cantons remained administratively separate. The practical implications of this administrative division were demonstrated by looking at the press and freedoms of movement: On the administrative level, the Jazirah canton had developed extensive monitoring of media institutions and regulating the press and work permits,[38] and on 19 December 2015, it introduced a law establishing a press council.[39] These regulations developed in response to a greater media presence and activity in the region due to its proximity to the KRI and to the political diversity within the population there. In comparison, the Kobani administration did not have a press council, which, in practice, complicated the movement of press, as well as NGOs, between the two regions.[40] International NGOs that operated in the cantons also needed permission from the separate canton administrations. A further administrative difference was the formation of a reconstruction board in Kobani in 2014 to manage rebuilding the city and dealing with the destruction. The decision reflected local needs not paralleled in the Jazirah.[41]

Other policies with administration-wide applicability have been applied at different times by the DAAs. When the Law on Mandatory Self Defence Duty (the PYD's term for military service) was adopted by the canton administrations on 14 July 2014, this was implemented in the Jazirah canton only on 20 November 2014.[42] The Kobani administration ratified the law much later, in June 2016, due to the considerable suffering that the population of Kobani had faced during the ISIS siege. The law was implemented when the need for manpower during the Manbij campaign necessitated it. Foreign relations, however, remained one area on which policy was not decentralized.[43] The development of foreign relations

---

[38] Media institutions included a press institution formed by the executive council, which dealt with granting permits – a duty previously handled by the Union of Free Media. See, for example, Hawar News 05/08/2015: 'Rûdaw and Orient TV's work permit cancelled in Cizîre Canton', *Hawar News Agency*, http://en.hawarnews.com/rudaw-and-orient-tvs-work-permit-cancelled-in-cizire-canton/ (last accessed 27 /03/2017); Reporters Without Borders (RSF) 20/01/2016: 'How Kurdistan's PYD keeps the media and news providers in line', *RSF*, https://rsf.org/en/news/how-kurdistans-pyd-keeps-media-and-news-providers-line (last accessed 27/03/2017).

[39] The Jazirah canton administration on 19 December 2015, passed a press law to create a press council, see, KurdWatch 30/06/2013: 'New press law for the Jazirah Canton', *KurdWatch*, http://kurdwatch. org/?e3885 (last accessed 05/05/2017).

[40] Kurdistan 24 reporter Ekrem Salih was temporarily banned from working in the Kobani canton in June 2016 despite having permission from the Jazirah and SDF forces based in Hasakah.

[41] The Independent Board for the Reconstruction of Kobanî, Dr. Musallam Talas 18/12/2014: 'The declaration of the independent board for the reconstruction of Kobanî', available on *Yekiti Media*, http://en.yekiti-media.org/declaration-independent-board-reconstruction-kobani/ (last accessed 05/05/2017).

[42] Danish Immigration Service 26/02/2015: 'Syria: Military service, mandatory self-defence duty and recruitment to the YPG', *Danish Immigration Service*, Copenhagen, available on http://www.refw orld.org/pdfid/54fd6c884.pdf (last accessed 05/05/2017), 16.

[43] IIST interview: Abdul Karim Omer, head of foreign relations, Qamishli, 11/05/2016.

was facilitated by the campaign against ISIS in Syria, and added a further dimension to administration, examined in Chapter 5.

Councils and communes

According to TEV-DEM officials, governance was a bottom-up system following the ideas of Öcalan grass-roots participation. 'It starts with the communes, then councils, and then self-administration', a TEV-DEM official said.[44] 'This is a concept of a new system: in Iraqi Kurdistan it is a centralized system because decisions are made by the top and, for us, it's different, since there will be relations between the bottom and up and if there is any suggestion from the communes it will reach the top', she said, suggesting that members of the communes could give papers to their councils which would be transferred as suggestions to the higher levels of governance. At each level suggestions should be discussed and voted on and, if passed, proceed upwards. Policy areas were similarly divided between the levels of the administration. Within the local communes, therefore, issues that directly affected the local community were addressed by the commune, and decisions on issues that had wider implications were made by the higher levels following representation by the lower councils.

The communes provide the mechanism for local grass-roots decision-making which fed upwards. Many observers commented on the democratic nature of this process and observed the development of initiative and responsibility within communities.[45] Communes could take decisions on local infrastructure, economic activities and local justice, as well as provide a mechanism for distributing services and basic supplies, community health services and military training. While serving the needs of local communities, communes also generated demand for and increased participation in their services. Their control over distribution of services and support for other institutions and philosophies connected to the DAA system, (such as directly supporting cooperative production and providing education) connected the councils with institutions of governance and reduced the space available for organization outside the system.

---

[44] IIST interview: TEV-DEM official Mizgin Amed, Amude, 19/04/2016.
[45] For example, Jason McQuinn 31/10/2015: 'Rojava dispatch six: Innovations, the formation of the *Hêza Parastina Cewherî* (HPC)', *Modern Slavery*, http://modernslavery.calpress.org/?p=949 (last accessed 24/03/2017); Knapp, Flach and Ayboga, *Revolution in Rojava*, 87–9.

The economy

Syria's economy was dramatically affected by the conflict, with a 50 per cent contraction in real terms after 2011. Within the war economy, autonomous economic spheres were created by the PYD in the north, as well as by ISIS in the south, which, together, controlled most of Syria's oil fields.[46] The areas controlled by the PYD-led administration included some of the country's most productive farmland and the richest areas in Syria in terms of oil resources. Economic activity was vital to the ability of the Administration to maintain its control in northern Syria and forming the democratic society through revolution went hand in hand with achieving ecological self-sufficiency or a semi-independent economy.[47] With the development of the model of governance, complementary security, legal, economic and educational structures were also developed and institutionalized. The administration and security services became primary sources of employment in northern Syria and the economy also became a central project of the Administration and economic practice was pursued within the community with the promotion of democracy at its core:

> It shouldn't be a capitalist system, one without respect for the environment; nor should it be a system which continues class contradictions and in the end only serves capital. It should be a participatory model, based on natural resources and a strong infrastructure.[48]

Cooperatives defined as the basic economic unit of the democratic society[49] were developed according to local environment and need and utilized vacant agricultural land and industry for local production and distribution. The economic system was directed at providing general welfare: Article 42 of the DAA social contract stated that 'it shall be aimed at guaranteeing the daily needs of people and to ensure a dignified life. The law prohibits monopoly. Labour

---

[46] State-controlled oil production dropped from 387,000 b/d to 10,000 b/d. David Butter 2015: 'Syria's economy: Picking up the pieces', Chatham House Research Paper, Chatham House, London, https://www.chathamhouse.org/sites/files/chathamhouse/field/field_document/20150623SyriaEc onomyButter.pdf (last accessed 13/01/2017), 2.

[47] TEV-DEM 16/02/2015 'The project of a Democratic Syria', available on *Peace in Kurdistan Campaign*, website: https://peaceinkurdistancampaign.com/resources/rojava/the-project-of-a-democratic-syr ia/ (last accessed 24/03/2017).

[48] Michael Knapp 06/02/2015: 'Rojava – the formation of an economic alternative: Private property in the service of all', Peace in Kurdistan Campaign, https://peaceinkurdistancampaign.com/201 5/02/06/rojava-the-formation-of-an-economic-alternative-private-property-in-the-service-of-all/ (originally published by Kurdistan Report: http://www.kurdistan-report.de/index.php/archiv/20 14/171/13-privateigentum-im-dienste-aller).

[49] Article 56 and 69.2 of the Draft Social Contract of the Democratic Federal System of Northern Syria.

rights and sustainable development are guaranteed.'[50] The Kurdish majority areas of Syria were rich in natural resources such as oil, water and agricultural products, which the social contract defined as the public wealth of the society. Although the right to private property was retained, the Administration also described all buildings and lands owned by the local administrations as public property and encouraged cooperative enterprise and ownership.[51]

Contextualized by the crisis in Syria, economic organization around the communes and development of cooperatives had, in many cases, eased economic pressures and facilitated necessary cooperation over the distribution of scarce resource and services. Fulfilling wider economic objectives, however, was hindered by the war, dependence on external supplies of goods and services, as well as by political divisions that prevented cooperation. Although the conflict itself provided the conditions for reorganizing local society and production around the democratic autonomy model, inevitable uncertainties about the future were obstacles to achieving the Administration's economic gaols and their longevity. Negative effects on salaries, prices, production and population migration, among other factors, increased general hardship and restricted incomes and resources. As a consequence, in parallel to organized cooperative economic activity, dependence on private enterprise, black and grey market trade and external remittances, to meet basic individual and family needs, was common.

The budget of the local administrations derived primarily from oil revenues, taxes on fuel and agriculture, and import duties.[52] Production within DAA areas continued but was negatively affected by the war. The local economy relied on imports of food and other products from other areas of Syria or from outside its disputed internal and sensitive international borders. PYD-held areas bordered Syrian government-controlled areas, as well as ISIS, FSA and Turkish held areas within Syria. Turkey closed all official border crossings with the PYD-led administrations in 2014 and began building walls to prevent smugglers from moving people and goods between the two countries.[53] Border closures and restrictions on trade by the KRG also negatively affected availability and prices

---

[50] The Charter of the Social Contract, 29/01/2014: Article 42.

[51] Ibid., Article 40–1.

[52] Tom Perry 28/07/2015: 'Syrian Kurds' spending plans reflect rising ambition', *Reuters*, http://www.reuters.com/article/us-mideast-crisis-syria-kurds-idUSKCN0Q21BK20150728 (last accessed 30/03/2017); Janet Biehl 25/02/2015: 'Rojava's Threefold Economy: A Presentation by Abdurrahman Hemo, adviser for economic development in Cizîre Canton, Dêrîk' *Biehl On Bookchin* http://www.biehlonbookchin.com/rojavas-threefold-economy/ (last accessed 18/12/2018).

[53] Interview: Salih Gheddo, leader of Kurdish Democratic Left Party, Qamishli, 11/05/2016.

of imported goods and the PYD claimed that there was a targeted embargo by both the KDP and Turkey to undermine its administration.[54] After the Duhok agreement between the KNC and the PYD broke down in 2014 the border became an area of political power plays between the two sides. For the KDP/KNC it provided some leverage over the PYD and closures were used in attempts to persuade the PYD to return to the terms of KDP-mediated power-sharing agreements and as a punitive response to arrests of KNC politicians. The PYD, however, often responded by arresting pro-Barzani and/or KNC politicians in Syria. In one such incident, in March 2016, the KDP closure of the Samealka border crossing in response to the PYD-led administrations arrest of KNC politicians caused the price of vegetables to skyrocket.[55]

Pre-war levels of production were not achievable and, even if hostilities ended, inevitable competition for control of strategic resources and settlements for their exploitation would certainly affect the ability of the Administration to develop self-sufficiency. Before 2011, the Hasakah Governorate was considered the 'breadbasket' of Syria, producing an estimated 1.8 million tons of wheat per year. Production decreased significantly due to fighting between Kurdish forces and ISIS, the migration of population away from farmland, the high costs of basic materials and farmers' reluctance to invest in production and necessary equipment. According to journalistic reports, however, wheat from Hasakah province continued to be bought by the Syrian government.[56]

The Rumailan, Souedieh and Karatchuk oilfields in Hasakah province, hosting 1322 oil wells and 25 gas wells,[57] were said to have produced one-third of the 380,000 b/d of crude in Syria. These fields fell under PYD control in 2012 and were governed by councils and managed by a workers' committee to

[54] See, for example, Fehim Tastekin 25/01/2017: 'Syrian Kurds rebuilding Kobani from rubble', *Al Monitor*, http://www.al-monitor.com/pulse/originals/2017/01/turkey-syria-isis-asked-kurds-to-se t-up-islamic-state.html (last accessed 31/03/2017); Wladimir van Wilgenburg 25/11/2013: 'Syrian Kurdish party calls on Turkey, KRG to end embargo', *Al Monitor*, http://www.al-monitor.com/puls e/originals/2013/11/syria-kurds-embargo-end-turkey-border-crossing-trade.html (last accessed 14/03/2017).

[55] A kilo of tomatoes increased from SP 150–200 in March to more than SP 800 in April 2016. Wilcox, Orion and Mohammed Abdulssatar Ibrahim 26/04/2016: 'As intra-Kurdish dispute drags on, protestors demand reopening of Iraqi border', *Syria Direct*, http://syriadirect.org/news/as-intra-kur dish-dispute-drags-on-protestors-demand-reopening-of-iraqi-border/ (last accessed 24/03/2017); Wladimir van Wilgenburg 28/05/2014: 'Rival Kurdish parties battle for power in Syria', *Al Monitor*, http://www.al-monitor.com/pulse/fr/originals/2014/05/kurdistan-kdp-pyd-erbil-barzani-ocala n-syria.html (last accessed 10/03/2017).

[56] See, for example, Drwish, Sardar Mlla 03/05/2016: 'Will Syria's Kurds succeed at self-sufficiency?' *Al-Monitor*, http://www.al-monitor.com/pulse/originals/2016/04/kurdish-areas-norther-syria-economy-self-sufficiency.html (accessed 05/05/2016).

[57] Hussein Almohamad and Andreas Dittmann 20/05/2016: 'Oil in Syria between terrorism and dictatorship', *Social Science*, Vol. 5, Issue 2, http://www.mdpi.com/2076-0760/5/2/20/htm (last accessed 04/04/2017).

produce cheap benzene for the cooperatives and the staff of the autonomous government. Refining and exporting this oil was dependent on downstream refineries and hindered by sabotage of the main pipeline from the Jazirah region, which forced the closure of 1300 wells in Rumailan.[58] Production was restarted and systematized with cooperation of the Assad government. The establishment of a company called Distribution of Al Jazeera Fuel (known as KSC) by TEV-DEM in November 2013 promised to further enhance production. By June 2015 the Rumailan field was reported to be producing 15,000 b/d.[59] Production remained limited, however; it depended on export to groups hostile to 'Kurdish rule' and revenues from sales within DAA area and to the government were not comparable to pre-war levels.[60] Black market trade with the Assad government, as well as with the KRG were reported and, while the PYD was not known to sell oil produced by ISIS, taxes on its transit through the YPG held territory were believed to contribute to the Administrations revenue.[61]

Businessmen in DAA-controlled areas also imported products through ISIS territories. An Administration foreign relations official said of the imports: 'A little comes from Daash [ISIS]. There is fuel from businessmen that pay a lot of tax to Daash to bring the goods [through Mabrouka] and they transport goods inside Rojava, but it's very expensive.'[62] The official added, however, that the amount imported in this way was not enough to cover 5 per cent of the needs of the people living in the Jazirah (Hasakah). Commenting on this trade, a PYD official said: 'This doesn't mean we are doing trade with ISIS. Civilians find their own ways to do trade. Sometimes goods also come from Iraqi Kurdistan, but not in the way we want.'[63] According to local media reports, the administrations had conducted illicit oil trade across the Syria-Iraq border to the KRG, which was believed to have generated revenue of around US $10 million per month.[64] One

---

[58] Almohamad and Dittmann, 'Oil in Syria between terrorism and dictatorship'.

[59] AFP 30/07/2015: 'Syrian Kurds refine oil for themselves for the first time', *The National*, http://www.thenational.ae/world/middle-east/syrian-kurds-refine-oil-for-themselves-for-first-time (last accessed 04/04/2017).

[60] Fabrice Balanche 24/08/2016: 'Rojava's sustainability and the PKK's regional strategy', *Washington Institute*, http://www.washingtoninstitute.org/policy-analysis/view/rojavas-sustainability-and-the-pkks-regional-strategy (last accessed 04/04/2017); Almohamad and Dittmann, 'Oil in Syria between terrorism and dictatorship'; Sirwan Kajjo 20/07/2016: 'US-backed Kurdish forces benefiting from oil in Syria', *Voice of America*, http://www.voanews.com/a/united-states-backed-kurdish-forces-benefiting-from-oil-syria/3427566.html (last accessed 04/04/2017).

[61] Rudaw 21/09/2015: 'PYD تتجاوز نفطية عائدات على يحصل 10 كوردستان اقليم عبر شهريا دولار ملايين', *Rudaw*, http://www.rudaw.net/arabic/kurdistan/210920156 (last accessed 04/04/2017).

[62] IIST interview: Abdulkarim Omer, Amude, 11/05/2016.

[63] IIST interview: PYD official, Netherlands, 15/02/2017.

[64] NOW 22/09/2015: 'Syrian Kurds earning millions from oil sales', https://now.mmedia.me/lb/en/NewsReports/565952-syria-kurds-making-millions-from-oil-sales (last accessed 04/04/2017); Rudaw: 21/09/2015: 'PYD تتجاوز نفطية عائدات على يحصل 10 كوردستان اقليم عبر شهريا دولار ملايين'.

PYD source even implied that direct oil sales to Nechirvan Barzani, of $25 per barrel, had occurred. 'He [Nechirvan Barzani] said "if you don't accept this price, you can try to sell it to someone else."'[65] This trade, however, was reported to have stopped due to pressure from Turkey: '[The Administration] traded last year with KDP. So Turkey pressured the KDP by shutting the pipeline for three weeks. They [the KDP] mixed oil from fields controlled by the PYD in Rojava with oil from the Ain Zalah field, and transferred it via a pipeline to Turkey', a consultant in the energy sector said.[66] Other Kurdish officials suggested that oil wells under PYD control were mostly idle.[67] Other exports to the KRG included sacrificial animals bought from rebel-controlled Idlib, on which the Administration levied taxes.[68] And in April 2017, local media suggested business was ongoing after a new border crossing opened between PYD-controlled territory and the KRG.[69]

Turkish hostility to the PYD increased the importance of land borders with Iraq, which became crucial to the Administration's resources and supplies. Frequent border closures by the KDP stimulated the need to establish a secure passage for goods and people further south. The Yaroubia-Rabia border crossing, captured by the YPG from ISIS in October 2013, was used to transport fighters and goods through Iraqi territory until June 2014, when the KRG Peshmerga took control of the border as the Iraqi army fled from ISIS.[70] The PKK presence in Sinjar after August 2014 was then reported to have facilitated smuggling between northern Syria and Sinjar. The KDP attempted to curtail this by limiting the movement of goods flowing into Sinjar through the Suhaila Bridge,[71] thus mitigating some of the benefits that influence in Sinjar held for the Administration. Further south, the Umm al-Jaris border crossing offered potential access to Iraqi government-controlled areas when the Iraqi Shia paramilitary, the Popular Mobilization

[65] IIST interview: PYD official, 15/02/2017.

[66] IIST interview: Alan Mohtadi. Head of T&S Consulting, 14/05/2017.

[67] Akram Hesso cited in Perry, 'Syrian Kurds' spending plans reflect rising ambition'.

[68] Fehim Tastekin 5/01/2017: 'Syrian Kurds rebuilding Kobani from rubble', *Al Monitor*, https://www w.al-monitor.com/pulse/originals/2017/01/turkey-syria-isis-asked-kurds-to-set-up-islamic-state. html (last accessed 18/12/2018).

[69] Hisham Arafat 22/04/2017: 'Business booming in Rojava after outlet opened with Kurdistan Region', *Kurdistan 24*, http://www.kurdistan24.net/en/news/1b332ce0-5791-4ca1-9bc1-1603fb830879/Business-booming-in-Rojava-after-outlet-opened-with-Kurdistan-Region

[70] See Wladimir van Wilgenburg 19/06/2014: 'Iraqi Kurds seize control of key Syria border crossing', *Al Monitor*, http://www.al-monitor.com/pulse/originals/2014/06/iraq-mosul-isis-pyd-pkk-kurds-barzani-kdp-peshmerga.html (last accessed 31/03/2017); AA 14/06/2014: 'Kurdish Peshmerga seizes control of Rabia, Mosul', *Anadolu Agency*, http://aa.com.tr/en/pg/photo-gallery/kurdish-peshmerga-seizes-control-of-rabia-mosul/0/68111 (last accessed 31/03/2017).

[71] Amberin Zaman 28/01/2017: 'Hope and fear for Syria's Kurds', *Al Monitor*, http://al-monitor.co m/pulse/originals/2017/01/northern-syria-kurds-rojava-ypg-turkey-kurdistan.html (last accessed 31/03/2017); HRW 04/12/2016: 'Iraq: KRG restrictions harm Yezidi recovery', *Human Rights Watch*, https://www.hrw.org/news/2016/12/04/iraq-krg-restrictions-harm-yezidi-recovery (last accessed 31/03/2017).

Units, expelled ISIS from areas bordering the SDF in May 2017.[72] Iraqi forces then took control of Sinjar, Rabia and other disputed territories in October, just one month after the independence referendum in the KRI.[73]

Within the DAA areas the fertility of the land and pre-existing industry had been an advantage for the Administration. Industry in the region of Afrin, famed for its olives and subsidiary products, as well as its textile industry, benefited from the movement of more factories and workshops from Aleppo city to Afrin during the Assad government advance on Aleppo in 2016.[74] According to the Rojava Minister of Economy in Afrin, the region was operating with fifty soap factories, twenty olive oil factories, 250 olive processing plants, seventy factories making construction material, 400 textile workshops, eight shoe factories, five nylon producing factories and fifteen marble processing factories. The majority of these industries existed prior to the outbreak of war in Syria. The canton administration had built a dam and two mills in order to regulate supplies of flour and, in addition, the return of many Kurds to the region from larger cities supplemented industrial production in the area.[75] Afrin region was also used to transport goods between ISIS-held areas around Raqqah and rebel-held Idlib in an 'oil-for-food' arrangement between the two sides. The PYD-led administration received 'taxes' and gained leverage through its ability to interrupt and block the passage of oil.[76] Surrounded by the Syrian government, rebel, and ISIS-controlled areas, as well as by the closed Turkish border, Afrin's isolation also contributed to inflated prices and restricted the availability of many goods and services.

Kobani's economy, known for livestock, cotton and wheat production, became dependent on the other Kurdish areas due to the destruction incurred during the ISIS siege on the town and because of the closure of its border crossing with Turkey. Although, significant reconstruction projects in Kobani, aimed at providing accommodation to the most vulnerable, provided employment

[72] Maher Chmaytelli 29/05/2017: 'Iran-backed Iraqi force says takes Islamic State villages near Syria', *Reuters*, http://www.reuters.com/article/us-mideast-crisis-iraq-mosul-idUSKBN18O0M2

[73] In October 2017 Sinjar fell under Iraqi control. See, Martin Chulov 17/04/2017: 'Iraqi forces drive Kurdish fighters out of town of Sinjar', *The Guardian*, https://www.theguardian.com/world/2017/o ct/17/iraqi-forces-drive-kurdish-fighters-out-of-sinjar (last accessed 01/05/2018).

[74] Sardar Mlla Darwish 03/05/2016: 'Will Syria's Kurds succeed at self-sufficiency?' *Al Monitor*, http://www.al-monitor.com/pulse/originals/2016/04/kurdish-areas-norther-syria-economy-self-sufficien cy.html (last accessed 31/03/2017).

[75] Sedat Yılmaz interview with Dr Amaad Yousef, 22/12/2014: 'Efrîn Economy Minister: Rojava challenging norms of class, gender and power', *Özgür Gündem*, available on https://rojavareport .wordpress.com/2014/12/22/efrin-economy-minister-rojava-challenging-norms-of-class-gender-and-power/ (last accessed 30/06/2017).

[76] Noura Hourani and Orion Wilcox 20/05/2016: 'Fuel prices soar as Kurds bloc oil-for-food trade in northwest', *Syria Direct*, http://eaworldview.com/2016/05/syria-feature-fuel-prices-soar-in-north west-as-kurdish-militia-blocks-oil-for-food-trade/ (last accessed 04/04/2017).

and development opportunity, they were hampered by the lack of necessary funding,[77] products and technology, which might otherwise have been imported from Turkey or from the Syrian interior. A member of the Kobani canton reconstruction board said: 'If we keep depending on ourselves, it will take a long time; reconstruction is difficult for us. We called the international community to help us, but obstacles always come from the same side: Turkey.'[78] Most financial support for reconstruction was believed to have come from private sources or NGOs and the slow progress prevented the return of the majority of Kobani's pre-war inhabitants to the area.[79]

The local administration paid the salaries to an estimated 35,000 people, excluding the YPG and SDF.[80] These salaries, in general, did not exceed US $50–100 monthly. According to the Administration's adviser for economic development in Cizîrê canton, 70 per cent of the Administration's budget was spent on security and the war, which cost $20 million per year.[81] Often Kurdish civilians received additional income from families in Iraqi Kurdistan, Turkey and Europe. '$100 is only enough to survive for 10 days', said Heybar Othman, the bureau chief of the Kurdistan 24 channel in Qamishli.[82]

Economic hardship and difficulties in meeting basic needs increased migration of Kurds from Syria to Europe, Turkey, and to the Kurdistan region and produced dependencies on alterative black/grey market trade or remittances from relatives abroad:

> Everything is very expensive, all the people, Kurds and Arabs are poor. We plant vegetables, but despite this they are expensive. The people are finished and have nothing to rely on. ... If my son was not outside in the Kurdistan [region], I would not be able to live. All people depend on their children outside. ... Some government employees receive 30,000 Syrian pounds, but it's very difficult to survive with this. (Bave Aras, a taxi driver from Qamishli)[83]

---

[77] Funding for such projects was limited and international aid largely confined to mine clearance operations and medical relief.

[78] Interview: Idris Nassan, member of reconstruction board, 11/10/2015.

[79] Sirwan Kajjo 27/01/2016: 'Year after liberation from IS, life in Kobani still tough', *VOA*, (online) http://www.voanews.com/a/year-after-liberation-from-is-life-in-kobani-still-tough/3165529.html (last accessed 31/03/2017).

[80] Fehim Tastekin 05/01/2017: 'Syrian Kurds rebuilding Kobani from rubble', *Al Monitor*, https://www.al-monitor.com/pulse/originals/2017/01/turkey-syria-isis-asked-kurds-to-set-up-islamic-state.html (last accessed 18/12/2018).

[81] Abdurrahman Hemo, adviser for economic development in Cizîrê canton, Dêrîk cited by Janet Biehl 25/02/2015.

[82] Interview: Heybar Othman, Kurdistan 24 office head. (From 2018 Heybar Othman worked for *al-Hurra*), 18/02/2017.

[83] IIST interview: Civilian, Qamishli, 26/06/2016.

Migration aggravated manpower problems for the YPG and put a further strain on the economy. Attempts were made by the local administrations to prevent migration and to address the negative consequences of it. In September 2015, the DAAs adopted a property law, which ruled that 'vehicles, real estate, land, and cash assets belonging to Syrians who have fled the territory that it governs' could be lawfully appropriated by the Administration.[84] This decision affected Kurds, as well as other ethnic groups living under the local administration control and increased criticism of the Administration. Locals suggested that some land and property, vacated as a result of migration of owners from Syria, had been seized by the Administration for communal use. This practice appeared to be regulated by laws that guaranteed appropriate compensation to the owner, or the return of property on the owners return. Interviews with Kurds with private property and land in the Afrin region suggested that the expropriation of land was an ongoing concern.[85]

Attempts to build the 'social economy' through cooperatives and developing self-sufficiency led to new economic initiatives such as trade companies and construction cooperatives.[86] Land which had been nationalized under Hafiz al-Assad was brought under the management of agricultural cooperatives. Doctors' committees worked to form a free health system.[87] The commune, also acted as a means of distribution of services and goods, such as basic staples, clean water and the use of generators. Participation in communes was optional and private ownership protected by the social contract.[88] Although the Administration offered a means of coping with the disruption of the Syrian crisis, research in Syria suggested this system was not without problems. The availability of these services to those who did not participate within the system was limited. Independent local businesses had also been negatively affected by price increases and embargos and economic incentives to migrate out of Syria remained a challenge to the local administration. Limited access to supplies from other governorates and neighbouring countries, however, hindered their development.[89] This economic system also required an ideological investment and was supported by specially developed academies designed to promote the

---

[84] KurdWatch 30/09/2015: 'Al-Qamishli: PYD takes possession of refugees' property', *KurdWatch*, http://kurdwatch.org/?e3605 (last accessed 30/03/2017).
[85] IIST interview: Afrin resident, 28/02/2016.
[86] Abdurrahman Hemo, cited by Janet Beihl 25/02/2015.
[87] Knapp, 'Rojava – the formation of an economic alternative'.
[88] The Charter of the Social Contract, 29/01/2014: Article 41.
[89] Ibid.

'cooperative mentality' and by companies that buttressed the development of cooperative agriculture.[90]

The lack of external recognition of the PYD-led administrations made it more difficult for the economy to survive, claimed the PYD officials. They maintained that the region's dependence on the Syrian government for official documentation, medicine, some salaries, and on the Qamishli airport was also a reason that the YPG and the SDF had not completely removed the Syrian government from its areas.[91] 'If we had guarantees [for our recognition], we would kick out the regime in 48 hours', one official said.[92] Initiatives to develop the social economy, and cooperatives and to distribute services according to this model, assisted regulating the war economy in northern Syria. The existence of layers of parallel economies, however, tied northern Syria intrinsically to the Syrian interior and to its neighbours undermining attempts to develop self-sufficiency.

The education system

The Kurdish language education system was not implemented straight away. Syrian state education continued to be provided until 2015 and teachers received state salaries. In 2015 the PYD-led administration introduced its own Kurdish language curriculum which it implemented in areas under its control.[93] The move further diminished and replaced the Syrian government's institutions and services in northern Syria. The Syrian government responded by cutting the salaries of teachers that taught the alternative curriculum.[94] The local administrations, however, paid them directly and trained new teachers to teach the Kurdish language. In October 2016 the state curriculum was completely removed, and parallel Arabic, Kurdish and Syriac curriculums were applied where appropriate.

According to the social contract the education system of the canton administrations was based on 'values of reconciliation, dignity, and pluralism' and was 'a marked departure from prior education policies founded upon racist and chauvinistic principles.'[95] Criminalization of the use of the Kurdish language

---

[90] Ibid.
[91] IIST interview: Aldar Xelil, Amude 02/05/2016.
[92] IIST interview: PYD official, Netherlands 15/02/2017.
[93] Ahmed Shiwesh and Ahmed Osman 02/10/2015: 'Kurds introduce own curriculum at schools of Rojava', *ARA News*, http://aranews.net/2015/10/kurds-introduce-own-curriculum-at-schools-of-roj ava-2/ (last accessed 30/03/2017).
[94] IIST interview: Abdulselam Ahmed, senior TEV-DEM official, Qamishli, 20/07/2016.
[95] The Charter of the Social Contract, 29/01/2014, Article 91.

and its teaching under the Baath Party government had resulted in high levels of illiteracy of their mother tongue among Syrian Kurds. The promotion of the Kurdish language and education system implemented in the cantons began to change this and Kurdish language teaching developed progressively after 2011.

According to Arshek Baravi, the founder of the Kurdish education system, preparations to introduce Kurdish language instruction started soon after the revolution broke out in Syria.[96] From a modest start in 2011, teacher training centres were slowly being set up across the PYD-controlled areas and in Damascus and work began on forming committees to develop a new curriculum and import new books from abroad. In a conference in Makhmour (KRI, where a heavily PKK-influenced refugee camp is located) a committee was set up to work on writing education books that were later used for the new education system.

Although a central directive on education was developed, the decentralization of the Administration also decentralized its implementation and organization: 'Every canton endeavours to build its own educational system on its own social structure', said Dorsin Akif, a lecturer in *Jineology* (women's studies) at the Mesopotamia Social Sciences Academy in Qamishli.[97] Decentralization of education highlighted the different experiences of DAA rule between the cantons. In the Afrin region, greater demographic homogeneity, absence of organized political opposition and geographic isolation allowed the education system to develop relatively quickly. By 2015, books for the new curriculum had been introduced up to the eighth grade and a university opened in August that year. By comparison, in the Jazirah new textbooks were introduced later and the university in Qamishli was being set up in 2016. Preparations to begin secondary school courses in the Jazirah were underway in 2018. The co-chairman of the Education Commission commented that 'this will be based on the [Öcalan's] philosophy of the democratic nation. ... [The ministry] will copy the courses and print it in books and start their work in the coming year.'[98]

As a central marker of culture and identity, Kurdish language teaching was widely welcomed as a positive development. Despite this, the educational system generated significant criticism. The Syrian government and the KNC denounced

---

[96] IIST interview: Arshek Baravi, founder of the Kurdish education system, Amude, 12/05/2016.

[97] Derya Aydin 21/01/2015: 'Education system in Rojava', *Kurdishquestion*, http://kurdishquestion.co m/oldarticle.php?aid=education-system-in-rojava (last accessed 30/03/2017).

[98] Fatma Abdulhalim, Jan Mohammed and Wladimir van Wilgenburg 15/08/2016: 'Rojava university seeks to eliminate constraints on education in Syria's Kurdish region', *ARA News*, http://aranews. net/2016/08/rojava-university-seeks-eliminate-constraints-education-syrias-kurdish-region/ (last accessed 30/03/2017).

the decision to introduce a new curriculum and school books. The Syrian government interpreted it as a challenge to its rule while the KNC stressed the importance of relevant expertise in drafting and implementing a curriculum and the need for competent teaching staff. Concerns also focused on the ideological content of the curriculum, its separation of education based on ethnicity and on the fact that the educational system was recognized neither internationally nor by the Syrian government. The KNC feared that its ideological content sought to diminish and remove alternative political and civil organization, that future generations would be taught Öcalan's ideas and produce a new generation of PYD supporters.[99] This worry was echoed by some civilians.

New Kurdish language books, while containing few pictures of Öcalan, taught students about the commune system and instructed them in the 'democratic nation' philosophy, which promoted the generation and maintenance of the 'moral society' and associated governance system. The language book, *Civak u Jiyan* (society and life,) mapped the administrative system and explained simply the organization of the communes to young children.[100] The text also set out their duties and responsibilities. At higher levels of education, ideology featured more heavily. For example, the Mesopotamia Akademya in Qamishli, a higher education institute, taught a system based on the ideology of Öcalan: 'We give them the general principles of a democratic nation and the confederalism of leader Apo [Öcalan] and how we can benefit from them', said a history teacher at the academy.[101] A co-head of the Education Commission, however, rejected claims that the system was ideological: 'We just teach that we should live together with all components [of society] learning in our own language. When necessary we mention the name of Öcalan – until now, the name of Öcalan has not been mentioned in our courses.'[102] In comparison, a teacher from Amude commented that 'it is a very bad, ideological system based on the ideology of Apo. ... The new teachers come from the PYD. They are not teachers, but PYD members. They get three months training.'[103] Interviews conducted with residents also suggested that the curriculum's ideological content had had a negative effect on school attendance. Some interviewees had chosen not to send their children

[99] IIST interview: Majdal Delli, senior Yekiti member, 12/04/2017; Hawar Abdulrazaq 15/90/2015: 'Syrian Kurdish party condemns PYD changing of school curriculum', *Bas News*, http://www.basnews.com/index.php/en/news/221870 (last accessed 04/04/2017).
[100] *Civak u Jiyan*, 2015, 3rd ed.: 44. Education Ministry. Jazirah.
[101] IIST interview: Reshan Shakr (25), history teacher at Mesotopmya Academy, Qamishli, 12/05/2016.
[102] IIST interview: Mohammed Salih Abdo, co-chair of education commission, Qamishli, 11/05/2016.
[103] Mohammed Shemo (54), a teacher from Amude Interview in Amude, 02/10/2015.

to schools because of its partisan character.[104] Others criticized this practice: 'I send my children to the new schools', said Manaan Kajjo, another teacher[105] and added 'Even if they don't want to, they have to send their children' referring to civilians who had rejected the school system. The gradual replacement of the state education system, however, meant that even those who did not support the PYD or accept its ideology could not avoid exposure to it.

In Kobani the education system appeared to have gained more acceptance due to denser support for the PYD and the destruction of the pre-siege infrastructure. Information about popular opinion in Afrin was scarce. Interviews that were conducted with residents, however, suggested that no alternative to the DAA education was available there. Some residents were reported to have removed their children from school, and attempts had been made to persuade officials to allow the establishment of independent schools. These requests had, however, been rejected.[106] In the Jazirah the education system had faced more open controversy and public criticism. Some Kurdish students were reported to have tried to join private Christian schools or government schools in Qamishli or Hasakah in order to avoid the new curriculum.[107] In November 2015, sixteen Assyrian and Armenian organizations (including churches) not aligned to the canton administrations, issued a statement rejecting the new system and any form of interference in the church's private schools.[108] For many the biggest concern about the education system was the fact that it was not recognized by Damascus. Parents feared that the education of their children was lost.[109] For the Administrations, this issue provided further impetus to work towards developing a comprehensive education system which included the secondary school system and universities, but officials recognized that this would take time.

A further strain on attendance of educational establishments was caused by the introduction of mandatory conscription. The consequent decline in availability of adult labourers produced greater demand for child labour.[110] Families placed labour and economic needs above schooling. Conscription was

---

[104] Interviews: Afrin resident 17/09/2016 (telephone); Rody Naso, ARTA FM radio manager, Amude, 04/05/2016.
[105] IIST interview: Manaan Kajjo, teacher in Amude, 05/10/2015.
[106] IIST interview: Afrin resident (telephone), 28/02/2017.
[107] IIST interview: Rody Naso, ARTA FM radio manager, Amude, 04/05/2016.
[108] AINA 11/02/2015: 'Assyrians, Armenians in Syria protest Kurdish confiscation of property', *AINA*, http://www.aina.org/news/20151102170051.htm (last accessed 04/04/2017).
[109] IIST interview: Rody Naso, ARTA FM radio manager, Amude, 04/05/2016.
[110] Unpublished Western NGO report: September 2015: 2, *Youth Labour Market Assessment, Northeast Syria*.

also reported to have negatively affected female education, as families prioritized the university education of sons as a means of postponing their conscription.[111]

The DAAs attempts to introduce new education, legal and economic systems furthered the local administrations' gradual replacement of Syrian government institutions and the institutionalization of parallel structures supporting the democratic autonomy project. The Kurdish origins of the system and the extension of its ideology into non-Kurdish areas, appeared, in many cases, to exacerbate political, ethnic and religious fissures within Syria's communities and no solution had been developed to address this. In other cases cooperation was, at least temporarily, facilitating the development of mechanisms of navigating the conflict in Syria and developing new forms of governance and representation. In the long run, however, the widespread fragmentation of education in Syria promised to deepen ideological, cultural and linguistic divides.

Media

After March 2011, Kurdish and opposition media in Syria expanded. Previously, journalists linked with the PKK and the KDP media had experienced problems working in northern Syria and often resorted to smuggling video material out of Syria. Under the Kurdish administration, new local media, radio stations and TV stations were established, most of which were dominated by either the PYD (PKK) or the KNC (KDP) because of funding needs. The most important TV stations locally were the PYD-linked Ronahi and Rojava TV, and the KDP-linked stations such as Zagros and Rudaw, which frequently encountered difficulties with the local authorities and PYD supporters. Other independent organizations, such as the radio station ARTA FM and the news agency ARA News,[112] were externally funded by Western NGOs. Another independent newspaper *Buyerpress* (formerly known as *Nudem*) operated in northern Syria and an independent radio station, Welat FM, operated in the Hasakah province.

From 2014, it became necessary to gain permission from the local administration to report from within the canton territories and reporting from the front lines required agreement from the YPG or the SDF. The legislative assembly passed a press law on 19 December 2015 in the Jazirah which further restricted media freedom and the press council established by it was authorized to impose fines and revoke publishing and broadcasting licenses, temporarily

---

[111] Ibid., 8.
[112] ARA news stopped operating in the summer of 2017.

or permanently.[113] While in some cases the Asayish (DAA police) pressured journalists, reporting from the Kobani and the Jazirah cantons was relatively widespread, if not unrestricted. Far less coverage was available of the Afrin region and respondents indicated that press freedom was more restricted there than in either Kobani or Hasakah and that reporters often worked anonymously.[114] Social media, such as Facebook, became a popular method of spreading news and issuing political statements and was used by Syrian Kurds both in and outside Syria.

As the administration developed, media freedoms within PYD-controlled northern Syria became a growing concern and reflected tensions between the PYD and the KDP/KNC. In August 2015 the DAAs banned the opposition-linked Orient TV and the KDP-linked Rudaw 'for enmity towards Kurdish people, institutions, and martyrs'.[115] Both Orient TV and Rudaw were highly critical of the PYD. Their reporters had been expelled from Syria, kidnapped by persons affiliated to the PYD or arrested by the Asayish.[116] Other more balanced local non-PYD media outlets were permitted to work in the DAA areas without issue. For example, the KDP-linked Kurdistan 24 operated freely and maintained an office in Qamishli, despite having been accused of association with KDP intelligence by TEV-DEM.[117] In KDP areas of Iraqi Kurdistan similar press restrictions were observed, and PKK-affiliated media were also subject to pressure from the Asayish.[118] Western media access to northern Syria was restricted by the KDP in March 2016. This was interpreted by the PYD as an attempt to prevent positive media coverage of the PYD-led administrations.[119]

---

[113] KurdWatch 30/06/2016: 'New document: Press Law for the Jazirah Canton', *KurdWatch*, http://kurdwatch.org/?e3885 (last accessed 04/04/2017).

[114] IIST interview: Adib Abdulmajid, ARA news founder, 02/02/2017.

[115] ANHA 05/08/2015: 'Rûdaw and Orient TV's work permit cancelled in Cizîre Canton', *Hawar News Agency*, http://en.hawarnews.com/rudaw-and-orient-tvs-work-permit-cancelled-in-cizire-canton/ (last accessed 04/04/2017). Some reports suggested that Rudaw later began operating within Rojava again. Ilham Ahmed was interviewed by Rudaw on 29 April 2018, see, Rudaw 30/04/2018: 'Kurdish official: Syrian regime attacking SDF permitted in Moscow meetings', http://www.rudaw.net/mobile/english/middleeast/syria/300420181

[116] RSF 01/05/2014: 'How Kurdistan's PYD keeps the media and news providers in line', *RSF*, https://rsf.org/en/news/how-kurdistans-pyd-keeps-media-and-news-providers-line last accessed 04/04/2017).

[117] IIST interview: Aldar Xelil, Amude, 02/05/2016.

[118] In August 2016, a PKK-linked journalist, previously subjected to numerous interrogations by the KRG Asayish about his work was killed under mysterious circumstances in the KDP stronghold of Duhok. HRW 25/08/2016: 'Iraqi Kurdistan: Kurdish journalist abducted, killed', *Human Rights Watch*, https://www.hrw.org/news/2016/08/25/iraqi-kurdistan-kurdish-journalist-abducted-killed (last accessed 03/06/2017); Rudaw 13/08/2016: 'Kurdish journalist killed in Duhok, evidence of torture', *Rudaw*, http://www.rudaw.net/english/kurdistan/130820161 (last accessed 04/04/2017).

[119] ARA News 27/03/2017: 'Syrian Kurds accuse Iraqi Kurds of preventing media covering Raqqa operation', *ARA News*, http://aranews.net/2017/03/syrian-kurds-accuse-iraqi-kurds-preventing-media-covering-raqqa-operation/ (last accessed 13/05/2017).

PYD co-chair Salih Muslim claimed: 'They don't allow journalists to come in, if they are serious they will allow journalists to write about the reality.' A KRG security official commented that 'the security situation in Syria is not safe. This why we are not letting the journalists to come in', and the KRG in Washington said that journalists were allowed in 'on a case-by-case basis'.[120]

As a consequence of wider political tensions, local Syrian Kurdish media faced pressure from both the PYD and the KNC. One casualty of these wider tensions was the independent ARTA FM radio station, funded by foreign donors. For some time the KNC refused to communicate with the station because they believed it was linked to the PYD-led administrations. Yet, the PYD also criticized radio station because it had refused to refer to killed YPG fighters as 'martyrs' and because of its 'controversial' reporting on DAA education.

> Five institutions affiliated to the [DAA] government issued a complaint in court against us. … Also they were angered when we reported that local civilians did not accept the education system. Many people did not send their children to school because they don't want to be influenced by the [PYD] ideology. (Rody Naso, ARTA FM's former local manager)

ARTA FM offices were burned down by supporters of the PYD, who were later imprisoned by the local authorities.[121]

While, independent press had developed and, aside from the temporary ban on Orient and Rudaw, media critical of the PYD could operate in DAA areas with the appropriate licenses and permissions, media appeared to be highly controlled and subject to wider inter-Kurdish political tensions.

The security of the administrations

The monopoly over the use of force gained by the PYD administration from the year 2012, and the role of the YPG in securing and defending Kurdish majority areas, established the security forces as primary institutions of governance in northern Syria. The centralized and disciplined YPG and Asayish (police) forces became key to domestic legitimacy claims and the Administration's ability to gain external assistance, secure territory from outside threats and maintain

---

[120] Ahed al Hendi 12/04/2017: 'Iraqi Kurds Restrict Movement of US-backed Anti-IS forces in Syria', *VOA*, http://www.voanews.com/a/iraqi-kurds-restrict-movement-of-us-backed-anti-islamic-state-forces-in-syria/3808191.html (last accessed 04/06/2017).

[121] IIST interview: Rody Naso, manager ARTA FM, Amude, 04/05/2016.

conditions within which the governance structures of the DAA and the federal system were applied.

The main security forces were organized as follows:

- Defence forces: People's Protection Units (YPG/YPJ), the Syrian Democratic Forces (SDF), the Self-defence Duty Forces (HXP).
- Internal security forces: The Asayish (security police), the Civilian Defence Forces (HPC).

The YPG and the Asayish were institutionalized by the DAA social contract of 29 January 2014, in which Article 15 defined the Asayish as the civil police force and the YPG as the sole military force. Although both were active before the establishment of the cantons and claimed to be independent of any political party, from 2014 they officially fell under the control of the DAAs. Each canton had a degree of autonomy to define and address security needs related to that canton, although the command structures remained centralized.

The Asayish

The police force of the DAAs was established on 25 July 2013 and was reported to have at least 15,000 members in early 2017.[122] Of this number 30 per cent were women and an estimated 300 were Turkmen. In the Jazirah, half of the Asayish forces were reported to be Arab. Within the DAAs, the Asayish came under the jurisdiction of internal affairs, while military forces fell under the defence office.[123] Ayten Ferhat, the co-head of the Asayish in the Jazirah canton, said:

> We formerly worked under the authority of the Supreme Kurdish Council. And after the announcement of the new administration we work under the ministry of interior affairs. ... We don't act as normal police; we are responsible for the protection of internal cities. Also if there are any social problems. The traffic police is also related to the Asayish. ... Internal protection is our job. Outside the cities we have the YPG, while on the borders we have new customs institutions.[124]

---

[122] Fehim Tasekin 30/01/2017: 'Does Syria really want to reconcile with Kurds?' *Al Monitor*, http://www.al-monitor.com/pulse/originals/2017/01/turkey-syria-kurds-are-working-to-build-a-state.html (last accessed 07/07/2017).

[123] At the time of writing, in the Jazirah, the Asayish fell under the interior affairs council led by Kenan Barakat, while the 'military forces' fell under Rezan Gullo, the head of the defence of the Jazirah. In the other cantons there was a similar system with defence in Kobani being led by Ismet Sheikh Hassan and interior affairs by Bozan Xelil. In Afrin the head of defence was Abdo Ibrahim and the interior body, lawyer, Hesen Beyrem.

[124] IIST interview: Ayten Ferhat, co-head of Asayish, Qamishli, 28/03/2014.

In 2016 the Asayish was reported to have 26 sub-divisions within it. The main units were the Checkpoints Administration, Anti-terror Forces (HAT), Intelligence Directorate, Organized Crime Directorate, Traffic Directorate and Treasury Directorate.[125] In areas of Assyrian majority within the Jazirah, the main police forces, however, were those connected to local political organizations, such as the Sutoro police (Syriac Security Office,) which cooperated with, but were subordinate to, the Asayish.

The Asayish police forces were established initially to fill a security gap and maintain public order. They became the most visible security services in the DAA regions. As with other institutions of the DAAs, the Asayish was established by the PYD but was, in theory, institutionalized further within the context of the democratic autonomy project. The PYD co-chair Salih Muslim said in 2013:

> It isn't independent. There are sides from which the YPG and Asayish are dependent, but they are connected to the Supreme Kurdish Council. It could be that the PYD supported it in the beginning, but then expert committees were formed and there is no longer dependence on the PYD.[126]

The institutional separation of the Asayish from the PYD did not silence concerns about partisanship. Its development from the democratic autonomy project and philosophy imbued the force with a social role and duty. Addressing social problems required the Asayish to work 'towards identifying the source of society's problems and solving these problems' – a factor that was said to set them apart from the police services of existing states.[127] Besides this ideological element to their mandate, their policing of demonstrations and arrests of numerous opposition activists led to suggestions that their obligation to the project made them an explicitly partisan force. Many accounts of arrests made by the Asayish suggested that due procedure was not followed, warrants were not presented, arrests were arbitrary and members of the Asayish had beaten detainees in custody.[128]

---

[125] Beritan Sarya-Cilo Jindar 06/06/2016: 'Rojava Asayish: Security institution not above but within society', *ANF*, http://www.anfenglish.com/features/rojava-asayish-security-institution-not-above-but-within-the-society (last accessed 02/04/2017).
[126] KurdWatch interview with Salih Muslim, 04/01/2013.
[127] Jindar, 'Rojava Asayish: Security institution not above but within society'.
[128] HRW 19/06/2014: *Under Kurdish Rule: Abuses in PYD-run Enclaves of Syria*, https://www.hrw.org/report/2014/06/19/under-kurdish-rule/abuses-pyd-run-enclaves-syria (last accessed 01/02/2017).

The YPG

In contrast to the Asayish, the YPG (and from October 2015, the SDF) acted as the army of the DAAs:

> The People's Protection Units (YPG) is the sole military force of the three Cantons, with the mandate to protect and defend the security of the Autonomous Regions and its peoples, against both internal and external threats. (The Charter of the Social Contract, Article 15)

The highly disciplined YPG operated primarily on the borders of PYD-controlled areas and on the frontlines. According to some sources, most YPG commanders were *cadro* members – professional soldiers trained in PKK camps in the Qandil Mountains[129] and dedicated to the 'revolution'. The majority of soldiers, however, were recruited from the Syrian Kurdish population and trained within Syria. The YPG bases were located outside the main cities and, in the Jazirah, it was uncommon to see YPG in the streets, unless they were attending funerals. Consequently, YPG commanders often had limited knowledge of affairs inside the cities. An exception was in Hasakah city, where the YPG had bases because of ISIS expansions and because the Syrian government-held areas in the city centre. The lack of YPG presence inside Qamishli meant that when clashes erupted between the Syrian government and Kurdish forces in April 2016, the Asayish did most of the fighting.

In frontline operations, in which additional manpower has been required, the Asayish has provided military assistance to the YPG. During the Manbij campaign in 2016 the Asayish from Kobani and Hasakah were moved to front lines. In this case, local security in the town of Kobani was maintained by the auxiliary HPC that normally acted as neighbourhood guards, assisted also by military conscripts within the HXP. While distinct institutional and administrative structures and duties separated the Asayish and the YPG, in practice maintaining security and defending the democratic autonomy project often blurred distinctions between 'external' and 'internal' security causing their roles to overlap.

Self-Defence Forces and Civil Defence Forces

The introduction of mandatory self-defence duty within the HXP (*Hêzên Erka Xweparastinê*) in July 2014 was followed, in March 2015, by the creation of a

---

[129] IIST interviews: Former US volunteer with YPG forces, 11/02/2017; Afrin residents, 08/10/2016. International Crisis Group, 04/05/2017.

system of armed neighbourhood civilian guards, the HPC (*Hêzên Parastina Cewherî*), based in the communes. Within these forces, units with specific purposes were also formed: HXP 'special forces' were recruited and trained in Afrin, with the first battalion graduating in Afrin in January 2017[130] and a special military police, the Military Discipline Units *(Yekîneyên Diziplîna Leşkerî)*, was made responsible for arresting YPG/HXP members who did not follow the rules.[131] According to the Duty of Self-defence law, all males aged between 18 and 30 years were required to complete six months of military service. Exceptions were made for those who had family members in the YPG or the Asayish, or whose family members were killed or 'martyred' in the 'Kurdish people's liberation movement' (PKK). It was clear that in some cases, individuals had avoided military service because they had personal connections with officials. Others attempted to hide or leave Syria to avoid conscription. This led to a wave of reports about military-aged men being arrested by the Asayish at checkpoints and in house raids as the Administration attempted to enforce compulsory conscription.[132]

According to the Administration laws, conscripts would only serve in their local areas and they should not be sent to the front lines, but they would have the option to voluntarily join the YPG.[133] Reports and field research, however, suggested that many conscripts had been deployed in battles against ISIS, outside Kurdish majority areas. In 2016, more conscripts were sent to front lines due to manpower needs created by the Manbij campaign and the expansion of YPG/SDF operations into Arab-majority areas. Similarly, conscripts were involved in active fighting in the 'Wrath of Euphrates' campaign launched on 5 November 2016 to isolate Raqqah. In February 2017, five hundred HXP members joined the campaign. It was unclear if this deployment occurred on a voluntary basis, but reports suggested that many youth had attempted to avoid conscription at

---

[130] Hawar News 04/01/2017: 'The first battalion of Special Forces HPX in Afrin graduated', *Hawar News*, 'http://en.hawarnews.com/the-first-battalion-of-special-forces-hpx-in-afrin-graduated/

[131] IIST interview: Abdulsalam Mohammed, Kurdish teacher, Qamishli, 16/02/2017.

[132] Peri Silo 05/02/2015: 'Compulsory military services raises concerns among Syrian Kurdish youth', *ARA News*, http://aranews.net/2015/02/compulsory-military-service-raises-concerns-among-syrian-kurdish-youth/ (last accessed 24/03/2017); ARA News 09/12/2014: 'PYD's conscription laws cause mass displacement among Syrian Kurdish youth', http://aranews.net/2014/12/pyds-conscription-law-causes-mass-displacement-among-syrian-kurdish-youth/ (last accessed 24/01/2017); ARA News 01/03/ 2017: 'Increased conscription of Kurdish youth in Kobane facing widespread criticism', *ARA News*, http://aranews.net/2017/03/increased-conscription-of-kurdish-youth-in-kobane-facing-widespread-criticism/ (last accessed 24/03/2017).

[133] YPG: 'Duty of self-defence', 13/07/2014.

this time, particularly concerned about fighting outside Kurdish areas in 'a battle that is not ours to fight'.[134]

The introduction of mandatory conscription and expansion of the YPG forces beyond Kurdish majority areas resulted in further emigration of military-aged men and those opposed to the PYD from Syria.[135] For the PYD and the SDF, sustaining international legitimacy by fighting against ISIS and gaining domestic legitimacy through attempts to connect the three DAAs, necessitated territorial expansion. This stretched its manpower and resources, however, and conscription became essential to achieving these strategic objectives. The conscription policy faced strong criticism from Syrian Kurdish communities as well as international observers, particularly as the YPG extended beyond Kurdish majority areas.

The HPC was established in March 2015.[136] It was affiliated to the communes but under the command of the Asayish. The co-head of a commune in Amude said:

> They protect the communes and neighbourhoods. ... If there is a funeral of martyrs, they go there to protect it. If there is something bigger, they call the police [Asayish]. There is also a commander of the Asayish responsible for them.[137]

The HPC regularly manned checkpoints when the Asayish was needed elsewhere. It had been involved in some clashes, such in the city of Hasakah, but in general, the forces were rarely involved in fighting.

Other military forces

With the expansion of the YPG territory and the development of military alliances against ISIS, particularly west of the Euphrates River, alliances with non-Kurdish groups became central to the Administration's attempts to gain and

[134] ANHA 05/02/2017: 'Self-defense fighters join Wrath of Euphrates', *Hawar News Agency*, http://en.hawarnews.com/self-defense-fighters-join-wrath-of-euphrates/ (last accessed 24/03/2017); Abdulrahman al-Masri 3/11/2016: 'Challenges surround the anti-ISIS Raqqa operation', *The Arab Weekly*, http://www.thearabweekly.com/Opinion/7035/Challenges-surround-the-anti-ISIS-Raqqa-operation (last accessed 24/03/2017).

[135] Unpublished Western NGO report: September 2015: *Youth Labour Market Assessment, Northeast Syria*, 17; Wladimir van Wilgenburg, 17/10/2015: 'Syria's Kurdish parties: Don't go to Europe', *Al Jazeera*, http://www.aljazeera.com/news/2015/09/syria-kurdish-parties-don-europe-150917061142096.html (last accessed 05/12/2015).

[136] ANHA 23/03/2015: '*Yekemîn Kongra Parastina Cewherî ya Kantona Cizîrê hate lidarxistin*', *Hawar News Agency*, http://ku.hawarnews.com/yekemin-kongra-parastina-cewheri-ya-kantona-cizire-hate-lidarxistin/ (last accessed 24/03/2017); McQuinn, 'Rojava dispatch six'.

[137] IIST interview: Leyla Hamza, co-president, Martyr Diyar commune, Amude, 02/05/2016.

maintain international legitimacy and military support. This, in turn, became central to the Administration's claims to domestic legitimacy and attempts to further institutionalize democratic autonomy across northern Syria. Several Christian and Arab militias groups operated within the DAA territories, either in cooperation with the YPG or under its command. Unlike the YPG and Asayish, such armed groups did not receive a legal status through the DAA social contract. Some of them, however, were required to license their political parties according to the canton law. Within the Jazirah, the Arab Shammar tribal militia, the al-Sanadid forces led by Bandar al-Humaydi, worked with the SDF and the YPG.[138] Furthermore, the Christian Syriac Union Party and the Assyrian Democratic Party had their own formally registered military wings and security police that operated within the Asayish and the SDF in Hasakah province.[139]

With the development of the federal system and the drafting of the federal social contract in 2016, the SDF, rather than the YPG, was institutionalized as the central armed force. Article 78 stated that the SDF would defend the democratic federal system in northern Syria and rely on volunteers and conscripts.[140] The YPG, however, remained the dominant force within the SDF and, while the federal system remained incomplete, the exact jurisdiction and command structures of each military force remained unclear. Conditions placed on US military support, however, required that in non-Kurdish majority areas, notably Raqqah, the role of local Arab forces were increased and direct US deals to involve additional Arab forces (Jarba's Syrian Elite Forces) were struck.[141]

Salaries

None of the armed forces received official regulated salaries. The HPC (neighbourhood guards) did not receive any financial support.[142] Several interviews confirmed, however, that since the DAAs were declared in 2014

[138] Mohamed al Hussein 11/09/2016: 'Clauses of agreement between al-Jarba movement and Kurdish Democratic society', *Zaman Al Wasl*, http://vvanwilgenburg.blogspot.nl/2017/02/clauses-of-agreement-between-al-jarba.html (last accessed 24/03/2017).

[139] For more information on Christian militia groups, see Aymenn Jawad al-Tamimi, 23/02/2014: 'Christian militia and political dynamics in Syria', *Syria Comment*, http://www.aymennjawad.org/14455/christian-militia-and-political-dynamics-in-syria (last accessed 24/03/2017).

[140] Hawar News 01/07/2016: 'al-kashaf 'an al-'qd al-ijtima'I lil-fidraliyyah al-dimuqratiyyah li rojava – shamal suriya' *Hawar News* http://hawarnews.com/الكشف-عن-العقد-الاجتماعي-للفيدرالية/ (last accessed 24/03/2017).

[141] Mahmoud Mourad 01/02/2017: 'Syrian Opposition figure to deploy all-Arab force in Raqqa offensive', *Reuters*, http://www.reuters.com/article/us-mideast-crizis-syria-jarba-idUSKBN15G51T (last accessed 08/05/2017).

[142] YPG Law of self-defense duty 13/07/2014.

members of the YPG who had a family to support received a monthly stipend of around 40,000 to 50,000 Syrian Pounds (SYP) equivalent at the time of interview to around US $180,[143] and that HXP conscripts received around SYP 25,000 ($115 per month).[144] YPG officials confirmed: 'There is small financial assistance offered to YPG fighters, and this is aid, not a salary, to help their families.'[145] Members of the Asayish also received SYP 40,000.[146] A former volunteer added that 'in the Kobani canton, YPG local volunteers had cell phones and got paid a small amount of money.'[147] Arab fighters of the SDF also received salaries. 'We provide salaries from independent sources, so we provide these salaries by ourselves', an SDF spokesperson said,[148] suggesting that financial contributions to armed groups remained decentralized and linked to political or tribal groupings.

Financial assistance provided an incentive to join the SDF and the YPG. According to a labour market assessment published in 2015, in Hasakah province the average income of a family's main breadwinner was between SYP 30,000 and SYP 42,000 (US $140–196 per month), supplemented by intermittent assistance from relatives abroad, which was often between SYP 5,400 and SYP 6,000, but would have varied with exchange rates.[149] Consequently, the stipend and assistance supplied to those in service were above average. Abu Ahmed, the pseudonym of an Arab from Deir al-Zour living in Qamishli suggested that this was an incentive to join: 'Some of them joined the FSA and Nusra and it was a failure, and some of them were jobless: and maybe that's why they join the SDF, because they need jobs. Others believe in it. We have both sides.'[150]

The move towards federalism

Several factors conspired to promote federalism as a means of organizing governance outside the canton structures that already existed in northern Syria.

[143] IIST interview: Abdulsalam Mohammed, Kurdish teacher, 16/02/2017.
[144] Online interview: Conscript from Kobani, 18/02/2017; IIST interview: Salih Gheddo, former foreign relations head of Jazirah canton, 11/05/2016; YPG Law of self-defense duty', 13/07/2014.
[145] IIST interviews: YPG official, 16/02/2017; Salih Gheddo, former foreign relations head of Cizere canton, 11/05/2016.
[146] IIST interview: Heybar Othman, Kurdistan 24 office chief, Qamishli, 23/02/2017. A conscript serving in Kobani said the YPG fighters normally received SYP 45,000/month financial assistance, but that that month it had been SYP 70,000 (around US $132) suggesting that financial assistance was subject to change. Online interview: Conscript from Kobani, 18/02/2017.
[147] IIST interview: Former US volunteer with YPG forces, 11/02/2017.
[148] IIST interview: Talal Silo, Hasakah, 25/04/2016.
[149] Unpublished Western NGO report: September 2015: *Youth Labour Market Assessment, Northeast Syria*, 11.
[150] IIST interview: Shop owner in Qamishli, 26/06/2016.

The immediate impetus behind the declaration was provided by the PYD's exclusion from the Geneva talks that commenced in February 2016, as well as by the need to maintain US military support against Ankara's increasing hostility to PYD domination on its borders with Syria. The formalization of governance alliances in northern Syria expanded the PYD agency in and influence over regional affairs, to the detriment of the main opposition groupings represented at Geneva. At the same time it diversified participation in governance. It led to the further broadening of the YPGs military alliances and the formation of new umbrella organizations patronized by the United States. Federalism also served long-term political objectives. Ethnically defined Kurdish aspirations made connecting the three Kurdish majority cantons central to the PYD's domestic legitimacy. The YPG military expansion into non-Kurdish areas in the Hasakah province and between Kobani and Afrin from 2013 onwards prompted the need to adapt the system to better incorporate non-Kurdish majority areas and populations in order to maintain control of strategic territories and resources. The coincidence of these factors, as well as the opportunity that the wider conflict provided to circumvent Turkish 'red lines' and consolidate the democratic autonomy project, made the move towards a federal system for northern Syria logical. Expansion into non-Kurdish majority areas, however, had consequences for the democratic autonomy project and its capacity to represent the diverse identities in northern Syria.

The proposal for federalism crystalized after the end of the siege on Kobani in January 2015 and with the subsequent expansion of the Kurdish cantons into many Arab-majority areas. Political and military alliances forged in these regions against the common threat of ISIS provided the basis and impetus for the institutionalization of multi-ethnic autonomous federal governance structures incorporating the three distinct DAA cantons. The SDF, formed in October 2015 with US support, offered that possibility, especially after liberating the town of Manbij. Extending further across the northern Aleppo border strip between Azaz and Jarablus (the Shahba region) and capturing it from Syrian rebel groups and ISIS could connect the cantons' territories. Meanwhile, military advances towards Deir al-Zour in cooperation with Ahmad Jarba's FSA group, the Syria Elite forces, and operations to isolate Raqqah, extended international support and leant international legitimacy to the project.

In February 2016, the YPG and YPG-aligned FSA rebels captured the town of Til Rifaat in Northern Aleppo. An assembly for the Shahba region was formed to govern these areas alongside the DAAs, and civilian and military councils for Manbij, Jarablus and al-Bab soon followed. Governance followed the DAA system of ethnic quotas and female participation through a co-chair system. These councils, however, often assumed a more tribal character due to the inclusion of figures from dominant local Arab tribes. In preparation for establishing coordinated councils, during the Manbij campaign, TEV-DEM officials had approached Arab tribal leaders from Jarablus. Sheikh Ali Jamili, a tribal leader who was supposed to head the new Jarablus council confirmed that, in May 2016, preparations were underway to establish a civilian council for Jarablus.[151] Other councils were created in the towns of Manbij and al-Bab, although at that time, in August 2016, only Manbij had been captured from ISIS, while al-Bab remained under ISIS control until February 2017 when it was captured by Turkish-backed forces.[152] Jarablus had also fallen under Turkish-backed rebel control in August 2016. In April 2017, the SDF had set up a council for Raqqah while its forces were still battling against ISIS to reach the city.[153]

The councils were to be managed under the administration for northern Aleppo that would be united with the three DAAs and, later, merged into the federal system. Mansour Saloum, co-head of the constituent council for the federal system said: 'The self-administration will stay like a service administration and include the bodies and institutions for schools and services etc. ... These administrations will be managed under the roof of one umbrella system.'[154] Other officials suggested that canton administrations could be turned into provinces and that Raqqah, once liberated, could join the system. There was no clear demarcation of borders to the federal entity and officials claimed that the model could be applied to other areas of Syria.[155] In practice, the territorial reach of this system was limited to areas controlled by the YPG and SDF forces and the reach of political alliances forged to support these military endeavours.

Institutions of federal governance were established to connect local councils. A constituent assembly for a Democratic Federal Syria (formed for purpose) held a meeting in the oil-rich town of Ramalan in order to establish a democratic

---

[151] IIST interview: Sheikh Ali Jamili, the Jarablus Council, 29/05/2016.

[152] Roy Gutman 23/02/2017: 'The ISIS stronghold of Al Bab falls to Turkish Backed Troops', *Daily Beast*, https://www.thedailybeast.com/the-isis-stronghold-of-al-bab-falls-to-turkish-backed-troops (last accessed 1/05/2018).

[153] Raqqah was eventually captured by the SDF in October 2017. Tom Perry 20/05/2017: 'Raqqa to be part of "federal Syria", U.S.-backed militia says', *Reuters*, https://www.reuters.com/article/us-mideast-crisis-syria-raqqa/raqqa-to-be-part-of-federal-syria-u-s-backed-militia-says-idUSKBN1CP16T (last accessed 1/05/2018).

[154] IIST interview: Mansour Saloum, the Arab co-head of the federal Rojava region, Ramalan, 21/04/2016.

[155] IIST interview: Sheruan Hussein, representative of the Rojava administration in the Netherlands, 16/02/2017.

federal system. It elected a 31-member organizing council to prepare a social contract and a comprehensive political and legal vision for the system. The resulting draft social contract was approved on 29 December 2016 by a council of 163 members.[156] The draft social contract stated that the region would be represented by a 'democratic peoples' conference':

> The democratic peoples' conference makes legislations and generally represents the peoples and groups in the 'Democratic Federalism of Northern Syria.'[157]

The Peoples' Conference itself would be administered by the 'presidency office' and work through committees on tasks such as electing co-presidents to the conference presidency offices, electing co-presidents of the executive committee, shaping general policy and deciding on strategic goals[158] and legislation on laws for the Democratic Federation of Northern Syria. At the time of writing this social contract was still a draft and, although the plan for federalism had been announced and denounced in March 2016 and the federation was soon referred to as an existing entity, the practical application of federalism made slow progress. Formulating and installing federal governing bodies was hindered and complicated by the Turkish military interventions in northern Syria in August 2016 and in January 2018 and by its support of Syrian rebels. Ankara's attempts to protect Turkey's interests in Syria by creating a buffer zone between the Kurdish cantons and by dislodging the PYD-led administration, thus prevented the realization of a contiguous Kurdish entity.

Achieving territorial contiguity was also complicated by the Syrian government's attempts to regain control over Syrian territory. The dominant power in the region, Russia, assisted the expansion of government forces towards Manbij, and land swaps (of some villages west of the city) were agreed with the YPG. To the west of the Shahba region, in Afrin, the YPG and Russian military were reported to have agreed on access to the region in March 2017, which resulted in a Russian military presence in Kafr Jenna, just thirteen kilometres north-east of Afrin town.[159] This development limited Turkey's ability to intervene against the Kurds but extended the Syrian government's

---

[156] ANF 18/03/2016: 'Final declaration of the Federal System Constituent Assembly announced', *Firat News Agency*, https://anfenglish.com/kurdistan/final-declaration-of-the-federal-system-constituent-assembly-announced (last accessed 24/03/2017); ANHA 29/12/2016: 'Northern Syria Constituent Assembly approves Social Contract draft', *ANHA*, http://en.hawarnews.com/northern-syria-constituent-assembly-approves-social-contract-draft/ (last accessed 25/03/2017).

[157] The Social Contract of the Democratic Federalism of Northern Syria (draft) 29/12/2016: Article 57.

[158] Ibid., Article 59.

[159] IIST interview: Afrin residents 17/04/2017; Tom Perry 20/03/2017: 'U.S.-allied Kurd militia says struck Syria base deal with Russia', *Reuters*, http://uk.reuters.com/article/uk-mideast-crisis-syria-r ussia-idUKKBN16R1GI?il=0 (last accessed 05/05/2017).

influence and its symbolic presence within Kurdish-controlled areas. A year later, in January 2018, Russia stood aside, allowing Turkey to enter Afrin region when the Kurdish administration refused to hand over Afrin completely to the Syrian government.[160] This led to the fall of Afrin to Turkish-backed forces on 18 March and demonstrated the volatility and ad hoc character of relations between the Kurds and international powers and the precariousness of the governance system and territorial control.

The move towards federalism and extension of governance structures across northern Syria, however, was also designed to install enduring political and representative structures, grounded in local alliances that could replace the central state. The cooperation of the PYD with other ethnic groups, or the incorporation of smaller local militias and factions within the administration's security and governance structures, dated back to 2013. Until 2016, however, cooperation had occurred within a framework defined by Kurdish majority areas, or Rojava, and had been driven, initially, by security needs and resources.

In October 2013, the PYD had allied with the Arab Shammar tribe to take control of the strategically important Yarubiyah border crossing and the town of Yarubiyah itself (also known as Tel Kocer in Kurdish) inhabited mainly by Arabs. The Shammar established the Sanadid militia in 2013 which cooperated with the YPG and later joined the SDF. In 2014, the PYD appointed an Arab Shammar leader, Sheikh Hamdi Daham al-Hadi, as co-governor for the province of Hasakah. His son, Bandar, also led the Sanadid militia.

> Shammar is the biggest tribe to work with the Kurds, but the other tribes worked with the regime. ... In the beginning of the crisis, [some] Shammar members were members of ISIS, [but] we called them to protect our land, so they left [ISIS] and [re-]joined their tribe. The Sheikh can influence tribes as a sheikh. (Bandar al-Humaydi of the Shammar)[161]

The YPG was also instrumental in forming other ethnically organized proxy militias such as *Jabhat al-Akrad* (the Kurdish Front) in 2013, which operated primarily in northern Aleppo with the FSA. It was expelled from northern Aleppo and from Tal Abyad by jihadist and FSA groups in the summer of 2013 after clashes had spread from Ras al-Ain to the Aleppo and Raqqah governorates. Although, before 2014, cooperation between jihadist groups and

---

[160] Wladimir van Wilgenburg 22/02/2018: 'Russia using Turkey to force Kurds back to Assad – Kurdish leaders', *Ahval*, https://ahvalnews.com/pyd-ypg/russia-using-turkey-force-kurds-back-assad-kurdish-leaders (last accessed 01/05/2018).
[161] IIST interview: Bandar al-Humaydi, head of Sanadid militia, Tal Alo village, 30/04/2016.

the FSA to attack the PYD and the YPG was common, ISIS's expulsion of non-jihadist factions from the Hasakah and Raqqah governorates changed this and initiated limited cooperation between some FSA groups and the YPG. Some of these smaller FSA groups had fled from ISIS to Kurdish-controlled areas and had formed alliances with the YPG, which led to the formation of the joint YPG-FSA operations room, Euphrates Volcano, in September 2014. The ISIS siege of Kobani and US-led military support cemented this alliance and it became the foundation for the larger SDF formed in October 2015.

By June 2015, the YPG territory included Tal Abyad which, with the removal of ISIS from the area, also connected the cantons of Kobani and Jazirah for the first time. After the formation of the SDF, which incorporated diverse military groupings,[162] large areas of Hasakah province were also taken from ISIS. This offered the possibility of incorporating many more Arabs towns (including Shadadi in February 2016) within the democratic autonomy project and extending its areas of control towards Deir al-Zour. In all Arab towns (such as Shadadi, al-Hawl, Tal Brak, Tal Hamees, Tal Abyad, Raqqah, and Manbij), through co-option or mediation by TEV-DEM, local Arab tribes were encouraged to form councils that followed the democratic autonomy model. Some of these tribes had previously worked with the Syrian government, with the Syrian rebels or with ISIS, but were convinced to join these councils and became part of the local canton administrations.[163] Under the PYD control, Arabs fighters and politicians were introduced to and taught Öcalan's ideology and the democratic autonomy model of governance by members of TEV-DEM and the YPG.[164] In Tal Abyad a council of 134 members was created, which included prominent Arab tribal figures. It then formed committees for services, women's affairs and justice, among others.[165] Some of the Arab members remained members of the Syrian Arab Baath Party and did not want to be interviewed fearing possible reprisals, while a Turkmen member said that

---

[162] Talal Silo, an ethnic Turkmen from Al-Rai, northern Aleppo (now controlled by Turkish-backed rebels), used to be in officer in the Syrian Army but joined the FSA operating in the Aleppo area in 2012. Later in 2015 he joined the YPG-affiliated FSA group Jaysh al-Thuwar formed on 3 May 2015 that included other groups that were defeated by jihadist groups. 'After the establishment of the SDF forces, I was requested to become an officer of the SDF in Hasakah, so we went from the Afrin canton through Turkey to Rojava, and I was part of the declaration of the SDF', he said. IIST interview: Talal Silo, SDF spokesperson, Hasakah, 25/04/2016.

[163] An example of previous cooperation with the Syrian government was in the Manbij civilian council, co-headed by Sheikh Farouq al-Mashi, whose uncle was the oldest member of the Syrian parliament.

[164] See Liz Slym 07/01/2017: 'U.S. military aid is fueling big ambitions for Syria's leftist Kurdish militia', *Washington Post*, https://www.washingtonpost.com/world/middle_east/us-military-aid-is-fueling -big-ambitions-for-syrias-leftist-kurdish-militia/2017/01/07/6e457866-c79f-11e6-acda-59924caa24 50_story.html?utm_term=.087a6285e0d4 (last accessed 27/03/2017).

[165] IIST interviews: Tal Abyad council members, 30/05/2016.

he had been imprisoned by the Assad government. Others had fled from ISIS-controlled Raqqah. These politically diverse alliances were secured by common threats and functioning military alliances. The cooperation of the SDF with the US-led coalition also encouraged greater numbers of Arabs to join both the YPG and the SDF. Increased Arab involvement in operations to remove ISIS from the Syrian interior was encouraged by the United States and, according to the US-led coalition, in January 2017 the SDF had about 50,000 fighters, including 23,000 Arab fighters: a fact which the US officials emphasized by referring to it as the Syrian Arab Coalition.[166]

The plans of the PYD-led administration, to formalize wider governance structures as well as military ones, were given incentive and provided impetus by US attempts to appease Ankara's domestic security concerns about the threat from PYD/YPG domination and US military assistance to the SDF. In December 2015, the first attempt to give political expression and structure to these military alliances was made. The SDC, although driven by security issues and overshadowed by its precursor and military branch, the SDF, was instrumental in designing the federal system. The coalition was created and co-headed by a Kurd and an Arab and included Kurdish, Christian and Arabic groups, as well as Kurdish political parties that had formed the Kurdish National Alliance.[167] It offered a structured council system that appealed to wider social groupings beyond the Kurds. Ibrahim al-Hassan, a Turkmen from Tal Abyad and the deputy of the SDC said that 'when the SDC was formed, it was very near our idea of forming assemblies [of the Syrian opposition]. We saw the self-administration as an example; we had a similar self-administration but we were forced to stay in Turkey.'[168]

The need to reform the administrative structures and to adapt to the territorial expansion into non-Kurdish majority areas was a strategic concern for the PYD-led administration and central to its move towards a non-ethnic federal system. Although ethnic pluralism features in the democratic autonomy ideology, the physical expansion of the project beyond Kurdish areas and the long-term goal of forming a contiguous territory led to pragmatic attempts to

---

[166] See, for example, Barbara Star 17/01/2017: 'Pentagon readies aggressive ISIS proposals for Trump', *CNN*, http://edition.cnn.com/2017/01/17/politics/pentagon-options-izis-trump/ (last accessed 27/03/2017).

[167] The Kurdish National Alliance became part of the federal system but forbade its members to be members of the canton administrations. In the past, Salih Ghedo and others had held official positions in the canton administration.

[168] IIST interview: Ibrahim al-Hassan, deputy co-chair of SDC and head of the judicial council in Tal Abyad, 31/05/2016.

create an administration that accommodated the demographic diversity of the region. Preparations for establishing a federal system continued: in January 2017 Kurdish and Christian co-heads were elected to lead the executive body of the federal system and drafting electoral laws and plans to hold elections proceeded.[169] The conflict, as well as Syria's diversity, while providing the opportunity to build and develop autonomy, also threw up significant obstacles and challenges to its realization.

Local obstacles to DAA control and federalism

The move towards federalism was hampered by several interconnected factors, including difficulties in bridging geographically and socio-economically rooted ethnic divisions, opposition from and non-recognition by the KNC, the intervention of Turkey in the northern Aleppo and Afrin, the strain on political alliances that the expansion of the Syrian Army towards Manbij posed, as well as by opposition to it from the Assad government, from Iran, and from regional and international powers. These latter regional factors are examined further in Chapter 5, while ethnic and political diversity, KNC–PYD tensions and political opposition are considered here.

Ethnic and political diversity

One of the main challenges for the development and maintenance of the multi-ethnic federal entity in northern Syria was the cooperation, integration and representation of non-Kurdish groups. The longevity and durability of these local alliances against changes to regional and local balances of power were uncertain. The federal project was rejected by much of the Syrian Arab opposition, which denounced its application as unilateral and a move towards separation from Syria. These alliances and oppositions generated political tensions within other identity groups, such as Arab, Christian, Turkmen societies, as they had done within Kurdish society. Cooperation based on security and resources, with political structures given secondary importance, also raised questions about

---

[169] Hubo 22/01/2017: 'ESU: Urgent appeal after many Christians fell in the struggle to liberate Raqqa', *Syriacs News*, http://www.syriacsnews.com/esu-urgent-appeal-many-christians-fell-struggle-liber ate-raqqa/ (last accessed 27/03/2017); ANHA 28/01/2017: '*intikhab maajlis al-fidraliyyah saytm bada' min al- kawmiinat* الكومينات انتخاب مجالس الفدرالية سيتم بدء من', *Hawar News Agency*, http://haw arnews.com/اللك-من-بدء-سيتم-الفدرالية-مجالس-انتخاب/ (last accessed 27/03/2017).

how these relationships might change post-ISIS or after a future settlement of the conflict in Syria.

Promoting wider local acceptance of the PYD's federal brand and multi-ethnic project was hindered by allegations about the displacement of Arab and Turkmen civilians and the destruction of homes during military operations. Human rights monitors and media organizations accused the YPG of destroying Arab houses and villages in the Hasakah and Raqqah governorates and preventing Arab civilians from returning to their homes.[170] These claims were seized on by Turkish officials who accused the Kurds of ethnic cleansing.[171] The Administration, YPG, as well as members of Arab councils established in 'liberated' areas, rejected allegations of collective punishment and accused the human rights group, Amnesty International, of deepening ethnic tensions.[172] They refuted the claims that the displacement and destruction of homes was deliberate and instead declared that the areas were destroyed in fighting. Evidence and interviews suggested that in many cases civilian populations of towns were prevented from returning due to security concerns because of the presence of mines, a suspected ISIS presence or ongoing fighting. The civilians affected were not exclusively Arab. The SDF and the YPG certainly justified the months of delays that civilians experienced before returning home in these terms.[173] In most cases, civilians were allowed to return after local councils were

---

[170] Amnesty International 13/10/2015: 'Syria: US ally's razing of villages amounts to war crimes', *Amnesty International*, https://www.amnesty.org/en/press-releases/2015/10/syria-us-allys-razing-of-villages-amounts-to-war-crimes/ (last accessed 27/03/2017); Vice 22/10/2015: 'Caught between the Islamic State and the Kurds: Exiled from Tal Abyad', *Vice*, https://news.vice.com/video/caught-between-the-islamic-state-and-the-kurds-exiled-from-tal-abyad (last accessed 30/03/2017).

[171] Humeyra Pamuk and Umit Bektas 16/06/2015: 'Turkey sees signs of "ethnic cleansing" by Kurdish fighters in Syria', *Reuters*, http://www.reuters.com/article/us-mideast-crisis-kurds-turkey-idUSKBN0OW1SA20150616 (last accessed 30/03/2017).

[172] ANHA 21/10/2015: 'YPG responds to Amnesty International report: It is contradictory', *ANHA*, http://en.hawarnews.com/ypg-responds-to-amnesty-international-report-it-is-contradictory/ (last accessed 30/03/2017).

[173] Although the town of al-Hawl was captured on 13 November 2015, the YPG allowed the return of civilians only on 2 May 2016 after it said it had cleared the city of mines. There were a number of protests by Arab civilians demanding to return to al-Hawl, such as in April 2016 in which a child was killed. Four YPG fighters were punished for damaging civilian property in al-Hawl by the YPG. (See KurdWatch 06/05/2016: 'al-Hawl: Residents return to the city', *KurdWatch*, http://kurdwatch. org/?e3826 (last accessed 04/04/2017); Etilaf 05/04/2016: 'PYD militias fire at protest in Hasaka, kill a child', *Etilaf*, http://en.etilaf.org/all-news/local-news/pyd-militias-fire-at-protest-in-hasaka-kill-a-child.html (last accessed 04/04/2017); Wilgenburg 05/06/2016(b): 'Senior Arab Leader backs return of civilians to Arab town', *ARA News*, http://aranews.net/2016/06/senior-arab-leader-backs-return-of-civilians-to-syrian-town-after-kurdish-ypg-dismantles-isis-explosives/ (last accessed 04/04/2017); Albin Szakola 19/01/2016: 'Syria Kurds put fighters on trial', *NOW*, https://now.mmedia.me/lb/en/NewsReports/566506-syria-kurds-put-fighters-on-trial (last accessed 04/04/2017).) IIST interview: YPG fighters in Tal Abyad, 17/10/2015, confirmed that delays had been caused by the presence of ISIS cells in Tel Abyad. According to Turkey and the Syrian opposition, civilians were massively displaced from Tel Abyad, but more than 3,000 families returned after the town was captured from ISIS. 'Some families had members with ISIS, another part of the population is still in Turkey for work. ... Those

established by TEV-DEM. In other cases, the continuation of hostilities between the SDF and ISIS in frontline areas, such as Ayn al-Issa in the countryside of Raqqah, had prevented civilians from returning.[174]

According to a foreign volunteer with the YPG near Tal Abyad, towns and villages were emptied of civilians in order to protect them from the fighting: 'In war things are like this; it was for a short time. They [ISIS] were fighting in the villages full of civilians and they [civilians] would be injured and killed. That's why we force them to leave.'[175] He added that houses were destroyed on front lines between 'Rojava and Daash [ISIS]' and implied that military objectives necessitated removing civilians from danger and obstacles from the line of sight:

> We don't want to destroy their homes and we don't want to force them to leave. We want them to agree and build up brotherhood between Arabs and Kurds. ... When these things happened nobody asked if this house belongs to a Kurd or Arab. It's not mass destruction. You need your point, some 100 meters to see [in front of you].[176]

Attempts to install local councils based on the PYD model certainly delayed the return of civilians. In the town of Slouk, captured in June 2015, civilians were not permitted to return until 26 January 2016. There were similar patterns in towns such as Tal Brak and Shadadi, where civilians returned only after local councils were formed. In comparison, in the Arab-majority town of Manbij, where a civilian council for it had already been formed, civilians returned on the day it was captured from ISIS while military operations were ongoing. ISIS mines that had not been cleared when the operation ended on 13 August 2016, however, caused civilian casualties.[177]

The differences in experience and procedure suggested that there was not a systematic displacement campaign against Arabs. The UN Independent

---

media reports about forced immigration is something wrong and a lie.' IIST interview: Hamdan al-Abad, Tal Abyad, 30/05/2016. The town itself was quite busy, but civilians were reluctant to talk about the situation.

[174] Ayn al-Issa was captured by the YPG and allied FSA groups on 23 June 2015 but temporarily recaptured by ISIS on 5 July. While Arab and Kurdish civilians were not initially displaced, they were forced to flee and prevented from returning when ISIS re-entered the town and it became a front line between the YPG and ISIS after 6 July and a base for SDF offensives towards Raqqah.

[175] IIST interview: Heval Jiyan, a foreign fighter in YPG, based close to Ayn al-Issa, 17/10/2015.

[176] Ibid.

[177] Suleiman Al-Khalidi, 14/08/2016: 'Thousands return to Manbij after IS militants flee city', *Reuters*, http://www.reuters.com/article/us-mideast-crisis-syria-manbij-idUSKCN10O0S2 (last accessed 04/04/2017); HRW 26/10/2016: 'Syria: Improvised mines kill, injure hundreds in Manbij', *Human Rights Watch*, https://www.hrw.org/news/2016/10/26/syria-improvised-mines-kill-injure-hundreds-manbij (last accessed 04/04/2017).

International Commission of Inquiry on the Syrian Arab Republic, in March 2017, stated that it

> found no evidence to substantiate claims that YPG [Kurdish People's Protection Units] or SDF [Syrian Democratic Forces] ever targeted Arab communities on the basis of ethnicity, nor that YPG cantonal authorities systematically sought to change the demographic composition of territories under their control through the commission of violations directed against any particular ethnic group.[178]

It was noted that 'there is regrettably little or no accountability on the ground in Syria for abuses and war crimes committed by all sides, and a comprehensive reckoning is unlikely to occur for the foreseeable future.'[179]

A primary factor influencing permission for civilians to return and the timescale involved appeared to have been the parallel political attempts to establish councils that cooperated with the democratic autonomy project, which would ensure that its governance structure was extended into non-Kurdish majority areas. The success of the federal plan depended on its acceptance by and application in non-Kurdish areas and, in particular, those located between Afrin and Kobani. Accounts of the processes, however, suggested that the establishment of councils and cooperative structures was, in some cases, coerced or that locals willing to cooperate were accommodated within the new governance structures, while other sectors of society were excluded. The primary manifestation of opposition to the PYD domination in Arab areas were rebel groups included within the Turkish-backed Euphrates Shield operation. The Turkish government also attempted to exploit existing tribal divisions by backing rival tribal military alliances, such as the Army of Al Jazirah and Euphrates Tribes, which was formed in Turkey in March 2017. Its members came mainly from within SDF-controlled areas and from Hasakah, Deir al-Zour and Raqqah, which had been affected by either ISIS or PYD domination.[180] In other areas of the Jazirah, there were still many Christians that remained loyal to the Assad government. The incorporation of Arab tribes and other groups within the PYD-led system and

---

[178] Wladimir van Wilgenburg, 15/03/2017: 'UN says no ethnic cleansing by Kurds in northern Syria', *ARA News*, http://aranews.net/2017/03/un-says-no-ethnic-cleansing-by-kurds-in-northern-syria/ (last accessed 14/04/2017).

[179] Aymenn Jawad Al-Tamimi 13/02/2017: 'Further response to Roy Gutman: Balancing the picture', *Syria Comment*, http://www.joshualandis.com/blog/response-roy-gutman-balancing-picture/ (last accessed 04/04/2017).

[180] The *Daily Sabah* 14/03/2017: 'Arab tribes to form army against PYD/PKK, Daesh in Syria', *Daily Sabah*, https://www.dailysabah.com/syrian-crisis/2017/03/14/arab-tribes-to-form-army-against-pydpkk-daesh-in-syria (last accessed 05/05/2017); Fergus Kelly 16/03/2017: 'Arab tribal leaders form "Army of al Jazira and Euphrates" to fight IS and PYD in Syria', *Grass Wir*, https://www.grasswire.com/2017/03/arab-tribal-leaders-form-army-al-jazira-euphrates-fight-pyd-syria/

the accommodation of these traditional power structures, however, implied that these alliances were not based on shared visions of political organization and social revolution. Rather, it appeared that alliances and enmities were determined more by acts of compliance, security, group interest, local inter-Arab/tribal power relations and politics, as well as the PYD's alliance with the US-led coalition and its strength on the ground. Certainly, for many, particularly non-Kurds, the ideology and central moral ethos of the PYD project was not a primary factor influencing cooperation nor did it dictate opposition to it within the particular political and security climate in Syria.

KNC–PYD tensions and political opposition

In this manner, local, sectarian and other tensions also translated into political ones. This was equally true within Kurdish areas. Although ethno-nationalism was rejected by the PYD and the creation of an ethnic Kurdish nation state was removed completely from the PYD and PKK agenda in 2005, organization around ethnic and local identities remained strong in Syria among both Arabs and Kurds. Differences between the models of federalism envisaged by the PYD and the KNC were highlighted and problematized with the extension of the YPG into non-Kurdish majority areas.

Hediya Yousef, the co-head of the federal system said:

> We don't want to make a Kurdistan border, maybe historically some of these areas belong to Kurdistan, but it doesn't matter to us if a region historically belongs to Kurds or Arabs. Our federal system is not based on geography, but based on communities. … If Raqqah is liberated it could also join. … We don't want a country to oppress the people. They can have their own self-administration.[181]

Nevertheless, expansion into non-Kurdish areas caused many Kurdish nationalists to criticize the PYD and the YPG for fighting in Arab areas that were not part of historic Kurdish lands. This led also to denigration from Syrian opposition groups, some of which suggested that the Kurds were 'occupying Arab areas' and displacing Arabs.[182] More generally, the PYD was seen to have removed Kurdish symbolism from its governance and followed a non-Kurdish

---

[181] IIST interview: Hediya Yousef, co-head of the federal system, 21/04/2016.
[182] See Amnesty International, 'Syria: US ally's razing of villages amounts to war crimes'. It appeared that the majority of Arabs returned to the town of Tal Abyad, despite accusations by the Syrian opposition, while others remained in Turkey.

project that prioritized coexistence with Arabs over unresolved, and specifically, Kurdish interests framed by the idea of the Kurdish nation and 'Kurdistan':

> They don't have a national project: not a Kurdish state nor Kurdish rights. …
> They are allied to the PKK and they are left-wing, not Kurdish. They have no
> project for Kurds. (Mohammed Ismail, a leading KDP-S politician) [183]

Concerns were expressed by Syrian Kurds over the large number of Arab refugees in Kurdish majority cities, such as Qamishli, which, it was feared, would produce irreversible demographic changes.[184] The DAA officials suggested that the Kurdish regions hosted over 1.8 million IDPs from all over Syria[185] in addition to thousands of Arab refugees from Mosul. The migration of Kurds out of northern Syria exacerbated Kurdish concerns about irreversible demographic change and its consequences for Kurdish nationhood. Some Syrian Kurds also expressed distrust of Arab fighters that worked with the YPG, suggesting that they could betray the Kurds or work with the regime in the future and further undermine and endanger efforts to secure Kurdish rights.[186]

This was not to say that the KNC sought an ethnically pure federal entity, or that those who were opposed to the PYD project did so because of a belief in ethnic exclusivity. On the contrary, the federal model proposed by the KNC also included recognition and representation of all ethnic and religious groupings. The formation of a federal unit akin to that in Iraqi Kurdistan was not considered geographically viable or, for the PYD, congruent with its ideology. The difficulties in forming such an entity in Syria had long been recognized by Kurdish politicians from diverse backgrounds.[187] Nonetheless,

---

[183] IIST interview: Mohammed Ismail, KDP-S official, Qamishli, 10/05/2016.

[184] IIST interview Majdal Delli, senior Yekiti member, 12/04/2017.

[185] Peace in Kurdistan Campaign 09/07/2015: 'Rojava, Kurdish autonomy and peace-building efforts in Syria: Report from a roundtable discussion', *Peace in Kurdistan Campaign*, https://peaceinkurdi stancampaign.com/2015/07/09/rojava-kurdish-autonomy-and-peace-building-efforts-in-syria-re port-from-a-roundtable-discussion/ (last accessed 04/04/ 2017).

[186] Aris Roussinos 2015: *Rebels: My Life Behind Enemy Lines with Warlords, Fanatics and Not-so-friendly Fire*, Random House, London, 280.

[187] For example, senior KDP-S member Abdulhakim Bashar told US officials on 25 November 2009 that it was impossible to unite the Kurdish regions: 'He also pointed out … that the issue of "territory" in no way appeared in any Kurdish party political platform; he further noted Kurdish areas in Syria were not contiguous. Kurds were concentrated in Aleppo, Afrin, Qamishli and other regions, all of which were "disconnected" from one another. It would be impossible, he stated, to unite them territorially.' (https://wikileaks.org/plusd/cables/09DAMASCUS826_a.html). Similarly, Ahmad Sulaiman, a politician of the *Pêşverû* party said it was impossible to create a Kurdistan region in Syria. 'If you go to the Kurdistan region [of Iraq], they don't even know Arabs, but if you go to our region everywhere there is an Arab village', he said. 'In Slemani and Hawler there are almost no native speakers, but in our region people are mixed. In Iraq, some cities like Kirkuk, Sinjar, and Khanaqin are disputed, but in our cities all regions are like that. Only Efrin and Kobani are pure Kurdish, but in Cizere [Hasakah], it is difficult, it's not majority Kurdish. … This self-administration is not only Kurdish, but also for Arabs, Christians, but in the Kurdistan region [of Iraq] you don't

issues of identity and representation continued to inform and ignite political tensions between the KNC and the PYD, and to divide the Kurds ideologically and prevent the development of representative forms of democracy. The model and implementation of federalism announced by the PYD-led administration in 2016 was denounced by the KNC despite its advocacy of a federal Kurdistan region for Syria. It further insisted that federalism should result from a political process involving all Syrians.

Tensions between the PYD and the KNC were increased by the latter's rejection of the DAA and federal systems and its political opposition. On 17 April 2014, the local administrations adopted a political party law that required political parties to register with the local administrations.[188] The KNC did not recognize this law and its parties remained unregistered but, nevertheless, operated under restrictions and faced occasional attacks on KNC party buildings and arrests of their politicians. Among many other examples of arrests and raids on party offices, on 24 April 2016 a KNC building in Girkê Legê (al-Ma'bada) in the Hasakah province was burned down. 'Who burned the KNC office? The PYD did it. They arrest people, take houses of people. The Turks don't do this,' Mohammed Ismail, a KDP-S official said.[189] In another example, on 13 August 2016, KNC chairman Ibrahim Biro was arrested and expelled to the Kurdistan region. 'This systematic persecution is one of the main reasons why, already, more than a million Kurds fled the area', the KNC said.[190] Several politicians, including many interviewed for this book, were imprisoned for extended periods because permission from the Administration was not granted for KNC gatherings, protests or for attending funerals of Peshmerga fighters who had died in Iraqi Kurdistan and who were buried in Rojava. Human Rights Watch criticized this policy of arbitrary arrests, and condemned the death, under suspicious circumstances, of a 36-year-old man in Asayish custody in Afrin in May 2014.[191]

Similar problems of discrimination against political opponents, and specifically against the PYD and the PKK, can be identified in areas under KDP control

---

even have one Arab minister.' (IIST interview: Ahmed Sulaiman, senior member Progressive Party, Qamishli, 6 May 2016).

[188] KurdWatch 30/09/2014: 'Rojava, Kurdish autonomy and peace-building efforts in Syria: Report from a roundtable discussion', *KurdWatch*, http://kurdwatch.org/?cid=185&z=en (last accessed 04/04/2017).

[189] IIST interview: Mohammed Ismail, KDP-S official, Qamishli, 10/05/2016.

[190] KNC 16/08/2016: 'President of the KNC abducted and deported by the PYD', http://knc-geneva.org/?p=657&lang=en (last accessed 21/10/2016).

[191] HRW 18/06/2014: 'Syria: Abuses in Kurdish-run Enclaves', *Human Rights Watch*, https://www.hrw.org/news/2014/06/18/syria-abuses-kurdish-run-enclaves (last accessed 05/04/2017).

in the KRI.[192] For instance Ahmad Sulaiman, whose party was independent of both the PYD and the KNC, said that both parties had the same mentality. 'In Shadadi, there are no Kurds but Arabs, and they have a big picture of Abdullah Öcalan. What will the Arabs say?' he questioned. 'There is also no democracy if you don't give sugar, if you don't join a commune.' He added, however, that the KNC had similar practises in the KRG. In 'the refugee camps [in the KRG] you don't receive help if you don't join KDP-S. What's the difference between the PYD and them?'[193] This claim could not be verified by the authors of this book. In March 2017, following military clashes between the PYD and the KDP in Sinjar, the Administration announced that vetting of all political parties would occur, and that any parties non-compliant with Administration laws would be closed.[194] A wave of closures of KNC offices and arrests of politicians followed[195] which were mirrored by arrests of PKK-affiliated activists within the KRI.

The KNC political position and activity within Syria and abroad placed it decisively in opposition to the PYD and its domination of governance. The regular actions taken against KNC activists implied that the control and suppression of the organization was important to the success of the PYD-led project. Policy towards Kurdish opposition parties that refused to legitimize the administrative had been called authoritarian and compared to a one-party rule.[196] In its defence, DAA spokespersons argued that they wanted to prevent a dual political system, similar to that in Iraqi Kurdistan, from emerging.

> We – for the Kurds – cannot make a division into two sides [two administrations].
> In the Kurdistan region thousands of people were killed in battles, and now they
> ask for a similar system and high positions. For sure we don't accept this, because
> these forces make so many problems between us. (Hediya Youssef)[197]

The fact that the KNC rejected the DAA and federal systems made elections more problematic for the Administration and unrepresentative of the population. When local municipal elections had been held in 2015 concerns about their

[192] See Campbell MacDiarmid, 02/11/2015: 'Journalists fear for freedoms in Iraq's Kurdish region', *Middle East Eye*, http://www.middleeasteye.net/in-depth/features/journalists-fear-freedoms-iraqs-kurdish-region-1281553919 (last accessed 04/04/2017).

[193] IIST interview: Ahmed Sulaiman, senior member Progressive Party, Qamishli, 06/05/2016.

[194] *Syrian Observer* 15/03/2017: 'Kurdish self-administration poised to ban Kurdish opposition parties', *Syrian Observer*, http://syrianobserver.com/EN/News/32472 (last accessed 04/04/2017).

[195] See, for example, ARA News 13/03/2017: 'Post-Sinjar tensions continue: Over 40 PYD rivals arrested in Syria, KNC offices burned', *ARA News*, http://aranews.net/2017/03/post-sinjar-tensions-continue-40-pyd-rivals-arrested-syria-knc-offices-burned/ (last accessed 04/04/2017).

[196] Robert Lowe 2014: 'The emergence of Western Kurdistan and the future of Syria', in David Romano and Mehmet Gurses (eds.), *Conflict, Democratisation and the Kurds in the Middle East*, Palgrave Macmillan, London.

[197] IIST interview: Hediya Yousef, co-head of the federal system, 21/04/2016.

legitimacy had arisen: Shaykh Ali's Kurdish Democratic Union Party, which operated within the DAAs and was the only other party to stand in municipal elections in Afrin on 10 September 2015, accused the election committees of bias after TEV-DEM won all positions. In general, all Kurdish parties claimed to have the support of the majority, but under the prevailing conditions in Syria this was impossible to ascertain decisively. 'If there is election, the KDP-S and KNC will get ten times more votes than the PYD', KDP-S politician Mohammed Ismail claimed.[198] Salih Muslim, then the co-head of the PYD, also said in 2016: 'We believe in elections and we trust in the people and respect their decision … but while the fighting is still going on you cannot do this.'[199] Elections were, nonetheless, held in September 2017, despite the then ongoing Raqqah operation.[200]

Further factors adding to tensions between the KNC and the PYD were international and regional relations, in particular, the relationships between Ankara and the KDP and the Syrian opposition, which are addressed further in the following chapter. Turkish influence over the Syrian opposition and over negotiations on peace settlements contributed to the exclusion of the PYD from the international peace talks in Geneva and in Astana. The relationship between Ankara and the KDP also provoked allegations of betrayal by the PYD supporters against the KDP and, by association, against the KNC, especially after the Turkey-PKK ceasefire broke down in July 2015. International condemnation of the KDP-led independence referendum on 25 September, however, led to a slight improvement of relations. But any return to the terms of the Erbil and Duhok agreements remained remote and tensions continued between the two blocs.

A new state structure?

While the Administration developed all the institutions and functions of a quasi-state, attempts were made to distinguish it from modern states in its rhetoric and terminology. It deliberately avoided the use of language associated with the

[198] IIST interview: Mohammed Ismail, KDP-S official, Qamishli, 10/05/2016.
[199] IIST interview: Salih Muslim, PYD co-head, Kobani, 26/05/2016.
[200] KurdWatch 17/09/2015: 'Afrin: Following elections all co-chair positions on the municipal councils are to be filled by TEVDEM', *KurdWatch*, http://www.kurdwatch.org/?e3600 (last accessed 04/04/2017).

nation state. The Administration described military service as a 'duty of self-defence' and introduced, not a constitution but a social contract:[201]

> The name itself distinguishes it from a Constitution, which generally defines the ground norm of States. The notion of the State, and of the nation-state in particular, is presented in the Preamble of the Social Contract as the root of the crises and problems of the people of Rojava.[202]

Although the language distinguished it from a nation state, in practice many of the institutions resembled modern state and electoral systems, with central decision-making and coordination, but with partially decentralized governing bodies, military and police forces. Likewise, hierarchies of power within and across the DAAs were identifiable. In all structures of government institutions TEV-DEM officials were represented. They also played central roles in setting up councils in non-Kurdish areas. And although hierarchies of political skill and intellect were dismissed in Abdullah Öcalan's ideology, levels of commitment and allegiance to the ideology itself formed alternative hierarchies embedded in the democratic autonomy governance system.[203] In line with Öcalan's theories of social revolution and the PKK policy, advancement within the system appeared to be based more on service, loyalty and commitment rather than on political or intellectual skills.[204] As a consequence, much decision-making was based on developing and preserving the democratic autonomy project and Öcalan's ideology rather than on local representation and popular mandates.

The ideological revolutionary project was where the administration abstracted from territorially based state systems. The network and structures that formed and included the PYD, KCK and associated political and military organizations existed in parallel to the state and to the local administration. Opponents of the PYD and associated governance structures accused the local administrations of taking orders from PKK camps in the Qandil Mountains in the KRI, rather than reaching their own internal decisions. Certainly, communications between the two regions existed and the wider governance structures testified to implicit connections. The PKK officials, however, denied direct agency in the development of Syrian Kurdish governance structures: "There is no coordination in the sense

---

[201] Many locals still used the Arabic term for military service.
[202] International Law Blog 24/10/2016: 'The 2016 Rojava social contract: A democratic experiment of civil and social rights in northern Syria', https://aninternationallawblog.wordpress.com/2016/10/24/the-2016-rojava-social-contract-a-democratic-experiment-of-civil-and-social-rights-in-northern-syria/ (last accessed 18/12/2018).
[203] Grojean, 'The production of the new man within the PKK', 7, 9.
[204] Ibid., 9.

of "this or that". We do not directly interfere there but rather offer suggestions, without giving specific instructions', said senior PKK official, Riza Altun, who also criticized the local administrations for moving too fast on federalism and urged them to stop using the name 'Rojava' for the federal system.[205]

The local administrations defined its model of governance and its institutions as democratic; as guiding a social revolution and developing a radical form of multi-ethnic direct democracy in Syria. Despite this rhetorical agenda – and alongside praise of its stated intentions, its practical management of a war-torn society and grass-roots mobilization – there has been much criticism of the PYD from within the Syrian Kurdish population, the Syrian opposition, the KNC, the Syrian government, local Christian and Arab organizations as well as from human rights organizations. Concerns about definitions of identity and channels of representation were evident at multiple levels and were contextualized by wider developments and events as well as by the parallel tensions between and within sub-state, state and regional loyalties. The PYD-led administration's representative structures faced many challenges, not least of which was the unravelling and clarification of its own institutions, power structures and decision-making in order to increase transparency.

At the time of writing, the model of government in northern Syria incorporated elements of the original interim administration that was a central administration of the three Kurdish areas; the DAA system, which decentralized administration to autonomous cantons; and the federal system, which, combining central and decentralized councils, had not been fully implemented in practice due to changes in frontiers and political and military alliances in the region between the Afrin and Kobani cantons. What had emerged was a multifaceted system in which different governance structures, developed since the start of the Syrian crisis in 2011, appeared to overlap. TEV-DEM, which dominated the interim administration, had become a governing body for the Kurdish territories and continued to act as a central organization managing and coordinating between the DAAs. The DAAs themselves were self-governed, as far as possible. The federal entity created in 2016 continued to be subject to development and appeared to be forming alongside these other two structures and expanded the core governance structures decisively into non-Kurdish areas. Furthermore, within these overlapping structures, the Syrian government continued to extend avenues of control into northern Syria and into sectors managed by the PYD-

---

[205] Mohammed Nouredinne 29/06/2016: 'PKK foreign relations head speaks out', *Al Monitor*, http://www.al-monitor.com/pulse/politics/2016/07/turkey-coup-pkk-kurds-rojava-us-intervention.html (last accessed 27/03/2017).

led administration. Finally, overarching these internal Syrian structures was the PKK/KCK network and edifice: combined, it formed a truly hybrid governance structure.

The model of governance and federalism had been denounced by the Syrian government, by the Syrian opposition, by the KNC, and by Syria's neighbours. Yet the PYD and TEV-DEM continued to benefit from the conflict and power vacuum in northern Syria. In the governance void, their legal, military, educational and political institutions following Abdullah Öcalan's ideology of a 'democratic autonomy' slowly developed and entrenched into the political and social infrastructure of northern Syria. Abuses of power were contextualized by the conflict and the existential threats that the Kurds faced, both past and present. Many observers celebrated the achievements of Administration and its ability to galvanize the Kurdish population. One comment on a Reddit forum suggested: 'Ultimately, the PYD has the support of the inhabitants of Rojava. It can't be authoritarian in a real sense so long as it has that support.'[206] And here we must return to those inhabitants and analyse the extent of support for the system.

---

[206] Comment in response to question: Is there any credibility to accusations of PYD authoritarianism?' on https://www.reddit.com/r/rojava/comments/5noqhf/is_there_any_credibility_to_accusations_of_pyd/ (last accessed 07/07/2017).

4

Identity and Representation II: The Democratic Autonomy Project

Democratic confederalism is based on grass-roots participation. Its decision-making processes lie with the communities. Higher levels only serve the coordination and implementation of the will of the communities that send their delegates to the general assemblies. For limited space of time they are both mouthpiece and executive institutions. However, the basic power of decision rests with the local grass-roots institutions.

(Abdullah Öcalan)[1]

The DAA system promised direct representation, freedom to express and practice personal beliefs and customs, and representations of identity through participation and the continuous appraisal of process. It was premised on participation and achieved through social revolution. At the time of writing this 'revolution' was incomplete and, as with the nature of revolution, it was unclear whether or not its goals would be achieved in Syria and beyond, or whether the pursuit of ideals and the maintenance of its governance system would embed new hierarchical power relations. Nevertheless, the administrative structures and state-like powers assumed by the PYD and associated organizations and institutions had established mechanisms and structures specifically designed to produce fair and equal representation. While for some outside observers and participants in the Administration it had already achieved much of what it set out to, field research in Syria suggested that, in terms of achieving majority participation and representation, the DAAs fell short of expectations.

In this chapter, the representative capacity of the administration is assessed through analysing the results of fieldwork conducted in the DAA regions. Surveys were completed by 180 randomly selected citizens, 87 from the Jazirah

---

[1] Abdullah Öcalan 2011: *Democratic Confederalism*, Transmedia Publishing Ltd, London, 33.

region and 93 from Kobani. Although it was not possible to distribute surveys in Afrin, a number of interviews with residents were conducted in an attempt to gauge the opinion there. While a sample of this size may not be large enough to draw firm conclusions, when combined with wide-ranging interviews and observations within the regions and with extensive open source research, the surveys provide a fascinating picture of opinions of identity and representation in northern Syria with which to compare images of the administration and revolutionary process. Although the Syrian conflict remained unresolved and expectations of perfect representation and participation would be unfounded, the experience of participants in the system and their opinions about it, particularly at this stage, highlighted areas in which the goals of the project had been achieved, where they had not and the main obstacles that faced both the DAAs and the population of areas under their governance. This chapter looks first at the commune system in more detail, examining participation and opinions about the system. Second, building on the examination of identity and representation in Chapter 1 and drawing on fieldwork within Syria, it looks at the effects of the crisis and the development of the DAAs on ideas of identity and representation between March 2011 and 2017. The third section returns to the question of how successful the 'revolution' has been in achieving democratic direct representative in the period in question.

Direct democracy in practice

> All groups of society and all cultural identities express themselves in local meetings, general conventions, and councils. Such a democracy opens political space for all social strata and allows diverse political groups to express themselves. In this way it advances the political integration of society as a whole. Politics becomes part of everyday life. (Abdullah Öcalan)[2]

The communes formed the foundations of the practice of 'direct democracy'[3] in the DAA system. Analysis and assessment of the communes, of participation in them and civilian's impressions of the system, therefore, can act as a test of direct

---

[2]   Öcalan, *Democratic Confederalism*, 26.
[3]   The exact form that direct democracy takes and what decisions the people are directly involved in can differ widely between models. In general, it should provide a system in which the people discuss and vote on laws and policy initiatives directly, often through referendums and on clearly defined topics of discussion at the local level.

democracy in practice and shed light on the overall capacity of the DAA system to represent the diverse sectors and identities of Syrian and Kurdish society.

According to representatives of the DAAs, the communes act on decisions and practices, primarily, at the local level and are concerned with meeting the needs of the local populace.[4] Commune meetings are open to everyone in a designated neighbourhood and are run by a commune coordinating board, consisting of two co-chairs and a representative from each commission (women, defence, economics, politics, civil society, free society, justice and ideology.)[5] They can take independent decisions on local issues that apply to constituent households and individuals and which can be addressed by the members of the commune themselves. On issues involving or affecting a number of communes, discussion and ideas expressed in the communes are fed upwards to the neighbourhood councils. In turn, these councils consult in order to produce policy.

> The system further prescribes that if decisions cannot be made at the commune level, they are relegated to the People's House (similar to a neighbourhood council), and then to the city councils. This form of local governance can be seen as an attempt at direct democracy, whereby all members of society are supposed to be involved with decision-making processes.[6]

Fieldwork in Syria included asking questions designed to assess democratic practice within the commune system: whether the participants believed that the administration was democratic and if the commune system gave them a role in decision-making processes. These questions were based on a common misconception that participation in the commune system was fairly widespread in the Jazirah and Kobani regions. The results revealed levels of non-participation not obvious from external observations and analyses or from pro-Administration sources. Answers to questions such as 'Do you believe that participation in local meetings gives you a direct involvement in local decision-making processes?' and 'Do you feel that your local administration acts as a tool for your social expression and participation in political life?' often included clarifications by respondents that they did not attend commune meetings, regardless of whether their opinion of the system was favourable or not. Of the 93 participants from

---

[4] Cinar Sali of TEV-DEM cited by Knapp, Flach and Ayboga, *Revolution in Rojava*, 87.
[5] Knapp, Flach and Ayboga, *Revolution in Rojava*, 87–91.
[6] Florence Bateson et al. 2016: *Gendered Alternatives: Exploring Women's Roles in Peace and Security in Self-administered Areas of Northern Syria.* Utrecht University and the Women's Commission of Rojava, http://www.kpsrl.org/browse/browse-item/t/gendered-alternatives-exploring-women-s-role-in-peace-and-security-in-self-administered-areas-of-northern-syria (last accessed 08/02/2017), 32.

Kobani 25 stated, without being asked, that they did not attend commune meetings and, of those in the Jazirah region, 36 out of 87 stated that they did not attend. A total of 61/180 or 34 per cent of survey participants volunteered this information. These numbers, therefore, do not imply that participants who did not mention non-participation actually attended commune meetings. Indeed, the real number of non-participants could be far higher. The data is given specifically to illustrate the fact that many participants in IIST surveys did not attend commune meetings. These results, as well as field observations and wider interviews, highlighted clearly that participation in the commune system was limited, even within Kobani where the PYD had gained greater popularity. Interviews suggested that participation in the Afrin region was an exception to low participation rates in Kobani and the Jazirah. In Afrin the control of the Administration over social, political and economic life was almost total and organization outside the governance structures was not possible. Respondents in Afrin said that there was an expectation on all civilians to regularly attend commune meetings and that non-participation was looked at unfavourably and could have negative consequences.[7] All local issues and problems were dealt with through the communes.[8]

Efforts of the Administration to increase participation in the Jazirah and Kobani were evident – posters encouraging participation, education about the revolution, re-education of women in particular, the proliferation of images and symbols of the revolution: martyrs and Abdullah Öcalan.

> Counterintuitively, we have the higher levels of this political system actively trying to expand the grassroots level of political participation. Lots of work is taking place to expand the numbers of communes numerically and geographically. It requires finding physical resources and educating people in the local community about the values of the revolution and the way the (sometimes complicated) systems work here. But perhaps the most visible element of the revolution is the role of women in society here.[9]

Nevertheless, this ideologization of the system and its extension downwards to the commune level hindered participation in what might otherwise have been successful institutions of direct democracy. Added to their partisan appearance was a perception that communes were for the poor or needy and that they were

---

[7] IIST interview: Afrin resident, 17/09/2017.
[8] IIST interview: Afrin resident, 28/02/2017.
[9] Rojava Solidarity Cluster 01/02/2017: "'A real revolution is a mass of contradictions": Interview with a Rojava Volunteer', *Novara Media*, http://novaramedia.com/2017/02/01/a-real-revolution-is-a-mass-of-contradictions-interview-with-a-rojava-volunteer/ (last accessed 12/06/2017).

ineffective as representative bodies on political matters. The control of communes over the distribution of subsidized products such as sugar, fuel and aid, also was seen by many as a tactic to force local participation and co-opt support.

Surveys as well as interviews with local residents demonstrated that the commune had limited scope for broad representation. The reasons for this were twofold: First, communes were widely reported to be dominated by PYD sympathizers (*hevals*), if not by members themselves, and the topics discussed and decisions made reflected the interests of the PYD-led administration.[10] Responses to survey and interview questions included many claims that decision-making was limited to those connected to the PYD administration and that commune organization and functions were overseen by individuals driven by the social revolution project and ideology of democratic autonomy. Claims that decisions were already made, that priority given to supporters[11] and that whether or not participants opinions were considered depended on their personal connections, implied that the communal discussions and processes were a façade.[12] For instance, in a meeting in Kobani in March 2017 civilians expressed widespread opposition to military conscription. The Administration was not obviously willing to respond positively to the demands of the civilians due to the overriding manpower requirements of the Raqqah operation.[13] Other survey participants thought that their opinions were not important to the Administration and that the system did not work.[14] Hassan Salih, *Yekîtî* party politburo member, went as far as to say that 'it is like the security forces of regime: to control everything in their eyes; to have their eyes in every place'.[15] In relation to this idea of the communes being a means of social control rather than of liberation, surveys also contained evidence that some people did not feel free to express their opinions if they might differ from PYD doctrine or ideology. Other participants suggested that they did not believe that their opinions or suggestions were considered and, even though they participated in the commune meetings, they could not make decisions as decision-making was 'only for some people'.[16]

---

[10] IIST survey comments; IIST interview: Afrin residents, 17/09/2016.

[11] IIST survey no. 60.

[12] For example survey no. 46.

[13] Hawar News 04/03/2017: '*al-idarah al-dtatiyah tustm'a li-rai ahali kubani*', *Hawar News*, http://aha warnews.com/الإدارة-الذاتية-تستمع-لآراء-أهالي-كوب/ (last accessed 24 March 2017).

[14] IIST survey no. 44; no. 62.

[15] IIST interview: Hassan Salih, 04/05/2016.

[16] IIST survey (166). At least 30/180 surveys contained comments about their opinions not being heard or not being considered important, and that they thought many decisions were made by people within the PYD or the administration or made regardless of the nature of the discussion and opinions of the people/communes. IIST surveys 2016.

Interviewees in the Afrin region suggested that positions of real power were held by Kurds who had been in the PKK and that important decisions about policy and organization came from 'outside Syria'.[17] Some voiced concerns that it was the military that drove decision-making, while others claimed that prejudice within the system existed, to the extent that only those sympathetic to the PYD and ideological project were provided with jobs, services and consideration in local decision-making. Some suggested that the administration was directed by the PKK itself and that local Syrian Kurds performed management roles and communes were used to control the local population.[18]

In contrast, however, other participants commented that the Administration was staffed by Syrian Kurds, some of whom had been in the PKK. Several participants expressed the belief that the communes were representative and tools for decision-making and empowerment, and recognized that their opinions were heard and considered. Some participants in commune meetings said that all opinions were expressed and heard and that everyone actively participated.[19] The absence of discrimination between peoples and groups was often cited as a positive aspect of the administrative system and discussion processes. Interestingly, many participants who said that they did not participate in the commune meetings still considered the system to be democratic. Conversely, others who recognized the democratic credentials of the administration also stated that they did not believe that their opinions were heard or considered in decision-making.[20]

The second reason that emerged from the surveys for the communes' limited scope for broad representation was the communes' inability to influence decision-making at the higher levels: it was restricted both by the dominance of the PYD and by constraints on their mandate. The decision-making capacity of communes concentrated on local issues and concerns and the resources at their disposal were limited.[21] Communes were involved in distributing services and aid, when available and when need dictated, and they ensued that families in need (in particular the families of martyrs) were appropriately supported. They regulated housing in the neighbourhoods and mediated in local disputes and conflicts. Consultations on more 'political' matters, however, were absent. Several interviewees commented that political issues were not discussed within

---

[17] ISST interviews: Afrin residents, 17/09/2016; 28/02/2017.
[18] Interviews: Afrin residents, 17/09/2016; 08/10/2016.
[19] IIST survey no. 42.
[20] For example survey no. 53; no. 50.
[21] Bateson et al., *Gendered Alternatives*, 55.

communes and that they had no influence over political decisions or matters. According to one Afrin resident, raising political issues or criticisms of the governance could lead to their removal from the commune.[22] The complaint that opinions, even if expressed within the system, did not reach the important people, appeared several of times within surveys. One participant suggested that, although she was satisfied with the sense of security and rights achieved for Kurds under the DAA, there was no political life – that there was just one political party and that the government did what it wanted.[23] This opinion was reflected in interviews and comments on surveys which suggested that communes engaged the population in local social issues and management but by doing so it also pacified them.

While grass-roots participation was encouraged by the administration and communes functioned for those involved in them at the local level, the downwards consultation from the drivers of the administration appeared to be lacking. Locals reported concerns that decisions were not driven by the processes or products of direct democracy, but rather that they were already made and discussion provided an illusion of consultation.[24] Certainly, the development of the administration after 2012 occurred from the top-down, from the PYD, and it was an attempt to stimulate and realize a grass-roots revolution. Its obvious strengths lay in its management of the region's economy and security and in its institutionalization of legal rights within the context of the conflict in Syria and multiple threats – more than in its claim to a grass-roots revolution. This was reflected in opinions expressed in surveys in which security, language and women's rights were highlighted as areas of success, far above any reference to representation or participation. This top-down, PYD-led implementation, however, led to distrust of its institutions by much of the population not politically sympathetic to the PYD and averse to the domination of one political party.

Herein lay a paradox for the administrative system and for the 'revolution' itself. For communes to operate democratically, people of diverse sectors of society and of differing political opinions had to believe that they were represented and come together and participate willingly in them. While communes were dominated by PYD supporters, or those ideologically sympathetic to it, the democratic process that the system promoted could only be experienced by its supporters. While participation was incomplete, the system simply served itself

---

[22] IIST interview: Afrin resident (m), 17/09/2016.
[23] IIST survey no. 122f.
[24] IIST survey comments.

in parallel to other sectors and structures of society. Identities and representative channels such as those discussed in Chapter 1 did not simply disappear but were challenged ideologically by the PYD-led system and the space available to them circumscribed. The state-like powers assumed by the DAAs meant that other options for representation and welfare were unavailable to those who did not recognize the political system or participate in it. For these sectors of society or individuals, their experience was one of unilateral and partisan decision-making that served an ideological project directed by the PKK.

Questions arose also about the effect that majority participation might have on the system. What would happen if a commune or council was dominated by a particular family or tribe or by a particular political party? All would appear to be realistic scenarios based on pre-existing socio-economic structures of Kurdish society and territorialization of political and social loyalties. Tribal divisions were already in evidence in Arab areas that fell under the council system. What might happen if these communes, or groups within them, armed through the right to self-defence, and the HPC engaged in conflict with another such group? Research suggested that at the time of writing the domination of the PYD prevented the manipulation of the communes for the promotion of interests inimical to the maintenance of the governance systems and the social project. The success of the commune system, it would appear, rested on the success of social restructuring and transformation – the social revolution – as envisaged in Abdullah Öcalan's theories and on a reorganization of personal references of identity and its representation in line with that.

Transformations in identity and understandings of representation, 2011–2016

Chapter 1 examined Kurdish identity and the channels of representation available before the start of the Syrian crisis. Profound changes in the political and social environments in Syria were triggered in March 2011 and were stimulated further by both the PYD takeover in June 2012 and the siege of Kobani in 2014–2015. These broad transformations of political, social and economic environments raised questions about how much choices of identity and ideas of representation had changed in response to the crisis and to the development of the PYD-led administrative system, and how far the PYD was from creating the 'democratic, moral society' that it spoke of and which was to form the bedrock of the democratic autonomy system.

Asked how they would describe their identity,[25] the vast majority of participants in IIST surveys chose 'Kurdish' (91.6 per cent).[26] Second to this, 'Muslim' was selected by 63.8 per cent of participants, followed by 'Syrian', 46.1 per cent. In terms of geographical entities 52.7 per cent identified with 'Rojava', 42.2 per cent with 'Kurdistan' and 18.3 per cent with Syria. Association with Syrian identity was higher within the Jazirah (56 per cent of participants from the Jazirah compared to 36 per cent of participants from Kobani chose Syrian to describe their identity) and the selection of 'Muslim' as an indicator of identity was slightly lower in the Jazirah then in Kobani (in Kobani 67 per cent of participants chose 'Muslim' compared to 61 per cent in the Jazirah).

Survey results showed that just over half of the participants recognized a change in how they defined their identity since the beginning of the crisis in March 2011.[27] Among this group, significantly more were from Kobani than from the Jazirah, reflecting the impact of the ISIS siege on social and political orders and on conceptualizations of identity there.[28] Explanations of and reasons for this change given by participants in surveys varied considerably. Examples included an increase in national identification, the achievement of Kurdish rights and self-realization, past and present threats posed by Arabs and ISIS, greater knowledge of issues, changed lives and displacement and even a loss of confidence. Among those that recognized a change in how they perceived of their own identity, there was a clear sense that the changes in Syria had stimulated reassessments of personal and group identities and most respondents indicated a degree of ethnicization of identity.

The extent that this ethnicization also reflected a parallel nationalization of political ideology was unclear. Looking at survey participants' ideologies, however, may shed some light on this. Almost all participants selected a political ideology when asked to do so, regardless of whether or not they supported a particular political party.[29] Participants were asked to describe their political ideology by selecting from several options.[30] The three most frequently selected

[25] Surveys were conducted between April and July 2016.

[26] All declared political party supporters chose 'Kurdish' as an indicator of identity.

[27] Around 52 per cent of survey participants said that their idea of their personal or group identity had changed since March 2011.

[28] About 63 per cent of survey participants in Kobani compared to 40 per cent of participants in the Jazirah claimed that their identity had changed since 2011.

[29] Approximately 69/180 (38 per cent) of participants in surveys identified themselves as supporters of a political party.

[30] The options, listed in no particular order, were: Communist, Öcalanism, Anarchism, Baathist, Nationalist, Democratic, socialist, conservative, Marxist, Socialist, Feminist, Religious, Left wing, Right wing, Centrist and Barzani.

options were: 'Democratic' (43 per cent of total participants),[31] 'Öcalani' (54/180 or 30 per cent) and Barzani (43/180 or 24 per cent). These latter two can be taken to represent the personifications of ideologies adopted and promoted by these two Kurdish political leaders – the ideology and project of democratic confederalism promoted by the PYD in the first case, and the more traditional nationalist politics based on the congruence of territory and people in the second. Because of this personification of ideologies, identifying how individuals perceived these two systems of ideas and what it was about each doctrine, or personality, that appealed to them was more complex and unclear in survey results. Were choices based on tangible achievements of individual political leaders, in terms of rights and representation of Kurdish identity, or were they based on the knowledge and understanding of deeper political doctrines and the social orders that distinguished them?

No options for identifying changes in ideology which might have gauged an increase or decrease in attachment to either ideology were included in the surveys. Broad ideological differences were apparent, however, between the two regions of the Jazirah and Kobani. Öcalanism (also referred to as Apoism) was chosen by 42 per cent of participants in Kobani compared to just 17.5 per cent in the Jazirah. In comparison, Barzani was chosen by 40 per cent of those in the Jazirah and by only 9 per cent in Kobani. This can be explained by the geographic proximity to sources of political ideologies, tribal territories and the fact that political affiliations were commonly inherited through families. TEV-DEM official Aldar Xelil also explained: 'For Cizere [Jazirah] canton, it's near Iraqi Kurdistan, that's why Barzani visited the canton sometimes, and there are people who follow the ideology of Barzani, but the people in Afrin and Kobani they didn't have this, it's far from the border.'[32] Abdullah Öcalan, in comparison, entered Syria through Kobani in 1980 and was sheltered by residents there[33] and greater support for the PKK in the area was a result of this. In addition it reflected the differences in personal experience between the two areas during the Syrian crisis. The YPG defence of Kobani against ISIS caused both an increase in support for the PYD in that area and a migration of its populace out of the area, leading to a heavier concentration of PYD supporters than might have otherwise existed.

---

[31] Roughly 78/180 participants selected 'democratic' to characterize their ideology. 'Democratic' was selected by 52 per cent of female participants, and 37 per cent of male participants.

[32] IIST interview: Aldar Xelil, Amude, 02/05/2016.

[33] IIST interview: Ayse Efendi, Kobani, 17/06/2017; Allsopp, *The Kurds of Syria*.

In terms of gender, a greater percentage of women chose 'democratic' as their ideology (52 per cent of female participants, compared to 37 per cent of male,) while more men chose 'Öcalani' than women (36 per cent of male to 11.5 per cent of female participants). Although the sample of female participants was relatively small, due to lower visibility of women in public in some areas, low support for the PYD ideology could point to a disparity between the image of women leading the social revolution projected by the DAA and the status of women outside it.

Significantly, 'nationalist' was selected by only eighteen participants and the combination of 'socialist', 'Marxist' and 'communist' was selected nineteen times in total. No participant identified their ideology as 'right wing'; only one as 'conservative' and two as 'Marxist.' Ideological identification such as 'religious' was selected by only eight respondents: one from the Jazirah, seven from Kobani, six of whom were female. These results demonstrated the 'monopoly' over ideology that the main political blocs and personalities had gained in Kurdish areas of Syria and their significance to ideas of identity and representation.

Returning to the general ethnicization of identity demonstrated by field research, the growth in support for the PYD during the crisis in Syria was stimulated by the practical application of rights previously denied to Kurds, by the military successes of the YPG, as well as by ideological persuasion. Despite clear mobilization around the Kurdish identity, this increased ethnicization of identity was not met or reflected in the policies and rhetoric of the PYD and the administrative institutions developed by it. On the contrary, the PYD and the Administration actively de-ethnicized their rhetoric and identity in response to changes in regional relations and local military fronts. The name of the party itself never included the word Kurd or Kurdish, nor did TEV-DEM, although its former political programme did. Cantons were referred to by local names and 'Rojava' (West), rather than 'Rojava Kurdistan', was used to describe the whole region. Over time, as the territory and character of the administration over northern Syria changed, its name also changed: from 'Transitional Administration' to 'Rojava' to the 'Democratic Federal System of Rojava-Northern Syria' and to the 'Democratic Federal System of Northern Syria.' The latter was announced in December 2016 after criticism from the PKK,[34] and involved the removal of the last remaining indirect reference to the Kurdish identity, 'Rojava', from the name. This was described by

---

[34] Mohamed Noureddine 29/07/16: 'PKK foreign relations head speaks out', *Al Monitor*, http://www.al-monitor.com/pulse/politics/2016/07/turkey-coup-pkk-kurds-rojava-us-intervention.html (last accessed 24/03/2017).

some critics as a dismantling of Kurdish rule in Syria[35] and as a decision directed by the PKK. Although no data existed that could shed light on whether the PYD and the Administration had lost support as a result of this de-ethnicization of its identity, many Kurdish critics deplored this ambiguity in its ethnic identity and questioned the interests of those driving the movement.[36]

The de-ethnicization of politics and governance can be explained as a product of both the political ideology of the party and system and the design for creating a 'democratic nation' not defined by ethnic identity and territory. As described in Chapter 3, it was also a response to the expansion of PYD territory outside Kurdish majority areas and to the development of military relations with the United States. The parallel ethnicization of popular identity and de-ethnicization of the DAA and the PYD might appear contrary and present an obstacle to gaining legitimacy as representatives of Syrian Kurds. The Administration's institutionalization of language and human rights and the rhetoric of the YPG, however, did much to maintain its vital support base in Kurdish society. Nonetheless, research demonstrated that popular belief in the representative capacity of the PYD and the DAA, however, did not match support for the ideology or the political party itself.

An ethno-nationalist model of achieving representation remained popular among Syrian Kurds. Rooted in traditional socio-economic networks and historic examples of Kurdish resistance, resisting state power remained central to its method and ideology. Outside the ideological and governance structures of the PYD and the Administration, the KNC parties continued to identify and pursue forms of representations based on Kurdish national identity and political capital gained in the pursuit of rights and freedoms.

Despite the existence of these different models of representation and identity, choices about representation in Syria were and remained limited and unfavourable for the Kurds. Survey questions about representation demonstrated a disparity between the people or institutions that participants said represented them and those that they wanted to represent them. The most frequently selected answers to the question 'Who represents you?' were: 'political party' (56/180), 'family connections' (46/180) and 'no one/myself' (39/180). State officials such as MPs, state functionaries or cabinet ministers were selected by only thirteen respondents in total. This gave an impression of the limited and sub-state nature

---

[35] See, for example, reader comments to the article: Rudaw 29/12/2016: 'Syrian Kurdistan drops Rojava word in its draft constitution', *Rudaw*, http://www.rudaw.net/english/middleeast/syria/28122016 (last accessed 20/01/2017).
[36] IIST interviews.

of channels of representation available to Syrian Kurds prior to and during the crisis in Syria. A marked difference was observable in the answers to the question 'Who do you want to represent you?' Here 'political party' remained high in respondents' choices (47/180), but there was a significant increase in the number that selected 'MP', which increased from 5/180 to 47/180. Parallel to this, there was a notable reduction in the number of times 'family connections' was selected (from 46/180 to 21/180). There were also significant differences in opinions about representation between the Jazirah and Kobani. The shift in favour of MPs between 'Who represents you?' and 'Who do you want to represent you?' was greatest in the Jazirah (1/180 to 31/180) compared to 4/180 to 16/180 in Kobani. Also in Kobani, 'political party' remained the most popular answer to the latter question selected by 30/180 (compared to 17/180 in the Jazirah). These results, in particular the shift towards MPs, arguably reflected a trust in electoral representation as a system and the continuing absence of representative channels available to Syrian Kurds.

The questions: 'Which, if any, political or military forces in Syria do you believe can represent you in the future?' revealed a strong preference for military forces above political ones. Overall, the YPG was selected most frequently (by 86/180 or 48 per cent of participants). Declared PYD supporters accounted for just 16 per cent of all participants that selected the YPG, demonstrating the broad appeal of this force and its popular separation from the PYD. The PYD itself was selected by a total of 60/180 participants (33 per cent), 41 of whom were from Kobani, demonstrating again the greater support for the PYD in this region. Here, the PYD was selected by 41/93; the PKK by 18/93; the KNC by only 7/93 and the KDP by just three participants. In comparison, data from the Jazirah displayed much more varied responses. Belief that military forces had a capacity to represent remained prominent, but selections of the YPG and the Peshmerga forces were roughly equal. In this region the YPG was chosen by 26/87 respondents and the Peshmerga by 24/87. Similarly the two political blocs were selected more evenly, with the PYD and PKK selected by a total of 21/87 participants, and the KNC and KDP selected by a total of twenty-two. The Administration's primary political and social institution, TEV-DEM, however, did not gain comparable support. TEV-DEM was selected by only 16 of all 180 participants (or 0.8 per cent) and ranked equal to the KNC and the KDP of Iraq, but below the PKK and the Peshmerga. This implied that the administrative system itself was not considered representative by many civilians and reflected, also, the low participation rates in the commune system and criticisms of decision-making procedures examined above.

The faith in the representative capacity of military forces above political ones can be explained by several factors related to the importance of security issues to Kurdish politics and popular conceptualizations of threat. Historically legitimacy had been imparted on political groups by military struggles associated with them rather than by the diplomatic engagements of their political leaders. Largely devoid of indigenous Kurdish armed struggle in Syria before March 2011, the crisis gave rise to a uniquely Kurdish experience of the conflicts and the threats posed by ISIS, the Syrian government, and by other non-Kurdish military forces in Syria. Military forces entered Kurdish identity politics decisively through the YPG and the Peshmerga successes in securing territory and defending it from those threats and through PYD propaganda glorifying the YPG/J and the sacrifice of martyrs. Added to this and distinguishing it from the PYD, the YPG maintained the use of Kurdish nationalist rhetoric alongside its role as protector of the democratic autonomy project. Most families had members in the YPG/J, regardless of their political affiliations, and its symbolic appeal and effectiveness on the ground made it appear representative of broad interests defined by the Kurdish identity. In practice, however, and as was shown in Chapter 3, the YPG/J role in politics was minimal and the group had limited representative capacity.

Pre-existing traditional and familial networks that provided sub-state channels of representation before 2011 were weakened significantly as the conflict caused rapid displacement, migration and the division of families. This was particularly true in Kobani where much of the social infrastructure of traditional channels of representation was destroyed along with Kobani's physical infrastructure. For those remaining in or returning to Kobani, in the absence of the state and other sub-state channels of representation, the PYD, and administrative system led by it, offered security, community, representation and services as well as resources needed to rebuild. In the Jazirah, surveys reflected a wider spectrum of political and social beliefs, and the lesser degree of migration from this region would suggest that pre-existing social networks remained stronger than in post-siege Kobani. Correspondingly, choices about representation were greater in Jazirah than in Kobani or in Afrin, where isolation from other areas gained the PYD-led administration comprehensive authority.

Women's representation

The experience of Syrian Kurdish women is of particular importance both in terms of the promotion of equal representation and rights and in terms of gauging the success of the 'revolution', the latter of which is examined in the following section on opinions about the system. For women a major shift in understanding of identity and representation was offered. The radical feminism of the PKK and the PYD, expressed also through the YPJ and other women's organizations, challenged deep gender divisions within Syrian society. While Kurdish society often boasted more liberal attitudes towards women, and some Syrian Kurdish women even mocked the ideological character of PYD inspired women's organizations, the PYD's policy and institutionalization of direct participation in all spheres of governance, defence and society, created a distinctly more open and public debate of women in Middle Eastern societies that encouraged responses from both women and men. Statements by women within the YPG or other institutions associated with the Administration reflected a sense of liberation of their identity and women in the YPJ became symbols of the revolution and radical liberation that were seized upon by observers around the world.

Changes in women's roles and visibility was not only on the military level but also in

> the slow, patient development of the women's political movement: political education for women to develop their skills and build the confidence of future organizers, forms of (re)education and intervention against abusive men, the activity of women's committees at all levels of the confederal system, and the tireless work of the *Kongreya Star* (star congress) – the organized expression of the women's movement here.[37]

The commune system and administrative laws highlighted the visibly positive and broadly inclusive effects of women's mobilization and the promotion, institutionalization and enforcement of gender equalities. The role of women in political and social life became significantly more visible in many areas due to legal rights, the proliferation of women's councils at every level of the administration and women's representation and women-led initiatives. Women were provided with safe spaces and mechanisms for countering threats emanating from the war as well as from pre-existing social inequalities. Survey questions determining what the 'Rojava' administration meant for individuals showed 'women's rights' to be ranked second highest out of twenty choices. Several interviews with Kurdish women reflected a substantive change in the experience of women, who noted

---

[37] Peter Loo interviewed by Rojava Solidarity Cluster 01/02/2017: "'A real revolution is a mass of contradictions": Interview with a Rojava Volunteer', http://novaramedia.com/2017/02/01/a-real-revolution-is-a-mass-of-contradictions-interview-with-a-rojava-volunteer/ (last accessed 24/03/2017).

that they were actively protected against gender discrimination and violence. At the same time, others expressed concerns about the rise in domestic violence experienced under the DAAs as a result of men fearing the loss of authority and feeling threatened by changes to gender relations.[38] Tensions generated from frictions between pre-existing social norms and new laws remained prominent and presented a challenge to achieving gender equalities.[39]

The central role taken by PYD-linked women's organizations (such as *Kongreya Star*) in directing women's participation and re-education, illustrated in the quote above, and their ideological and political doctrines were also significant factors preventing wider development and acceptance of gender equalities:

> Women in Rojava are visible and active in local governance, social services and security. Overall, this is received positively across ethnic backgrounds. However, political affiliations seem to be a restricting factor for participation in local governance and access to social services, thereby affecting perceptions on (the effectiveness of) female led initiatives negatively.[40]

The intrinsic connection of women's liberation to Abdullah Öcalan's ideology, examined in Chapter 2, threatened to alienate women who wished to avoid ideological indoctrination from participation in communes and women's institutions. Similarly, while equality in the workplace was evident, division of labour itself was gendered to some degree, with many women being employed specifically on women's issues and in women's organizations.[41] As a result, while positive steps towards gender equalities and their institutionalization had taken place, drawing firm conclusions on the real extent of gender equality in the DAAs and about their substantive effect on society and ideas of identity and representation was more difficult.

A revolution in representation? Opinions about the system

While participation is a critical test of the success of the representative system and looking at changes in opinion about identity and representation can help

---

[38] Bateson et al., *Gendered Alternatives*, 40–1.
[39] See, for example, Wilgenburg 15/11/2016: 'Syrian Kurds tackle conscription underage marriage and polygamy', *ARA News*, http://tr.aranews.org/2016/11/syrian-kurds-tackle-underage-marriages-p olygamy/ (last accessed 24/03/2017).
[40] Bateson et al., *Gendered Alternatives*, 68.
[41] Ibid., 50.

gauge the direction of social change, examining whether people believe that the system is democratic and representative is equally intrinsic to an assessment of its claims to legitimacy. With limited data available and access to the region problematic, analysing opinions of survey participants and interviews, alongside actions and outputs of the administration can help provide a clearer picture of the system and its capacity to represent Syrian Kurds.

Broadly speaking, survey results showed a fairly even divide between those who were satisfied with the PYD-led administration and considered the system of governance to be democratic and representative, and those who did not. Comments elaborating on reasons for opinions varied significantly and did not reflect a clear-cut division between those who supported it and those who did not. Opinions were nuanced with detail of, often diverging, personal views on various aspects of its governance and the situation in the regions.

The surveys demonstrated clearly that among those who were satisfied with the Administration or aspects of it, security was a primary factor for considering the credentials of the administration and their level of satisfaction with it. Analysis of the Administration itself and its rhetoric also suggested that the relative peace in northern Syria, the fight against ISIS and the loss of martyrs and their sacrosanct character were fundamental factors supporting its claims to legitimacy and were used to muster both domestic and international support.[42] Of 180 survey participants, 105 (58 per cent) associated 'security' with the administration. Security also featured heavily in the reasons participants gave about why they were satisfied with the Administration: 'They are the ones that protect us', 'They provide safety and security', 'They saved our lives', 'They are fighting terrorism', 'They got rid of the Baathists and the Islamists', 'Stability' and 'The Administration is the power that protects us and sacrifices martyrs.' The broad appeal and recognition of this aspect of the Administration was also demonstrated by the fact that only forty-six participants were declared PYD supporters and fifty-four identified their ideology as Öcalanist.

The six most selected answers to the question 'What does "Rojava" mean for you personally?'[43] were: 'Security' (selected 105/180 times); 'women's rights' (98/180 times); 'freedom' (70/180); 'language rights' and 'democracy' (both

[42] Rana Khalaf 2016: 'Governing Rojava: Layers of legitimacy in Syria', Chatham House Research Papers, Chatham House, London, https://www.chathamhouse.org/sites/files/chathamhouse/public ations/research/2016-12-08-governing-rojava-khalaf.pdf (last accessed 24/03/2017), 22, 12–15.

[43] Security (selected 105/180 times), women's rights (98 times), freedom (70), language rights (67), democracy (67 times), human rights (54), education (46), a voice (42), employment (37), control (31), silence (30), exclusion (28), religious freedom (27), representation (25), services (25), national rights (24), progress (21), participation (16), leadership (13), regression (13).

selected 67 times); and 'human rights' (54/180). All were positive reflections on the rights and freedoms secured as a result of the retreat of the Assad government from northern Syria, the establishment of the PYD-led administration and the securing of territories against external threats. Answers to this question also echoed positive comments made to illustrate why participants were satisfied with the Administration. As an answer, however, 'representation' was selected by only 25 of 180 participants and 'participation' by just 17. This may illustrate the lack of popular engagement with the direct democracy project, but it also reflects the political importance that obtaining rights associated Kurdish identity gained under the Assad regime and their inextricable association with achieving democracy. The withdrawal of the Syrian government provided the opportunity to realize rights of expression and representation of Kurdish identity. This marked a substantive change in governance in the regions, immediately recognizable and experienced by the population. Reasons given within surveys about why participants were satisfied with the Administration also underlined this association of the DAA with identity rights. Examples included the following: 'Because they are Kurdish', 'we speak in our own language', 'the government uses our language', 'I have national rights', 'it achieved our rights and goals', 'our rights are protected' and 'they are Kurds – better than Assad'. The numerous survey samples citing the achievement of rights and security are testimony to the importance of the Kurdish identity and its representation to the Kurdish population and how it translated into popular legitimacy.

In the long term, however, the Kurdish identity and ethnic rights may also prove an insecure source of legitimacy for the Administration if it cannot deliver more widely accepted forms of representation and democracy. The realization of these basic identity rights were connected directly to the roll-back of the Assad government, which had relied on Arab nationalism at the expense of Kurdish identity and representation. Legitimacy gained through providing security was made possible, again, by the retreat of the government from northern Syria and by the resources immediately available to the PYD through the PKK and then through military cooperation with the US-led anti-ISIS coalition. This left unanswered crucial questions about the popularity of the social project, the politics of the PYD and the overall popular legitimacy of the administration. How much of its popular legitimacy was gained through security, the YPG and the wider context of conflict and sectarian divisions in Syria? How can that legitimacy be maintained in peacetime, or if/when vital resources are withdrawn by the international coalition, by the PKK, or are reclaimed by the Syrian government? To what extent would the DAA be able to continue to provide vital social services to the population[44] if efforts were made by the Assad government or other external forces to isolate it and dissolve its powers?

Gauging the popularity of the PYD, Öcalanism and the social project, as well as opposition to its ideology, was complicated further by the diverse understandings and range of meanings that the Administration had for different people. Many who expressed satisfaction with the structures and methods of governance did not participate in it. And satisfaction with the Administration did not always correspond to a belief that the system was democratic or that participation provided a role in decision-making processes. Many participants said that they were satisfied with the Administration but that it was not democratic; one said that it was corrupt, one that it did not represent all people, and another that it monopolizes trade and politics. The ideology of Öcalan and the Administration encouraged participation but the relatively low levels of participation evident from field research suggested that there was a popular detachment from the ideological groundings of the administrative system and a gap between the theory and practice of governance. Indeed, evidence within surveys and interviews suggested that the transformation of social norms and values that the social project envisaged and entailed continued to meet with resistance from within the Kurdish society.

Immediate resistance to the PYD encroachment on territory and authority occurred after March 2011 and came, not only from other political parties, but from tribal forces, communities and individuals that opposed the PYD rule and were unwilling to abandon established social networks, hierarchies and customs that, for many, were intrinsic to the Kurdish identity. The PYD/PKK ideology reinvented 'the Kurd' as pure, enlightened, free and truly Kurdish only when liberated through self-criticism and reinvention in accordance with Öcalan's teachings.[45] The appeal of that doctrine appeared to be limited to those invested in Abdullah Öcalan as a leader and in the PYD as a political party and an instrument of revolution. While many Syrian Kurds were prepared to cooperate with the system of governance in northern Syria, particularly because of the ongoing crisis in Syria, internalization of its ideology was less common.[46]

By 2017, the longevity of the Syrian conflict, the Administration and the military struggle against ISIS had aided gradual internalization of aspects of

---

[44] See Rana Khalaf, 'Governing Rojava: Layers of legitimacy in Syria', 17–21, for more details of the service provision and its connection to governance legitimacy.

[45] Grojean, 'The production of the new man within the PKK'.

[46] IIST surveys and interviews demonstrated that support of the system was commonly not driven by ideology and political affiliation but by an interest in securing basis rights and security of the regions against threats defined in broadly sectarian terms.

its social project through the normalization of governance structures and institutions. The Administration actively sought to re-educate the population through educational institutions, women's organizations, communes, laws, security, as well as through symbols and rhetoric. The YPG/J training included education about democratic autonomy and self-criticism to instil a commitment to protect the project and to sacrifice for it. Likewise the legitimacy and political capital gained through the YPG's military activities, dramatic victories against ISIS and ensuring the security of Kurdish regions reflected onto the administration. The military campaign also gained the YPG/J international legitimacy which was capitalized by the Administration and by the PYD domestically.

The relative weakness of other Kurdish political parties and the restrictions on their activities also worked in the Administrations favour. Divisions within the KNC parties and within the organization, their limited access to resources, dependence on the KDP and their side-lining by the PYD all worked to reduce their capacity to represent Syrian Kurds, to present practical alternatives to local governance or offer viable opposition to PYD domination. Survey results demonstrated that for many participants political and organizational divides between Kurdish political parties did not impact decisively on beliefs they expressed about identity and representation. For many people, concerns for security far outweighed other ideological beliefs about representation and the choices associated with it. Although conditions in northern Syria had been relatively more peaceful than in many other areas of Syria, the need for security and stability had had a decisive impact on individual choices and opinions about the Administration, and these choices were not determined entirely by political ideologies. The need for security and the belief in the representative capacity of armed organizations crossed political and ideological divides with many survey participants identifying both the PYD and the KNC or the YPG and the Peshmerga as capable of representing them in the future. The belief in the capacity of military organizations to represent, particularly among those who said they did not support any political party, also developed despite clear partisanship in Kurdish military organizations.

According to laws produced by the Administration, however, the YPG/J was 'the sole military force of the three cantons with the mandate to protect and defend the security of the Autonomous Regions and its peoples, against both internal and external threats'.[47] Coupled with the active prevention of

---

[47] Charter of the Social Contract, A.15.

KNC parties from taking up arms, this legal and security framework denied opposition parties capacity to gain, or capitalize on, legitimacy through participation in armed opposition, except outside Administration-controlled areas. It also channelled mobilization around Kurdish identity and rights into the YPG, particularly in the first few years of the Syrian crisis, feeding popular investment in the Administration.

The ability of the YPG and the PYD to retain popular support and legitimacy imparted through armed struggle, however, was threatened by the extension of YPG military operations beyond Kurdish areas after 2015. The sacrifice of martyrs in operations in Manbij in 2016, Raqqah (2016–2017) and near Deir al-Zour (February 2017), well outside 'Kurdish' territory and interests, was far less comprehensible to Syrian Kurds. One resident of Afrin complained that they believed their children were being sent to die in foreign areas, not at home.[48] Indeed, mandatory or forced conscription was an issue on which organized protest and opposition to DAA policy was more visible, even among supporters of the PYD. Making conscription obligatory caused a barrage of criticism against the PYD and the Administration from within Kurdish communities and from other Kurdish political parties. Several participants in surveys commented that this policy had caused a wave of migration of male youths out of northern Syria. Reports by Human Rights Watch (HRW) and Amnesty International highlighted the recruitment of underage youths to the YPG. The YPG signed a 'Deed of Commitment' with the NGO Geneva Call pledging to demobilize child soldiers within the YPG. While 149 were demobilized after a month, reports of underage recruitment continued to appear from within the PYD-controlled areas and HRW documented ten cases between July 2014 and July 2015.[49] Reports of forced conscription continued to appear from Kurdish areas as did protests against it, most originating from the Jazirah, due to more press freedoms and greater ability to organize independently,[50] but also from Kobani.[51]

[48] IIST interview: Afrin resident, 28/02/2017.
[49] HRW 15/07/2015: 'Syria: Kurdish forces violating child soldier ban', https://www.hrw.org/news/2015/07/10/syria-kurdish-forces-violating-child-soldier-ban-0 (last accessed 24/03/2017).
[50] Reports from the Jazirah: *Syria Direct* (online) 22/11/2015: 'Syrian Kurdish refugees in Iraq protest PYD conscription', *Syria Direct*, http://syriadirect.org/news/syrian-kurdish-refugees-in-iraq-protest-pyd-conscription-%C2%A0/ (last accessed 07/02/2017); Zaman al-Wasl 21/05/2016: 'PYD, regime militarize Hasake to fight ISIS, U.S., Russia ignore forcible conscription', *Zaman al-Wasl*, https://en.zamanalwsl.net/news/15946.html (last accessed 07/02/2017); National Coalition of Syrian democratic and opposition forces Media Office 26/05/2016: 'Amude protests against PYD child recruitment', http://en.etilaf.org/all-news/local-news/amuda-protests-against-pyd-child-recruitment.html and; Etilaf, 'Qamishli residents protest against PYD practices', *Etilaf*, http://en.etilaf.org/all-news/local-news/qamishli-residents-protest-against-pyd-practices.html (last accessed 07/02/2017).
[51] Reports from the Kobani region, Wilgenburg 21/06/2016: 'Kurds launch conscription campaign to protect Kobane from ISIS attacks', *ARA News*, http://aranews.net/2016/06/kurds-launch-consc

Interviewees, and news reports from organizations monitoring Afrin, claimed that youth between the ages of 16 and 35 were being forcibly recruited into the YPG. Families of individuals that had fled to avoid conscription claimed that they were required to pay a fine to the Administration for each child not attending military service.[52] In January and February 2017, (as part of what appeared to be a new training round and renewed efforts to build up military regiments in Afrin) two respondents in Afrin reported that children aged fifteen were being forcibly recruited to the YPG, not to self-defence units in which military service was compulsory for those over eighteen. One respondent declared that 'the women of Afrin are crying into the wind' referring to their distress and failed attempts to prevent their children from being conscripted.[53] In this instance, it was reported that communities had attempted to block the authorities from taking individuals for military service by forming a barrier of armed people. In addition, mothers of youths taken to military service had repeatedly protested at YPG offices. The same respondent reported that as a result efforts to conscript youths had reduced.[54]

Respondents in Afrin, the Jazirah and Kobani expressed concerns about the representativeness of the Administration and about its practice of restricting activity outside sanctioned organizations and associations. Some, not affiliated to the PYD, claimed that authority and decision-making in the Afrin region was dominated by Kurds from Turkey and by Syrian Kurds who had been based in the Qandil Mountains. By comparison, ministers appointed to the Administration from within the local communities were considered powerless in terms of decision-making. Unions, communes and other associations were all said to contain at least one member of the party, or *heval*, who relayed orders or direction to the organizations. Political issues were not discussed within the commune, and interviewees from Afrin suggested that doing so would warrant arrest or questioning.[55] Organization outside the commune, or other institutions of the administrative systems, was reported to be very difficult and risky. Representatives of the Bihar Relief NGO in the Afrin region were arrested by the local security services and imprisoned. After negotiation, the organization was permitted to continue operating, but only under the guidance

ription-campaign-to-protect-kobane-from-isis-attacks/ (last accessed 24/03/2017); ARA News, 'Increased conscription of Kurdish youth in Kobane facing widespread criticism'.

52 IIST interview: Afrin residents, 08/10/2016.

53 IIST interview: Afrin resident, 28/02/2017.

54 The individual had confirmation from other sources that the child was in a YPG training camp in the Afrin region. Interview Afrin resident, 28/02/2017.

55 IIST interview: Afrin resident, 17/09/2016.

of the Administration.[56] Intelligence services linked to the Administration were reported to have a heavy presence, particularly in Afrin canton, with every area having at least ten to fifteen masked individuals observing and informing, enforcing control through their presence.

In general the institutionalization of gender equality was looked upon favourably within Kurdish society.[57] Criticisms of it focused primarily on the dominance of one political party, the constraints of traditional gender relations and the double burden experienced by women. The institutionalization of the ideological critique of gender relations embedded within the administrative system itself attached this feminist movement directly to the PYD, to Öcalan and to the wider political project. Agency for women's emancipation was placed ultimately with Öcalan and political institutions driving the 'revolution'. The model of women's liberation and social space created for women was dictated and directed by Öcalan himself rather than being developed by women for women. Women became the revolutionary subjects responsible for the movement and for realizing and implementing an ideological project. This raised questions about whether a 'genuine' women's revolution could occur while it was under the control of the PYD, and whether women's organization outside parameters of the social revolution could occur. Surveys conducted in Syria reflected deep divisions in society. The ideological and political doctrine itself divided society between critics, supporters and ideologues, and between participants and non-participants. While women's rights ranked high on the achievements of the Administration, survey results also suggested that women were less likely to support political parties, including the PYD, and research on gender equality suggested that women's participation in the communes remained very low.[58]

Some women connected non-participation with their childcare responsibilities, constraints imposed by their husbands and also with exclusion due to their political affiliations.[59] Comments on surveys supported suggestions that aspects of, and transitions required by, the social revolution were unwelcome with many sectors of society. Gender equality was among them. The belief that the laws, migration and the breakdown of traditional leadership roles were causing an erosion of the family and of values and customs associated with traditional kin networks and gendered power relations was expressed several times.[60] The

---

[56] Ibid.
[57] IIST surveys and interviews; see also Bateson et al., *Gendered Alternatives*, 50, 60.
[58] Ibid., 50.
[59] Bateson et al., *Gendered Alternatives*, 50–2.
[60] IIST surveys (April–June 2016). Bateson et al., *Gendered Alternatives*.

disruption caused by the crisis in Syria as well as by the top-down ideological conditioning had broken down local social networks and affected customary behaviours. Similarly, attempts to restructure pre-existing social networks that governed the resolution of local disputes, mediation and communal discussion within the commune system involved disruption and the breaking of traditional social hierarchies. The system appeared to have created an intellectual hierarchy attched to enlightenment in the theories of Öcalan and in their correct application, which ensured that PYD supporters dominated decision-making. Alongside this, however, the DAA system and traditional organization appeared to overlap to some extent, providing some pre-existing power networks with an alternative source of authority.[61] In some cases, traditional leaders appeared to have been integrated into the commune system[62] suggesting that communes continued to provide mechanisms for retaining pre-existing power relations, rather than replacing them. Nevertheless, traditional gender divisions and social norms remained powerful constraints to women's emancipation and the realization of the 'moral society' envisaged by Abdullah Öcalan.

Despite the reductions in, co-option of, and limitations on, alternative channels of representation available to the Kurds, it was clear that the population in general, with the exception of Afrin region, was exercising some choice about representation – even if only by choosing not to participate in the commune system or by attempting to retain certain benefits by cooperating with it. The experience of PYD rule was different for different groups of people and individuals alike and decisions to resist, subsist, cooperate or migrate had been based on diverse reasons. Surveys demonstrated that, for many people, political loyalties and beliefs that they held before 2011 had remained steadfast throughout the subsequent period of conflict and change. Others had had little interest in, experience of, or exposure to, the politics that the Kurds in Syria had developed. Some expressed a sense of realization of identity due to the changes that had occurred in Syria after March 2011. While many participated in the administrative system through communes, others did not consider them representative or inclusive.[63] Nevertheless, by all accounts, there was a widespread support for the decentralization of governance of Syria and for federalism as a model of achieving that. This was a product of both the history of Kurdish struggles for official representation in Syria and the experience of quasi-autonomy during the Syrian crisis.

---

[61] IIST surveys comments
[62] Bateson et al., *Gendered Alternatives*, 51.
[63] IIST Surveys.

But here we must attempt to separate desires for representation of the Kurdish identity and democracy and decentralization from the parallel revolutionary project that had achieved versions of these goals in northern Syria. In general, surveys demonstrated recognition of both positive and negative aspects of the system. Positive comments concentrated primarily on rights and on security and the sacrifices made by the YPG. Some welcomed these aspects of the Administration but also claimed the system was authoritarian and repeated criticisms about unqualified people occupying powerful positions within the system of governance and about unilateral decision-making. Other comments recognized mistakes made by the Administration, but expressed hope that these could be overcome with time.[64] Some rated the Administration's democratic credentials as, for example, 70 per cent;[65] 'not 100 per cent democratic' or recognized that it was 'sometimes democratic'.[66] Many of the criticisms gave an impression of a group (the PYD/PKK bloc) holding and monopolizing power within the Administration and that ideological affinity and personal connections were instrumental in persons benefiting from and within the system and that the voices of people within that group were considered above others. Criticisms that other political parties were not permitted to operate, or comments indicating that participants did not believe in the politics or ideology of the PYD and the Administration raised questions about its representative capacity. Certainly, the social transformation envisaged by the 'revolution' had not been achieved, and in the absence of this, the representative capacity of the DAA was limited.

A fundamental paradox within the administrative system was the seizure of power by the PYD: its clear domination over governance and the top-down approach to the 'revolution'. Although the PYD directed attention to its participatory project and to the inclusion of different parties and institutions in decision-making processes in the practical governance of the regions,[67] the system itself was initiated by the PYD and its social project was based on Abdullah Öcalan's ideology. For a social revolution to occur without resort to vanguard authority, initiative and participation had to be bottom-up, voluntary and have a transformational effect on the dominant values and myths of society as a whole as well as on the institutions that governed them. While the PYD

---

[64] IIST survey no. 34.
[65] IIST survey no. 32.
[66] IIST survey no. 29.
[67] See, for example, comments made in the PYD response to the 2014 HRW report: https://www.hrw .org/sites/default/files/related_material/The%20Democratic%20Self-Rule%20Administration%E2 %80%99s%20Response%20to%20the%20Report%20of%20Human%20Rights%20Watch%20Orga nization.pdf.

and DAA had attempted to avoid the trappings of vanguard authority through processes of continuous criticism and appraisal and had actively supported participation, to all intents and purposes, the PYD had seized power in northern Syria, albeit in a political vacuum, and had created the space and institutional framework for a social revolution to occur and flourish. Although important universal and specific rights had been realized under its rule and attempts to diminish inequalities based on race, gender or religion had been made and the socialization of justice and security had penetrated society, the monopoly of the administrative councils and structures over services and goods, social organization and, indeed, identity framing and representation, implied that participation was to some extent compelled. The absence of real political opposition and unobstructed opportunity to canvas alternative political ideas and leadership within the system undermined the social values championed by the system. Examples of restrictions on the emergence of opposition implied a degree of intolerance to attempts to organize representation and identity criteria outside DAA governance and ideological structures.

The crisis in Syria – itself an expression of the need for dramatic changes in this country – the multitude of conflicts within it and the retreat of the government from northern Syria did engender social changes among the Kurds. Attempts by the PYD and associated organizations and institutions to direct the current of social change in the regions had effects on conceptualizations of identity and on ideas about representation, but not in a linear or homogeneous manner. Nor had they been the only forces affecting change among Syrian Kurds. Surveys demonstrated the extent that some participants had stayed true to long-held views about Kurdish identity and nationalism and about how that should be represented. Many had further embraced the Kurdish identity and forfeited religious beliefs because of the threat of ISIS. Some had found purpose and truth through the administrative system. Others placed the YPG and Peshmerga above any political party. The majority positively recognized the gains in rights and recognition that had been made since 2011 and the benefits of these to Kurdish representation in the long term, whether or not they envisaged or desired the formalization of the existing administration or the fulfilment of the social revolution.

5

The Role of Regional and International Actors

The involvement of regional and international actors in the Syrian conflict and within Kurdish politics in Syria were both a benefit and a detriment to the Kurdish struggle for representation. The exact nature and effect of these relations depended largely on the agency and agendas of the parties involved. The multiple foreign actors involved in the crisis formed an intricate and tangled web of alliances and hostilities involving local, regional and international actors and powers. Agendas overlapped or diverged irrespective of historic animosities and alliances. Among these tangled geopolitical interests, Syrian Kurdish political organizations increased their agency in regional and international affairs but, simultaneously, become dependent on and subject to wider political agendas.

During the war in Syria, non-state actors developed their own regional and international relations in attempts to gain external support and recognition. Syrian Kurdish political parties and military organizations were no exception. From emerging as the armed wing of a pariah political party in 2011, the YPG (and with it, the SDF) became key local partners in the US-led coalition against the ISIS in 2014. For the PYD and the KNC, relations with the main political parties in the KRI deepened; foreign relations developed with other regional states and with international actors. The PYD-led administrations developed its international presence by opening representative offices abroad: in Russia, the Netherlands, France, Sweden and Germany, although these did not obtain official diplomatic status. Furthermore, the PYD established relations with parties and other governments in the region, such as in Egypt and Lebanon. The KNC, through its partnership with the SNC in 2013, joined the international effort to develop a solution to the Syrian crisis, and opened its offices in Geneva in 2016 and in Berlin in 2017. Nevertheless, the agency of both the PYD and the KNC was undermined due to their historical domination by external regional power centres located in the KRI: the PKK in Qandil Mountains, the KDP in

Erbil and the PUK in Sulaymaniyah.[1] This also embedded their fate within the wider regional relations and geo-politics forged around both controlling and exploiting the Kurdish question and influencing the balance of powers within Syria. International powers involved in the conflict, directly or indirectly, also employed often contradictory rhetorics of regime change; of promoting democratic development; of national and international security; and of domestic security. The United States and Russia, whose interests in Syria both overlapped and conflicted, dramatically affected the balance of local powers within the country and remained set to significantly influence what might emerge from the war.

The roles of regional and international actors in the Syrian Kurdish affairs, examined here, highlight both the ways these tangled agendas and intrigues have affected the Kurds and the consequences that these changes to them might have. Although separating interlocking relationships territorially is not without consequences, this chapter looks at these relations and intrigues at the intra-Kurdish, regional and international levels in turn.

Intra-Kurdish power relations

Tensions between traditional rivals, the PKK and the KDP, played out within the Syrian Kurdish region. Historic rivalries and methodological differences between these parties always played a significant role in Syrian Kurdish politics but, during the Syrian crisis, these tensions deepened a fundamental cleavage in Kurdish politics in Syria, between different understandings of Kurdish identity and models of political representation. Tensions between these two blocs translated into power plays within Syrian Kurdish politics. Involvement within it became a means of extending regional agency and influence but, alongside this, also increased and heightened competition for representation of the Kurds at all levels.

As discussed in Chapter 2, ideological differences between the PKK, KDP and PUK divided Kurdish political blocs and defined the political spectrum within Syria. Historically, their competing political agendas contributed to marginalizing independent Syrian Kurdish political movements and, most significantly after March 2011, youth groups that sympathized with the Syrian

---

[1] IIST interview: Riyaad Heme, member of *al-Wahda* Party, Erbil, 05/04/2016.

opposition and led the street protests.[2] Organization outside the orbit of these main political groupings remained isolated, unable to gain either the financial support or the capacity to break the prevailing order. More often, they were co-opted and neutralized by the main Syrian Kurdish political parties. 'Qandil wants all Kurdish parties to be allied to be loyal to the PKK, the KDP wants all the Kurdish parties to be KDP, and the PUK wants all the Kurdish parties to become *Peshveru* [Abdulhamid Haj Darwish's party]', a Syrian Kurdish activist said.[3] This domination over Syrian Kurdish agency contributed towards the establishment of a third or neutral Kurdish position in the Syrian civil unrest of 2011: between the mainstream opposition and the Syrian government and defined by agendas rooted in distinct understandings of Kurdish national identity (the KNC) and of Kurdish liberation (the PYD). While this also reflected the often tense Kurdish–Arab relations, it also contributed to the failure of many Kurdish organizations to develop a democratic agenda that incorporated and represented all Syrians regardless of ethnicity or religion.

Following the seizure of power by the PYD in 2012, Turkish- and Iraqi-Kurdish parties' relations with, or reproofs of, the PYD informed their own attempts to increase their agency in regional and international affairs. The KRI was closely involved in events in northern Syria from the beginning, not only because of national affinity and relations with Syrian Kurdish political parties but also because of the affect that it had on its domestic politics. The renewed impetus given to the PKK movement, combined with the opportunity for expansion that ISIS provided, extended the PKK presence and influence within the KRI as well as in Syria. Relations developed between the PYD and PUK increased tensions within the KRG. Refugees fleeing Syria added to its economic burden as well as to its political responsibility to Syrian Kurds, and checking the increasing influence of the PYD/PKK also became central to the KRG–Ankara relations.

The relationships between the parties within the two main pan-Kurdish political blocs were fundamentally different. The PYD–PKK relationship was defined by their common 'revolutionary' project and a single spiritual leader, Abdullah Öcalan. This facilitated coordination and sharing of resources across international borders. In comparison, the relationship of the KNC with the KDP was shaped by Iraqi sovereignty, which restricted the support available to the KNC and the ability and willingness of the KDP to interfere in issues that might threaten Syrian sovereignty. Rooted firmly within state sovereignty, inter-state

---

[2] Bradost Azizi 17/05/2013: 'Kurdish Youth Groups in Syria Blame opposition parties for divisions', *Rudaw*, http://www.rudaw.net/english/middleeast/syria/17052013 (last accessed 08/03/2017).
[3] IIST interview: Sipan Seyda, former member of the SNC and Kurdish activist, Erbil, 11/03/2016.

relations and recognizing nationhood (or statehood) as an ultimate achievement for the Kurds, this relationship lacked the flexibility of that between the PKK and the PYD. The consequence of these differences for the representation of Syrian Kurds was significant. The PYD-led project in Syria had yet to gain any official external recognition. The PYD's recognition of state sovereignty and adherence to it were central to its engagement with the international community but its connection to a wider, non-state, agenda problematized external recognition of the autonomy developed in northern Syria. The pragmatic approach of the PYD, however, which limited the project to the Syrian state, promoted de-ethnification of nationhood and extended participation into non-Kurdish areas, helped to dissipate non-Kurdish concerns about their wider agenda. But, as Chapter 4 has shown, this came at the expense of support from nationalist Kurds. The more nationalist KNC's dependence on Iraqi Kurdish parties and limited resources, however, prevented them from obtaining real agency in their own politics.

A major factor affecting PYD–KDP relations was the dealings between the KDP and Ankara. The breakdown of the Kurdish–Turkish peace process in July 2015 intensified the pressure on the KDP to control its borders with PYD-controlled Syria. As noted in Chapter 3, Ankara's closure of its own border with PYD territory increased the importance of land access to Iraq. The PYD's relations with the central Iraqi government and the position of the PKK in Iraq, therefore, had significant bearing on PYD's ability to successfully govern in northern Syria. Tensions between the KDP and the PYD/PKK over the border and broader regional relations and ambitions, however, prevented both the KNC and PYD from using the Kurdish-controlled border crossing in Fish Khabour, necessitating politicians from both sides to smuggle themselves in and out of northern Syria. 'Our KNC-head Ibrahim Biro did not go [in to Syria] through the Kurdistan border gate. He went on foot, because [the PYD] didn't allow him to go through the gate', a *Yekîtî* Party member said.[4]

The control of borders of YPG- and PYD-held areas by the KDP and by Turkey made Sinjar central to power struggles between the KDP and the PKK. In the political vacuum caused by the ISIS occupation of the area in August 2014 and by its subsequent expulsion both parties competed for support and influence among the Yezidi communities. The PKK presence in Sinjar provided the party with a pocket of support deep in Iraqi Kurdish territory and its geographical position offered potential to open a corridor to Baghdad after PYD access to Iraq was cut off when the Peshmerga took over the Rabia border crossing. The effect

---

[4] IIST interview: Majdal Delli, Yekiti politician in Qamishli, 01/03/2016. Border tensions decreased in 2017 following the Raqqa operation and the KRI independence referendum.

of clashes between the KDP-affiliated Rojava Peshmerga and the PKK-linked Sinjar Resistance Units (*Yekîneyên Berxwedana Şengalê* or YBS) on 3 March 2017 were felt inside Syria. Relations between the KNC and the PYD worsened significantly and many KNC members were arrested in northern Syria and their offices shut down.[5]

The PUK also lent support to the PYD and provided a safe space for it within in its strongholds in Iraq. This relationship developed from a nominal convergence on more leftist political positions, their mutual rivalry with the KDP and from a concurrence of Iranian interests in both these parties. The internal divisions experienced by the PUK after Jalal Talabani suffered a stroke in December 2012 led TEV-DEM official, Aldar Xelil, to say that the support the PUK could give them was limited; 'Talabani is sick and the PUK is not strong now because of Mam Jalal's sickness.'[6] He also played down the role of the PUK in Syrian affairs suggesting that the PUK's support for the PYD had limited effect: 'The [KRG] government is controlled by the KDP and the KDP controls the border between Rojava [northern Syria] and Basur [Iraqi Kurdistan]. The PUK has no decision-making power in Baghdad or Erbil.'[7] Nevertheless, the PUK's military cooperated with the PYD and the PKK in Kirkuk and even in Sinjar, where PKK and PUK bases were adjacent to each other. A PUK Peshmerga fighter from Kirkuk affirmed: 'We have good relations with the PKK in Kirkuk and Sinjar, but not with the KDP, since the KDP is with Turkey.'[8]

Within Syria the PUK had an historic and enduring relationship with Abdulhamid Darwish's *Pêşverû* party which influenced its positions on the Syrian Kurdish political spectrum. The convergence of PUK–PYD/PKK interests in Syria also influenced the position of Darwish's party within the Syrian crisis and on Kurdish autonomy.[9] After a period of cooperation, Darwish stopped working with the PYD when civilians were shot in the town of Amude in July 2013.[10] The PUK, however, continued to support the PYD. The Kurdish National Alliance in Syria, an alliance of parties that left the KNC and enjoyed good relations with TEV-DEM, was also sympathetic to the PUK. 'Mam Jalal has a great role, a lot of

[5]   KNC 16/03/2017: 'PYD's repression of the KNC reaches new climax', *Kurdish National Council – Geneva/Berlin*, http://knc-geneva.org/?p=1059&lang=en, KNC Geneva (last accessed 10/03/2017); HRW 16/03/2017: 'Kurdistan region of Iraq: 32 arrested at peaceful protest', *Human Rights Watch*, https://www.hrw.org/news/2017/03/16/kurdistan-region-iraq-32-arrested-peaceful-protest, HRW (last accessed 11/03/2017).
[6]   IIST interview: Aldar Xelil, Amude, leading TEV-DEM official, 02/05/2016.
[7]   Ibid.
[8]   IIST interview: Peshmerga member of the CTG forces in Erbil, 16/03/2017.
[9]   Wladimir van Wilgenburg 11/12/2013: 'The Kurdish PUK's Syria policy', *Carnegie Middle East Centre*, http://carnegie-mec.org/diwan/53884?lang=en (last accessed 11/03/2017).
[10]   IIST interview: Peshmerga member of the CTG forces in Erbil, 16/03/2017.

Kurds like him', said Salih Gheddo, one of the main politicians in this alliance.[11] It was the PUK's relationship with the PYD-led administration in Syria, however, that allowed it to increase its agency in Syrian Kurdish affairs, where, previously, the KDP had held greater influence.

The PUK appeared to be making a concerted efforts to move closer to the PKK and the PYD, which became evident with several events: Lahur Talabani, director of the Kurdish Counter-Terrorism Group (CTG), claimed to have brokered US assistance for the YPG in Kobani and the PUK claimed that it had provided weapons, through US mediation, to the YPG during the Kobani siege;[12] Lahur Talabani later visited Kobani in June 2016 providing medical aid and called on the KDP to open its border with Rojava;[13] and during the 2014 Newroz celebrations held in Diyarbakir, the PUK joined PKK and pictures of both Abdullah Öcalan and Jalal Talabani were widespread.[14] Within the KRI, the PUK also facilitated PYD/PKK organization, movement and recruitment. In PUK-controlled areas, such as Sulaymaniyah and Kirkuk, the PYD and YPG operated freely and had been known to support local Peshmerga forces against ISIS. The DAAs, the PYD and the Kurdish Red Crescent all had representative offices in the region and foreign fighters who joined the YPG in Syria often transited through Sulaymaniyah (where a YPG representative tasked with orientating foreign fighters was based) before travelling on to northern Syria by land.[15] The operational space that the PUK provided the PKK and the PYD in Iraqi Kurdistan supported both the PYD logistically and expanded the PKK presence.

The PYD also had connections with the Iraqi Kurdish opposition Gorran (Change Movement) Party, which was closer politically to the PUK than to the KDP. The Gorran supported the establishment of the canton administrations in

---

[11] IIST interview: Salih Gheddo, ex-KNC politician and head of Kurdish Democratic Left Party, 11/05/2016.

[12] David Ignatius 25/10/2016: 'Why the Middle East knows not to trust the United States', *Washington Post*, https://www.washingtonpost.com/opinions/why-the-middle-east-knows-not-to-trust-the-un ited-states/2016/10/25/09c00c52-9afa-11e6-b3c9-f662adaa0048_story.html?utm_term=.4f0dbce5e e96 (last accessed 13/03/2017); PUK Media 20/10/2014: 'Lahore Sheikh Genki: 24 tons of weapons and ammunition sent to Kobani', *PUK*, http://www.pukmedia.com/EN/EN_Direje.aspx?Jimare=2 2293 (last accessed 11/03/2017).

[13] Millet Press 08/06/2016: 'KDP partially re-open border with Rojava', *Millet Press*, http://www.mill etpress.com/Detail_EN.aspx?Jiamre=1041&T=KDP+Partially+Re-Open+Border+with+Rojava (last accessed 13/03/2017).

[14] *Slemani Times* 30/03/2014: 'A PUK-PKK-YPG alliance in the making?' *Slemani Times*, https://ww w.facebook.com/SlemaniTimes/posts/709348175775550 (last accessed 11/03/2017).

[15] Seth Harp 14/02/2017: 'On the front lines of Syria with the young American radicals fighting ISIS', *Rolling Stone*, http://www.rollingstone.com/politics/features/american-anarchists-ypg-kurdish-mi litia-syria-isis-islamic-state-w466069 (last accessed 13/03/2017).

2014[16] and had met several times with the PYD in Sulaymaniyah.[17] KNC parties had not developed significant relations with Gorran, in part, because they considered the Gorran to be linked to Iran.[18] Gorran publicly backed the PKK following clashes between the KDP-affiliated Rojava Peshmerga and the PKK-linked YBS on 3 March 2017 and, again, following PKK protests against the KDP on 14 March.[19] While Gorran's position added support to the PYD, Aldar Xelil of TEV-DEM said simply that 'they are sometimes with us'.[20] Gorran's agency in these wider Kurdish politics was limited by its eviction from the KRG, its limited territorial support base and lack of dedicated security forces.

The PKK had more support in PUK-held territories, such as Sulaymaniyah and Kirkuk, than in KDP-held territories. This was due to the leading parties' territorially derived support bases. Both the PUK- and Gorran-affiliated media agencies backed the PKK against the KDP and gave more legitimacy to the PYD. Within the domestic tensions between the KDP and both the PUK and Gorran, rhetorical and logistical support for the PYD/PKK served to check and undermine the dominance of the KDP. Increased tensions between the KDP and PUK facilitated the PYD agenda in Syria, which in turn fomented and maintained wider tensions between the PKK and KDP and, consequently, between the KNC and PYD. The PYD/PKK was able to exploit unresolved domestic issues within the KRG, shore up wider support and legitimacy across the Kurdish regions and retain territorial havens necessary for logistical requirements.

Inter-Kurdish relations and divisions were also bound inextricably to wider regional power relations, particularly between Turkey, Iraq, Iran and Syria. Historic cooperation between these four countries on the Kurdish issue, in order to foment and maintain divisions between the various political movements, contributed to preventing a unified Kurdish discourse and movement from developing across and within Kurdish areas. Similarly, playing the 'Kurdish card' in hostilities between them allowed relationships to develop between Kurdish sub-state organizations and regional state powers.

---

[16] Rudaw 02/02/2014: 'Gorran backs PYD autonomy in Rojava', *Rudaw*, http://www.rudaw.net/engl ish/middleeast/syria/02022014 (last accessed 13/03/2017).

[17] Gorran 08/11/2016: 'PYD, Change Movement discuss several pressing issues', *Gorran Movement*, https://www.gorran.net/En/Detail.aspx?id=11497&LinkID=135 (last accessed 13/03/2017).

[18] Wladimir van Wilgenburg 24/05/2017: 'Syrian Kurds divided on relations with Iraqi Kurds', *ARA News*, http://aranews.net/2016/05/syrian-kurds-divided-relations-iraqi-kurds/ (last accessed 13/03/2017).

[19] NRT 15/03/2017: 'Gorran: KDP responsible for killing, wounding protesters in Sinjar', *NRT*, http://www.nrttv.com/En/Details.aspx?Jimare=13186 (last accessed 14/03/2017).

[20] IIST interview: Aldar Xelil, Amude, 02/05/2016.

Regional relations

Turkey

Turkey played a central role in fomenting divisions and tension between Kurdish parties and preventing resolutions of Kurdish issues regionally. Rival states, such as Syria, Iran and Russia, provided patronage to the PKK amid tensions with Turkey. This support was used to pressure and influence Ankara and its domestic and regional policy. The PKK and, since 2011, the PYD, were central to Ankara's domestic security concerns and its ongoing conflict, and the unresolved Kurdish issue in Syria lay at the heart of Turkey's regional relations.

The DAA territories were land-locked between Turkey, the KRI, Iraq and the Syrian interior. As shown above, tensions and competition between the PKK/PYD and the KDP prevented cross-border cooperation between the DAAs and the KRI. The DAA's longest border was with Turkey and the enmity between Ankara and the PYD had profound impact on the decision-making of the PYD within Syria and on its foreign policy considerations. Cooperation between Damascus and Ankara against the PKK after 1998 was ended by the turnabout in Turkish foreign policy towards Syria in 2011. Ankara called for the removal of Bashar al-Assad's government and began supporting Sunni and armed rebel groups against it. It was not clear whether the Assad government's decision to withdraw from northern Syria in 2012, and not to challenge the PYD seizure of power, was premised partly on this breakdown of Damascus–Ankara relations. Hostility from Ankara, however, and the threat posed to the government directly or indirectly from Turkey played a significant role in the government's concerns as the rebellion militarized in 2012. Leaving PYD control unchallenged presented it with an opportunity to exploit Turkey's domestic security concerns and limit the territory available to rebel forces. Even without a formal agreement, the Kurds and the Administration became a geographic and strategic buffer against further Turkish intervention in Syrian affairs and a means for the Syrian government to gain leverage over Ankara.

For Ankara, the PYD was considered a greater threat to its domestic security than ISIS. A contiguous PYD/YPG-controlled territory, encompassing Syria's northern border with Turkey had the potential to become a haven for the PKK from which attacks against Turkey might be launched, which could dramatically increase the leverage of the PKK over Ankara and potentially increase the levels of conflict there. Ankara's involvement in Syria and in regional attempts to contain and degrade ISIS could be contextualized by its primary agenda of disrupting PYD ambitions in Syria: Ankara's support of the Syrian opposition, its reluctance to support international campaigns against ISIS, its closure of borders and support of de-militarized zones, its military intervention in August 2016, its rapprochement with both Moscow and Damascus after 2015 and its military operation in Afrin in 2018. All these hindered the ability of the PYD to achieve territorial contiguity in Syria and, the latter three in particular, weakened its prospects of surviving, unscathed, a post-war settlement.

The PYD's focus on political agency within Syria and its organizational separation from the PKK did little to abate Ankara's concerns. Evidence of mutual support between the PYD and PKK existed: during clashes between the PKK-affiliated Patriotic Revolutionary Youth Movement (YDG-H) and Turkish security forces in February 2016, the YDG-H received weapons through a tunnel from Syria (most likely from PYD-held Qamishli).[21] The Turkish army also claimed that they had captured 'PYD fighters' with ammunition smuggled across the border, although this was not confirmed by independent sources.[22] For the PYD, Turkey was always defined as the primary threat to Kurdish interests and existence and featured heavily in its political rhetoric. The PYD accused Turkey of using Syrian FSA rebel groups, ISIS and *Jabhat al-Nusra* to attack Kurds,[23] and its derogation of both the Syrian and Kurdish opposition was commonly framed in terms of perceived cooperation with Ankara.

Ankara's support for the Syrian opposition, however, preceded the rise of the PYD in Syria. Its influence over the composition and agenda of the nascent opposition groupings, cradled in Turkey from the beginning of the Syrian crisis, influenced decisively the course that Kurdish political organizations would take. Kurdish political parties of the 1957 genealogy and independent activists involved in those early assemblies reported that Kurdish issues were shunned in favour of Arabist and Islamist agendas and that their representation was not proportionate. This was blamed on both the constituent parties within the new opposition alliances (which was then dominated by the Muslim Brotherhood) and on Ankara's support and influence. Its influence on the Syrian opposition prevented dialogue on and representation of the Kurdish issue within it

[21] Katrin Kuntz 12/02/2016: 'The growing intensity of Turkey's civil war', *Der Spiegel*, http://www.spie gel.de/international/world/escalating-turkish-civil-war-sees-young-fighters-on-front-a-1076663. html (last accessed 14/03/2017).

[22] Radikal 07/02/2016: 'TSK: PYD terrorists caught in Nusaybin with large amount of ammunition', *Radikal*, http://www.radikal.com.tr/turkiye/tsk-nusaybinde-pydli-teroristler-cok-sayida-muhimma tla-yakalandi-1506615/ (last accessed 14/03/2017).

[23] Wladimir van Wilgenburg 28/07/2013: 'What does the PYD want from Turkey?', *Orsam*, http://www .orsam.org.tr/index.php/Content/Analiz/3796?s=guvenlik%7Cenglish (last accessed 14/03/2017).

and contributed to the decision of all Kurdish political parties to organize independently of the wider opposition. Ankara was also believed to have pressured Syrian opposition groups it supported to shun relations with the PYD. 'The opposition was founded in Istanbul and Turkey does not allow the Syrian opposition to support the Kurdish people', said a former Kurdish member of the Turkish-backed Syrian opposition.[24] Although negotiations and talks between the Syrian opposition groups and the PYD did occur, by 2017 their strategic objectives and political alignments did not converge sufficiently to provide a basis for further cooperation.

Despite its clear objection to PYD authority in Syria, Ankara was also engaged in negotiations with PYD officials and with the PKK. Before the Kurdish–Turkish peace process failed in July 2015, Turkish officials had met with PYD representatives, including Salih Muslim, several times.[25] The PYD was asked to join the Turkish-backed opposition.[26] Turkey also allowed Peshmerga fighters to enter Kobani through its territory to assist the YPG in November 2014 and it appeared to have turned a blind eye to Turkish Kurds travelling to Kobani to join the YPG.[27] The YPG was reported to have facilitated the relocation of the Suleyman Shah tomb, belonging to the father of the founder of the Ottoman Empire, in February 2015, although Turkey denied this.[28] Abdullah Öcalan was also said to have proposed, in 2014, a strategic alliance between the PYD, FSA and Turkey, and cooperation in the region between Azaz, Bab, Tal Abyad and Jarablus to end Syrian rule.[29] However, after the breakdown of the PKK-Turkey ceasefire in July 2015 relations worsened significantly.

Turkey's border with Syria became a supply route to support Syrian rebels and was also used by ISIS for these purposes. All border crossings with PYD-

[24] IIST interview: Sipan Seyda former member of the Syrian National Council (SNC) and Kurdish activist, Erbil, 11/03/2016.

[25] Hurriyet 02/09/2016: 'No re-launch of PKK peace process but normalization with Syria, Egypt on agenda: Turkish PM', *Hurriyet*, http://www.hurriyetdailynews.com/no-re-launch-of-pkk-peace-process-but-normalization-with-syria-egypt-on-agenda-turkish-pm.aspx?pageID=238&nID=103518&NewsCatID=338 (last accessed 14/03/2017).

[26] Kom News 16/03/2017: 'PYD not engaged in violence against Turkey, court document reveals', *Kom News*, https://komnews.com/pyd-not-engaged-violence-turkey-court-document-reveals/ (last accessed 14/03/2017); Aliza Marcus 01/10/2013: 'No friends but the Kurds', *National Interest*, http://nationalinterest.org/commentary/no-friends-the-kurds-9161 (last accessed 14/03/2017).

[27] IIST interview: Anonymous YPG foreign fighter, 23/03/2017.

[28] Hawar News Agency 23/02/2015: 'YPG: We are informed of and participated in operation for Suleyman Shah Tomb', *ANHA*, http://en.hawarnews.com/ypg-we-are-informed-of-and-participated-in-operation-for-suleyman-shah-tomb/ (last accessed 14/03/2017).

[29] IIST interview: Walter Posch, National Defense Academy (Vienna, Austria) by e-mail, 24/03/2017; Tunca Öğreten 11/02/2016: 'From Öcalan to Erdoğan, who says "PYD is my red line": "Like Hitler invading Soviets?"', *Diken*, http://www.diken.com.tr/ocalandan-pyd-kirmizi-cizgimdir-diyen-erdogana-hitlerin-ani-bir-kararla-sovyetlere-girmesine-benziyor/ (last accessed 14/03/2017).

held territories, however, were closed and Ankara began to build concrete walls along its 900-kilometre border with Syria, which was interpreted by Kurds as a deliberate policy to isolate the PYD.[30] Ankara was believed to have exploited tensions between FSA groups and the PYD and encouraged them to confront the YPG.[31] Politically also, Turkey opposed participation of the PYD in the wider negotiations on Syria that were held in Geneva and Astana.[32]

In August 2016, Turkish-backed groups launched Operation Euphrates Shield, aimed at capturing the border town of Jarablus from ISIS. Ankara officially emphasized that its goal was to remove 'terror groups' from the border. More importantly for Turkey, however, was preventing the PYD from connecting the Kobani and Afrin cantons and reducing its political and military power.[33] With tacit agreement from Moscow and the United States, a coalition of Syrian rebels and the Turkish army captured over 2000 square kilometres of territory. Ankara gained substantial influence in this zone and, with support from Turkmen and Islamist groups, the Turkish army inflicted significant losses in conflicts with SDF and YPG fighters. In an attempt to increase this presence and influence inside Syria, Ankara pressured the Trump administration to end its support for the SDF and, instead, coordinate with the Turkish military and Turkish-backed rebels to capture Raqqah at the beginning of 2017.[34] In March 2017, however, American support to the SDF was renewed with the suggestion that an additional thousand US soldiers be deployed to assist in the Raqqah campaign.[35] In a further slight on the role of the Turkish military in Syria, in May 2017 the United States announced that it would arm Syria's Kurdish fighters 'as necessary' in order to defeat ISIS in Raqqah.[36] The US dependence on the SDF for implementing anti-ISIS policy,

---

[30] van Wilgenburg, 'Syrian Kurdish party calls on Turkey, KRG to end embargo'.
[31] IIST interview: Sipan Seyda former member of the Syrian National Council (SNC) and Kurdish activist, Erbil, 11/03/2016.
[32] Rudaw 04/02/2017: 'Turkey tells Syrian opposition that PYD should not attend Geneva talks', *Rudaw*, http://www.rudaw.net/english/middleeast/syria/04022017 (last accessed 14/03/2017).
[33] Patrick Cockburn 26/08/2016: 'Turkey could be overplaying its hand with Syria ground offensive as civil war reaches crucial point', *The Guardian* (online), http://www.independent.co.uk/voices/turk ey-syria-civil-war-ground-offensive-us-russia-un-peace-a7211941.html (last accessed 06/10/2016).
[34] ARA News 04/02/2017: 'Turkey demands US to stop supporting Kurdish YPG forces in Syria', *ARA News*, http://aranews.net/2017/01/turkey-demands-us-stop-supporting-kurdish-ypg-forces-syria / (last accessed 14/03/2017); Wilgenburg 26/09/2017: 'Kurdish stronghold in eastern Syria defies assaults by Islamic State', *Jamestown Foundation*, https://jamestown.org/program/kurdish-strongh old-in-eastern-syria-defies-assaults-by-islamic-state/ (last accessed 14/03/2017).
[35] Thomas Gibbons-Neff 15/03/2017: 'U.S. military likely to send as many as 1,000 more ground troops into Syria ahead of Raqqa offensive, officials say', *Washington Post*, (online) https://ww w.washingtonpost.com/news/checkpoint/wp/2017/03/15/u-s-military-probably-sending-as-m any-as-1000-more-ground-troops-into-syria-ahead-of-raqqa-offensive-officials-say/ (last accessed 14/03/2017).
[36] AP 09/05/2017: 'US to arm Kurdish fighters against Izis in Raqqa, despite Turkish opposition', *The Guardian*, (online) https://www.theguardian.com/world/2017/may/09/us-arm-kurdish-fighters-syria-izis-raqqa-trump (last accessed 15/05/2017).

therefore, provided some protection for the PYD against threats from Turkey. But the strain that these relations put on long-established US–Turkish relations and on regional balances of power meant that YPG-US relations had limited scope and endurance.

While the PYD's agency in regional and international affairs was not comparable to Ankara's, the role and agency offered to it by the United States sidelined Turkey within the anti-ISIS campaign: the PYD gained and maintained US military support despite Ankara's objections; the YPG took the lead in the Raqqah operation; military support was extended to allow it to take control of Manbij despite vehement objections from Ankara and threats to intervene militarily against the YPG and; it coordinated with the Syrian government against Turkish-backed Syrian rebels around Aleppo.[37] This increased agency was facilitated by the United States but, as examined in more detail later, was limited to the military field and contextualized by the campaign against ISIS. Politically, Ankara's own agency in regional and international affairs enabled it to keep the PYD isolated from wider negotiations on Syria's future and stall international recognition of PYD-governance structures. On the ground in Syria, Ankara's agency increased again with its rapprochement with Russia in 2016, its indication that it accepted that Bashar al-Assad would be part of any peace settlement and transition period and with its role as one of three 'guardians' of the de-escalation zones proposed by Moscow and agreed during the Astana talks on 4 May 2017. Turkey's involvement in establishing de-escalation zones suggested that the country could gain a role in defining 'terrorist' groups in Syria. This development, along with Turkish military intervention in Syria, was followed up with a change in the Syrian government's rhetoric on the PYD and YPG: on 19 August 2016 the Syrian military's General Command referred to the Asayish as 'the military wing of the PKK'.[38]

Ankara's intervention in Syria increased uncertainties about the future of Kurdish self-governance there, in particular, for PYD dominance. While the PYD/YPG remained in northern Syria further military actions against it were a realistic and palpable threat to its governance. The international legitimacy gained through alliances with the United States and Russia provided the PYD/YPG with

---

[37] Cengiz Candar 09/11/2016: 'Why Turkey's hostile stance doesn't worry PYD leader', *Al Monitor*, http://www.al-monitor.com/pulse/en/originals/2016/11/turkey-syria-operation-raqqa-salih-muslim.html (last accessed 10/11/2016).

[38] Ayse Wieting 20/08/2016: 'Turkey: Assad can be part of transition in Syria', *AP*, https://apnews.com/ef6fa94895854d96abb111ccc11986d0/turkey-assad-can-be-part-transition-syria (last accessed 15/05/2015).

some means of halting a confrontation with Ankara, which was demonstrated in US and Russian intervention around Manbij in August 2016. The long-term durability of these alliances with the YPG was, however, questionable and, as detailed further below, US commitment to defeating ISIS was not a corollary of a commitment to the PYD political project, or vice versa. But while ISIS remained strong in Syria, US support for the YPG and SDF prevented any concerted Turkish challenge to the PYD: and while Damascus and Ankara remained at odds, the PYD could still use that to its advantage.

Iraq

Iraq, like Syria, experienced the 'Arab Spring' protests and an intensification of sectarian tensions that further weakened the central government. It was the country in which ISIS developed and from which it expanded. Unlike in Syria, centralized efforts to combat ISIS triumphed over local unrest and local populations were galvanized better against the expansionist radical group. But like Syria, it was uncertain how disparate militarized and empowered sub-state groups could be brought back within a centralized governance system. Iraq and Syria stepped up military cooperation in 2017 against ISIS strongholds in border areas between Iraq and Syria.[39]

Iraq's relations with Tehran influenced its relations with the PYD and its position on Kurdish autonomy in Syria. From mid-2014 Iran provided substantial military aid, advice and support to Iraq's Shia militias fighting against ISIS, as it did for the Syrian government. Iraq, therefore, formed part of an axis of alliances that extended from Tehran to Baghdad to Damascus and which incorporated relations with Hezbollah and Russia in Syria. Limiting the influence of Turkey regionally also united these forces after 2011 and support for the PYD and PKK provided a means of affecting Turkey domestically.

The PYD's relations with the Iraqi government developed after July 2012, as Iraq's relations with Ankara worsened and as the PYD's need to secure unhindered land access to the cantons and bypass hostilities from both Ankara and the KDP increased. In December 2012, as part of the National Coordination Body (NCB) delegation, the PYD co-chair, Salih Muslim, met with Nouri al-Maliki in Baghdad. He was also reported to have visited Baghdad secretly to

---

[39] Mustafa Saadoun 07/04/2017: 'Is Iraq poised for large-scale military involvement in Syria?' *Al Monitor*, http://www.al-monitor.com/pulse/originals/2017/04/iraq-syria-isis-us-raqqa-mosul-terrorism.html (last accessed 20/05/2017).

meet the Iraqi prime minister, Haider al-Abadi, in June 2015.[40] Aldar Xelil of TEV-DEM confirmed: 'We have good relations with the Iraqi government, we have met Maliki and Abadi also.'[41] Land access to Iraqi territory was essential to supply PYD-controlled areas with both resources and PYD/YPG fighters. The border gradually became more fortified and restricted as the conflict in Syria escalated, making negotiating and maintaining access a central strategic and logistical issue for the DAAs. The YPG, in coordination with the Iraqi government, captured the Yarubiyah Syrian-Iraqi border crossing from jihadist groups in October 2013, but the Iraqi side of the border crossing fell under Kurdish Peshmerga control in June 2014, preventing PYD transit.[42] The YPG presence in Sinjar, following the defeat of Peshmerga forces by ISIS in August 2014, allowed a route from Sinjar into Syria to be established through which besieged Yezidi populations were rescued. The subsequent formation of the YBS, affiliated to the YPG and the PKK, secured the area and allowed freer movement across the border into Syria.[43] Between January 2016 and February 2017, the YBS received salaries from Baghdad.[44] This funding was stopped due to US and Turkish pressure on Baghdad.[45] Sinjar, however, remained a strategic asset to the YPG, the PKK, the KNC, the KDP and to the Iraqi government, despite it being isolated from the Iraqi interior by ISIS-held areas. Syrian Kurdish officials suggested that the YPG and PYD hoped to link DAA territory to Iraq through Sinjar or the Syrian-Iraqi border after the defeat of ISIS in Mosul.[46]

Control over Sinjar was, however, contested. Yezidi Peshmerga forces, loyal to the KDP, were also present in the region. Fierce competition between the KDP

[40] Bilgay Duman 26/06/2015: 'What PYD leader Muslim's Baghdad visit means', *Orsam*, http://www .orsam.org.tr/index.php/Content/Analiz/4432?s=orsam%7Cenglish (last accessed 14/03/2017); NOW 17/06/2015: 'Syria Kurdish chief reportedly in secret Iraq deal', *NOW*, https://now.mmedia. me/lb/en/NewsReports/565450-syria-kurdish-chief-reportedly-in-secret-iraq-deal (last accessed 14/03/2017).

[41] IIST interview: Aldar Xelil, Amude, 02/05/2016.

[42] Wladimir van Wilgenburg 19/06/2014: 'Iraqi Kurds seize control of key Syria border crossing', *Al Monitor*, http://www.al-monitor.com/pulse/originals/2014/06/iraq-mosul-isis-pyd-pkk-kurds-barzani-kdp-peshmerga.html (last accessed 14/03/2017).

[43] HRW 04/12/2016: 'Iraq: KRG restrictions harm Yezidi recovery', *Human Rights Watch*, https://ww w.hrw.org/news/2016/12/04/iraq-krg-restrictions-harm-yezidi-recovery (last accessed 14/03/2017).

[44] Wladimir van Wilgenburg 08/01/2016: 'Baghdad-Erbil competition complicates battle against ISIS in Sinjar', *NOW*, https://now.mmedia.me/lb/en/commentaryanalysis/566454-baghdad-erbil-co mpetition-complicates-battle-against-isis-in-sinjar (last accessed 14/03/2017).

[45] TRT World 13/02/2017: 'Iraq cuts off support for PKK, vice president says', *TRT World*, http:// www.trtworld.com/mea/iraq-cuts-off-support-for-pkk-vice-president-says-296722 (last accessed 22/03/2017).

[46] Christine van den Toorn and Wladimir van Wilgenburg 15/06/2016: 'Sinjar after S: Returning to disputed territory', *Pax for Peace*, https://www.paxforpeace.nl/stay-informed/news/sinjar-after-isis-r eturning-todisputed-territory (last accessed 14/03/2017). ISIS was removed from Mosul by Iraqi forces on 21 July 2017.

and the PKK erupted after ISIS was expelled from Sinjar in November 2015.[47] KDP 'embargos' on the PYD were extended to Sinjar in order to restrict access of the PKK and its affiliates to goods and funds.[48] In March 2017 clashes erupted between the PKK-affiliated YBS and the KDP-affiliated Rojava Peshmerga over control of the border, which further territorialized PYD/PKK–KDP/ KNC tensions. Plans to link the DAAs with Baghdad through Sinjar remained incomplete and depended on the successful removal of ISIS from Mosul: an outcome that could also allow the KDP to increase its efforts to remove the PKK presence from the region. By late May 2017, the Shia paramilitary Popular Mobilization Units (PMU) affiliated with the Iraqi government had reached the Iraqi–Syrian border making the establishment of a trade corridor between northern Syria and Baghdad more feasible and likely.[49] The arrival of the PMU in South Sinjar, however, resulted in greater tensions between the PMU and the KDP-linked forces. In October 2017, Iraqi forces took over most of Sinjar from the KDP while the local YBS maintained a presence in the area. Then in March 2018, PKK forces also withdraw from Sinjar and additional Iraqi forces were deployed to deter possible Turkish attacks.[50]

For the Iraqi government, the PYD/PKK mitigated and balanced the authority gained by both the KDP and Ankara in the KRI. The drive for Kurdish independence, pursued largely by the KDP, threatened the territorial integrity of Iraq and, therefore, any check on its authority might have appeared beneficial to long-term Iraqi interests. Yet, although mutually beneficial relations between the PYD, Baghdad and Tehran and between Ankara and the KDP existed, none of the Turkish, Iraqi, Iranian or the Syrian governments supported the long-term success of the PYD entity in Syria. Their dealings with the PYD were defined in terms of their own domestic policies, regional strategies and the trans national dimension of the Kurdish issue. The formalization of Kurdish autonomy in Syria would have profound consequences on domestic politics, claims to legitimacy, power relations and governance structures within these four states.

---

[47] Al Jazeera 13/11/2015: 'Iraqi Kurd leader declares Sinjar "liberated" from ISIL', *Al Jazeera*, http:// www.aljazeera.com/news/2015/11/iraqi-kurd-leader-declares-sinjar-liberated-isil-1511131432203 84.html (last accessed 16/03/2017).

[48] HRW 04/08/2016: 'Iraq: KRG Restrictions Harm Yezidi Recovery', *Human Rights Watch*, https://www w.hrw.org/news/2016/12/04/iraq-krg-restrictions-harm-yezidi-recovery (last accessed 14/03/2017); Christine van den Toorn and Wladimir van Wilgenburg 15/06/2016: 'Sinjar after ISIS: Returning to disputed territory', *Pax for Peace*, https://www.paxforpeace.nl/stay-informed/news/sinjar-after-isis-r eturning-todisputed-territory (last accessed 14/03/2017).

[49] Chmaytelli, 'Iran-backed Iraqi force says takes Islamic State villages near Syria'.

[50] Fehim Tastekin 26/03/2018: 'Erdogan keeps finger on trigger as PKK exits Sinjar', *Al Monitor*, https://www.al-monitor.com/pulse/originals/2018/03/turkey-iraq-sinjar-pkk-withdraw-from-ya zidi-region.html (last accessed 3/05/2018).

The Syrian government

Although PYD relations with the Syrian government were addressed in Chapter 2, for several reasons, it is also discussed within this section on regional relations. First, Syria had coordinated with Turkey, Iraq and Iran on regional policy on the Kurdish issues. Second, the government engaged in direct relations with the PKK from 1980–1998. Third, the Syrian government was dependent on both Iran and Russia for the success and maintenance of its military and political campaigns. And fourth, the distinct DAA governance system and territorial regions made examining relations with non-allied groups or regions within Syria through the lens of regional or international relations (as well as in terms of Syrian domestic and sub-state relations) analytically logical.

The Syrian opposition, the KDP and the KNC all accused the PYD of working under the influence of Bashar al-Assad and Iran.[51] Aside from direct denial by the PYD, evidence to the contrary included occasional localized clashes between the PYD-affiliated security groups and the Syrian government; the Syrian government's denunciation of the PYD's federal and education system, and; the PYD boycott of government elections in Kurdish towns in June 2014 and April 2016, when the Asayish also confiscated ballots papers. PYD officials, however, stated that they would cooperate with whomever necessary to realize their interests. The PYD claimed it followed a 'third way': 'From the beginning of the revolution of Rojava, we took a third line: not with the regime and not with the Syrian opposition', Ayse Efendi, co-head of the People's House in Kobani said.[52] As a result, the PYD and YPG had cooperated and fought with both Syrian rebels and the Syrian government depending on strategic objectives, local power balances and pragmatic alliances.

The interests and territory of the PYD and the Syrian government converged increasingly following Russian intervention in 2015 and the siege of eastern Aleppo in 2016. Government forces extended northwards into the coveted region between Kobani and Afrin. The subsequent Turkish extension southwards towards SDF-held Manbij, in March 2017, led the SDF to relinquished control of several villages west of the town to the Syrian government in accordance with an agreement with Russia that was forged to prevent Turkish-rebel attacks against the PYD. This was reported to have been preceded by an agreement between Turkey, Iran and Russia to hand control of Aleppo to the Syrian government in

---

[51] For instance, Hassan Salih, of the political bureau of the *Yekiti* party, suggested the PKK was under the influence of Bashar al-Assad and Iran. IIST interview: 04/05/2016.

[52] IIST interview: Ayse Efendi, co-chair of People's Assembly of Kobanê Canton, 17/06/2016.

August 2016 and to allow Turkey to occupy large parts of the northern Aleppo countryside and prevent the Kurds from uniting their cantons.[53]

The PYD interests in dominating the areas under its control and connecting the cantons to create a contiguous autonomous zone underlay its pragmatic alliances and agreements. The absence of a clear international policy on Syria and the increased Russian and Iranian support for the government made confronting government forces increasingly problematic without guarantees for recognition. International policy on the government and on Kurdish autonomy in Syria were not comparable with Iraq before the overthrow of Saddam Hussein, where Iraqi Kurds received security guarantees from the Americans and federalism was recognized in the Iraqi constitution. The PYD position on the Syrian government was informed by circumstances and practical considerations: 'Our primary goal is not to kick out the regime. We just build the society, and don't let the regime effect their people: they are weak and can't do anything', TEV-DEM executive member Aldar Xelil said.[54] The Russian military intervention in Syria had shifted the balance of powers in the country and the rhetoric of regime change gradually gave way to that of transition. The Syrian government aimed to reassert control over Syria. The short-term pacification of the Kurds, control of both Syrian rebels and ISIS and the buffer against Turkey that PYD domination inadvertently provided the Assad government had facilitated its campaign against rebel-held areas. With successive gains against rebels, secured with Russian military support, the question of how long Assad would continue to tolerate a de facto Syrian federal region in northern Syria became more pressing. Would Assad make a deal with the PYD to curtail Turkish influence? Or could Russian mediation facilitate cooperation between Ankara and Damascus against the PYD: either way, it was likely that the control of the PYD over northern Syria would be challenged.

Iran

Iran's geopolitical rivalry with Turkey and its disagreement about core regional policy and interests in Iraq and Syria placed the PYD between these regional powers. Tensions between them allowed the party to be used by Iran to check Ankara's and the Syrian rebels' ambitions in Syria, while their common interest

---

[53] Ragip Soylu 24/03/2017: 'Why Turkey needed Russia's partnership in Syria', *Daily Sabah*, https://www.dailysabah.com/columns/ragip-soylu/2017/03/24/why-turkey-needed-russias-partnership-in-syria (last accessed 18/12/2018).

[54] IIST interview: Aldar Xelil, Amude, leading TEV-DEM official, 02/05/2016.

in containing and weakening Kurdish autonomy in Syria provided the incentive to cooperate. The Iranian position towards PYD autonomy was contextualized by Iran's geopolitical interests in preserving Bashar al-Assad's government, which led it to conduct an extensive, expensive and integrated effort to bolster its power.[55]

Both the PYD co-chair Salih Muslim and the prominent KDP-S politician Abdulhakim Bashar were invited to Teheran in August 2013.[56] According to a Kurdish politician, Syrian Kurds were asked to support the Syrian government.[57] The outcomes of the meetings were unclear: Kurdish officials denied any cooperation but allegations about PYD collusion with Iran and the Assad government were common. According to analysis by the International Crisis Group, Iran had tried to exploit historic competition between Kurdish parties and bring its own favoured Kurds – the PKK in Turkey, the PYD/YPG in Syria, and Talabani's PUK in Iraq – into a broad alliance against Barzani's KDP.[58] There were even suggestions that Tehran, with PUK's assistance, brokered a deal between the PYD and the Assad government through which Assad had surrendered control of northern Syria to the PYD in 2012 in exchange for it remaining neutral in Syria's domestic conflict.[59] Critics of the PYD frequently alluded to Iranian agency in PYD actions and ambitions. KDP-S leader Abdulhakim Bashar said 'The PYD is with the regime and their decision is in Iranian hands.'[60] These claims connected back to the ceasefire between the PKK-affiliated Kurdistan Free Life Party and Iran in 2011, which was interpreted as a rapprochement between the PKK and Iran that had allowed the KCK to concentrate its regional efforts on fighting against Turkey and developing the democratic autonomy project in Syria.[61] The PKK commander Agid Kalari said, 'We don't want to fight against the Iranian government. We stopped because they asked us to stop fighting ... but they started to kill Kurds again. We don't want to fight against Iran, because we have to fight against Turkey.'[62] He suggested that

---

[55] Will Fulton, Joseph Holliday and Sam Wyer, May 2013: 'Iranian strategy in Syria', *Understanding War*, http://www.understandingwar.org/report/iranian-strategy-syria (last accessed 19/03/2017).

[56] Kurdpress 06/08/2016: 'Syrian Kurdish leaders to visit Iran', *Kurdpress*, http://www.kurdpress.com/En/NSite/FullStory/Print/?Id=5114 (last accessed 20/03/2017).

[57] IIST interview: KNC politician 15/02/2016.

[58] Joost Hilterman 19/05/2016: 'The Kurds: A Divided Future?' *International Crisis Group*, https://www.crisisgroup.org/middle-east-north-africa/gulf-and-arabian-peninsula/iraq/kurds-divided-future (last accessed 14/03/2017).

[59] Orsam 04/04/2017: 'Federalism in Syria, PYD and ambivalent position of Iran', *Orsam*, http://www.orsam.org.tr/index.php/Content/Analiz/5094?s=orsam%7Cenglish (last accessed 08/07/2017).

[60] IIST interview: Abdulhakim Bashar, Erbil, 15/02/2016.

[61] High-level KRG official including KRG prime minister Nechirvan Barzani were involved in brokering the PKK-Iran ceasefire.

[62] IIST interview: Agid Kalari, PKK commander in Sinjar city, 15/04/2016.

the KDP media was accusing the PKK of links with Iran but that it was mere propaganda intended to discredit the party: 'The KDP is saying that there are places in Shingal [Sinjar] to attack Israel by missiles and that Iran will control Shingal Mountain to attack Israel.'[63] Some Iranian links with the PKK-affiliated YBS militia in Sinjar were evident: representatives of the YBS had visited Iran in January 2017[64] and its members had received salaries from the Iranian- and Baghdad-backed Shia PMU in 2016.[65] The PKK, however, denied links to Iran and PKK commander Zeki Shingali said, 'When the YBS was created in 2014 there was no KDP, Iran, or Iraq [in the region]. ... The YBS is just for protecting the Yezidis.'[66] There were some suggestions, made by KDP officials and the Turkish media, that Iran wanted to carve a land corridor into Syria.[67] These were given weight by Iranian president Hasan Rouhani's announcement, in March 2017, that railway construction would be extended to connect Iran to the Syrian Mediterranean coast, via the KRI.[68] Allegations of PYD collusion in the Iranian corridor plan, however, were undermined after PMU units reached the Syrian border and the Asayish chief, Ciwan Ibrahim, warned that they would not allow the PMU and the Syrian government to connect territorially.[69]

The Iranian government's primary interest in Syria was the survival of the Assad government and in the words of YPG official Redur Xelil, 'Iran regards the Kurdish issue as a secondary and a trivial matter.'[70] Tehran opposed the declaration of federalism in March 2016 and the Syrian government was reported to have employed Shia paramilitary groups to fight against the Kurds

---

[63] Ibid.

[64] Baxtiyar Goran 25/01/2017: 'PKK-military wing in Shingal, Hashd al-Shaabi vizit Tehran', *Kurdistan 24*, http://www.kurdistan24.net/en/news/46357dad-e6bb-4626-aad9-1f49b63cd926/PKK -military-wing-in-Shingal--Hashd-al-Shaabi-visit-Tehran- (last accessed 14/03/2017).

[65] van Wilgenburg, 'Baghdad-Erbil competition complicates battle against ISIS in Sinjar'; TRT 13/02/2017: 'Iraq cuts off support for PKK, vice president says', *TRT World*, http://www.trtworld. com/mea/iraq-cuts-off-support-for-pkk-vice-president-says-296722 (last accessed 14/03/2017); *Al Monitor* 27/12/2016: 'Transcript of Al-Monitor interview with KRG Prime Minister Nechirvan Barzani', *Al Monitor*, http://cabinet.gov.krd/a/d.aspx?s=040000&l=12&a=55246 (last accessed 14/03/2017).

[66] IIST interview: Zeki Shingali, 15/04/2016.

[67] See, for example, Mira Rojkan 06/03/2017: 'PKK Serving Iran's Shi'ite Crescent: Peshmerga Official', *Bas News*, http://www.basnews.com/index.php/en/news/kurdistan/334553 (last accessed 14/03/2017) and AA 20/03/2017: 'PKK secures Iran's "Shia Corridor" project', *Anatolia News Agency*, http://aa.com.tr/en/info/infographic/5355 (last accessed 14/03/2017).

[68] Rudaw 26/03/2017: 'Train line to connect Iran to Mediterranean Sea through Kurdistan Region, Syria', *Rudaw*, http://www.rudaw.net/english/middleeast/iran/26032017 (last accessed 14/03/2017).

[69] NRT 31/05/2017: 'YPG warns Hashid al-Shaabi of not entering areas', *NRT*, http://www.nrttv.com/ EN/Details.aspx?Jimare=14804 (last accessed 06/06/2017).

[70] Zanyar Omrani 23/05/2015: 'Interview with Redur Xelil, the Spokesman of the People's Protection Units (YPG)' *Countercurrents.org*, https://www.countercurrents.org/omrani230515.htm (last accessed 18/02/2018).

during the brief clashes in Hasakah in August 2016.[71] The former PYD co-chair, Salih Muslim, claimed that Iran was 'making obstacles for Kurdish rights in Syria'[72] and suggested that Kurds in Iran should fight for their rights, just as the Kurds in Syria did.[73] In May 2015, however, Redur Xelil had implied that the Administration was open to relations with Iran.[74] For its part, the Iranian government had opposed Turkey's attack on Afrin in January 2018 and Iranian-backed militias went to the area to prevent it.[75] Simultaneously, however, Iran-backed militias attacked SDF-held positions in Deir al-Zour in February 2018.[76] These events confirmed the fluidity and locally rooted nature of policy as well as the separation of PYD/YPG policy from Kurdish ambitions in other states, which allowed them to make strategic alliances according to their specific and immediate interests. While Kurdish and Iranian interests coincided to some degree in the short term, and these were exploited by both parties, their long-term strategic interest and priorities diverged and prevented deeper cooperation that could promote and secure Kurdish representation, locally or regionally.

International relations

The United States

US policies on Syria and the Assad government were central to the prospects of maintaining a PYD-led administration in Syria despite its somewhat ambiguous position on Kurdish ambitions. US policy and its role in Syria were tied intrinsically to its key regional partners, Turkey and Saudi Arabia, its past investment in the federal system in Iraq, its global security role and historic tensions with Russia and Iran, as well as to the fight against ISIS that was framed by domestic policy concerns. Where the Syrian Kurds and Kurdish representation lay within these

---

[71] Wladimir van Wilgenburg 22/08/2016: 'Syrian regime using Shia militias to fight the Kurds in Hasakah', *ARA News*, http://aranews.net/2016/08/syrian-regime-using-shia-militias-fight-kurds-ha sakah/ (last accessed 14/03/2017).

[72] IIST interview: PYD co-chair Salih Muslim, 02/08/2016.

[73] Wladimir van Wilgenburg 08/08/2016: 'Kurdish parties in Syria supporting Iranian Kurds in struggle for democracy', *ARA News*, http://aranews.net/2016/08/kurdish-parties-syria-supporting-iranian-kurds-struggle-democracy/ (last accessed 14/03/2017).

[74] Omrani, 'Interview with Redur Xelil, the Spokesman of the People's Protection Units (YPG)'.

[75] Fars News Agency 21/02/2018: 'Iran asks immediate halt to Turkey's attacks in Afrin', *Fars News Agency*, http://en.farsnews.com/newstext.aspx?nn=13961101001651 (last accessed 07/05/2018).

[76] Christoph Reuter 02/03/2018: 'The truth about the Russian deaths in Syria', *Der Spiegel*, http://www .spiegel.de/international/world/american-fury-the-truth-about-the-russian-deaths-in-syria-a-119 6074.html (last accessed 07/05/2018).

interests, alliances and hostilities remained somewhat ambiguous and US policy was, at times, contradictory.

From 2014 the SDF and the YPG were recognized as the most effective US allies against ISIS in Syria and US military assistance added significant strength to the legitimacy claims of the wider PYD-led administration. The US position towards the PYD and the YPG, however, highlighted the dual strategies employed by it in Syria: first, backing the Syrian opposition against the Assad government. This stance was informed by its interest in regional stability and the benefits of this to US interests in the region. The second, and the one that was prioritized from 2014 onwards, was the campaign against ISIS. The Islamic State was defined as an immediate threat to the United States that trumped longer-term regional interests. Consequently, the American government's military and political policies within Syria diverged from each other. These dual policy trajectories, however, converged in their affect in Syria and added significant uncertainty to the future status of the DAAs and to the political groupings it involved.

Until 2014, US support for the main Syrian opposition groupings and for its long-standing NATO-partner, Turkey, defined its political agenda in Syria and underlined its opposition to any form of Kurdish autonomy there. Political relations with the PKK-linked PYD or any other related institution were avoided. US officials publicly expressed concerns about PYD ambitions and actions in Syria: In mid-July 2013 US State Department spokesperson, Jen Psaki, said 'We're also very concerned by press reports indicating that the Kurdish Democratic Union [PYD] might declare an independent Kurdish region in Syria; such a declaration is highly provocative, as it will certainly exacerbate tensions between Arabs and Kurds.'[77] Condemnation of the PYD's 'deadly response' to peaceful demonstrations in Amude in July 2013 also followed[78] and in December 2013 the United States indefinitely withheld a US visa for the PYD co-chair Salih Muslim. In parallel with Ankara, it increased its pressure on the PYD to 'break its ties' with the Assad government and join the Syrian opposition.[79]

[77] Roy Gutman 23/07/2013: 'Kurdish-Nusra battle becoming war within a war in northern Syria', *McClatchy*, http://www.mcclatchydc.com/news/nation-world/world/article24751405.html (last accessed 18/03/2017).

[78] United States State Department 01/07/2013: 'Situation in Amude, Syria', *US State Department*, https://2009-2017.state.gov/r/pa/prs/ps/2013/07/211430.htm (last accessed 19/03/2017).

[79] Cengiz Candar 15/08/2013: 'US, Turkey to rethink Syria policies', *Al Monitor*, http://www.al-monitor.com/pulse/originals/2013/12/turkey-syria-kurdish-pyd-policy-united-states-redefine.html (last accessed 14/03/2017).

Robert Ford, former US ambassador to Syria (2011 to 2014) said: 'We really had no [official] contacts with the PYD until after I left in 2014.'[80] However, backchannel talks, between the PYD and the United States, involving a Syrian intermediary based in Europe, had begun in 2012.[81] According to Ford, it later transpired that the intermediary was an active PYD member. 'There was no discussion of military cooperation', Ford said. 'Prior we had very little information what the PYD was and its affiliation to the PKK. We knew the Turks would vehemently object if we talked to the PYD.'[82] Consequently, these talks were declared to Ankara. The fact that the PYD called for a decentralized state and was fighting against the FSA and Islamist elements was also problematic for the United States and Robert Ford claimed that this was one reason that they did not push for the PYD to be part of the Geneva II conference (January–February 2014):

> Within a post-war constitution discussion it would be very difficult to put PYD with rest of the opposition, especially since there was tacit cooperation between the PYD and the Syrian government that didn't exist with other elements of the opposition. We tried to get them as an independent delegation, but the Turks were strongly against it. ... To try to get the PYD in the opposition would delay the conference for months. (Robert Ford)

Ford noted that Turkey also pressured the Syrian opposition to exclude the PYD. Due to Turkish opposition, the PYD and related organizations were excluded from all such talks.

In 2014 the focus of the Barack Obama administration shifted on to fighting terrorism in both Iraq and Syria and, in September 2014, a multi-country coalition was created to degrade and defeat ISIS.[83] The change in policy was noted on the ground in Syria and, in the same month, the YPG formed a joint operations room calling for international support. 'The PYD/YPG resistance in Kobani was kind of a tactical alliance against a common enemy', Robert Ford said about US cooperation with the PYD that developed after ISIS besieged Kobani

---

[80] IIST interview: Robert Ford, 15/03/2017.

[81] Jake Hess 07/10/2014: 'Washington's secret back-channel talks with Syria's Kurdish "terrorists"', *Foreign Policy*, http://foreignpolicy.com/2014/10/07/washingtons-secret-back-channel-talks-with-syrias-kurdish-terrorists/ (last accessed 14/03/2017).

[82] IIST interview: Robert Ford, 15/03/2017. Ford said that when he had had briefings on the PYD, before he became the US ambassador, it was surprising how little the CIA and US intelligence knew about the Kurds. 'They knew who Salih Muslim was and that they were a member of the NCB. There was almost no information about the armed wing.'

[83] The Global Coalition against Daesh: a coalition of sixty-eight partners committed to degrading and defeating Daesh through military action. See, for example, https://www.gov.uk/government/topic al-events/daesh (last accessed 14/05/2017).

in September 2014. The intervention by the United States, however, was by him explained in terms of an opportunity seized by officials involved at the time: 'Military officers and commanding generals were beginning to get involved in Kobani. It was not planned before. They were watching and fighting ISIS with drones and saw a lot of ISIS fighters on the ground and started to bomb them.' Another anonymous US official stated that 'the ISIS convergence on Kobani provided a clear opportunity to halt ISIS expansion.'[84]

Coordination with the YPG was, nonetheless, convoluted and initially directed through the KRG, avoiding direct negotiation with the PYD. Robert Ford stated that 'they started to coordinate through Erbil with YPG fighters.' According to another US official:

> The PUK is the one that helped to establish the relationship between the US and the YPG during the Kobane episode. We were looking for a force that could defend Kobane and then use Kobane as a launch pad to clear ISIS off the Turkish border; the PUK approached us with the YPG and the KDP approached us with the Peshmerga. We then arranged for the defence of Kobane with both groups.[85]

Then in October 2014, 150 Iraqi Kurdish Peshmerga fighters entered Kobani via Turkey and direct communications between the US-led coalition and the YPG were established. As the conflict continued and the US role in Syria increased, these direct relations were further developed. International mediation and intervention, in this case, facilitated short-term inter-Kurdish cooperation against an imminent common threat.

For the US government, the YPG had proved to be a local force willing to undertake the fight against ISIS and offering support to the Kurds in Kobani had several benefits, such as countering ISIS's expansionist and jihadist narratives, preventing it from capturing a further border crossing and diminishing its numbers and capabilities. According to an anonymous US official, Kobani had a symbolic importance:

> The longer the ISIS siege of Kobane persisted, the more significant the narrative of a victory became – the danger of ISIS being able to say: 'We prevailed after four months of U.S. airstrikes!' ... With every month that went by, the U.S. therefore had an increased interest in ensuring that ISIS suffered a big, public defeat. The international media was also intently focused on the battle. (Anonymous US official)[86]

---

[84] IIST interview: Off-the-record US official, 12/02/2017.
[85] Ibid., 05/03/2017.
[86] IIST interview: off-the-record US official, 12/02/2017.

The border itself was of great strategic importance to ISIS. A US official stated 'By autumn 2014 the U.S. Government had a good understanding of just how much ISIS traffic transited the Turkish border. … An ISIS capture of Kobane would have provided ISIS a new major transit route into/out of Syria close to Raqqah. This would've been a big strategic gain for ISIS.'[87] Kobani was calculated into wider US efforts to defeat ISIS in Syria and in Iraq, but close media coverage of the siege, from across the Turkish border, increased the moral imperative to intervene. From a military perspective, Kobani provided opportunity to expose ISIS forces and for US forces to target high concentrations of its fighters. 'There was a clear, visible frontline between the YPG and ISIS. U.S. pilots and targeters knew that only ISIS fighters were present south of the frontline. U.S. forces could therefore inflict significant losses on ISIS relatively easily and without the danger of striking the YPG or civilians', he said.[88]

The continuation of this anti-ISIS alliance after the Kobani siege was a definitive victory for the PYD/YPG that supported its subsequent legitimacy claims and expansion beyond Kurdish majority areas. The intervention was predicated largely on coincidence of military interests in the region and on the preparedness of forces to cooperate, rather than on political decisions about Syria's future. The aforementioned US official stated candidly that

> the U.S. would have come to the defence of Kobane even if the city had been held by the Syrian opposition; there was nothing special about the YPG or the fact that the city is Kurdish. … However, once the U.S. air campaign in defence of Kobane started, the YPG quickly proved itself to be a proficient military partner capable of coordinating ground operations with U.S. pilots. U.S. pilots would strike an ISIS-held building on the frontline, watch YPG fighters advance to occupy it, then strike the next building, and watch the YPG advance again. The YPG's ability to coordinate effectively with U.S. pilots made the U.S. air campaign more effective, allowing the U.S. to inflict greater losses on ISIS. … Clearly, this is also what distinguishes the YPG from the Syrian opposition and is the basis for the US tactical partnership with the YPG for the counter-ISIS campaign.[89]

US support for the YPG was not without consequences and repercussions for the future of the Kurds, for Syria and for regional balances of power. The exclusive focus on ISIS, direct support to the Kurds and disregard of wider Syrian and

---

[87] Ibid.
[88] Ibid. According to ISIS defector, Abu Khaled, ISIS lost between 4,000 and 5,000 fighters in Kobani. Michael Weiss 15/11/2015: 'Confessions of an ISIS spy', *The Daily Beast*, http://www.thedailybeast.com/longforms/2015/isis-weiss/confessions-of-an-isis-spy.html (last accessed 14/03/2017).
[89] IIST interview: Off-the-record US official, 12/02/2017.

sub-state politics by the United States helped undermine what remained of the Syrian rebel groups and allowed the PYD to further entrench its governance project. The connection of the PYD to the PKK added regional consequences to US policy and, while attempts were made by the United States to nuance its support and distance itself from specific political actors and agendas, the long-term consequences of this policy looked significant. US support for the YPG dramatically increased the PYD's agency and extended its administrative and military domination territorially and into society.

One of the most significant attempts to distance the United States from the PYD and the PKK was the establishment of the SDF. After ISIS was defeated in Kobani in January 2015, military cooperation continued and led to the transformation of the Euphrates Volcano Operations Room into the SDF in October 2015. The SDF was designed to facilitate the recruitment of Arabs and to address Ankara's concerns about what was, to all intents and purposes, indirect US support to the PKK. Both the United States and the PYD/YPG adopted appropriate rhetoric to support the image of an ethnically mixed military force. A US official said, 'The U.S. encouraged the creation of an umbrella anti-ISIS coalition in Syria that unites groups willing to fight ISIS. The SDF was the result. We knew that an exclusively Kurdish group, including the YPG, may not have the desired optics effect.'[90] Under the banner of the SDF and the Syrian Arab Coalition, using a Kurdish YPG force to confront ISIS in Arab-majority cities like Manbij, in May 2016, or Raqqah in 2017, was made possible. Talal Silo, an ethnic Turkmen and spokesperson for the SDF (who later defected in 2017),[91] said 'Our target for the SDF is not to only liberate Kurdish regions. … We liberated Shadadi, and the southern region of Hasakah, which was controlled by ISIS. And these forces were not only Kurds, but also Arabic, Syriac, and Turkmen people. The SDF is for all people.'[92] In the absence of a cohesive and broadly representative alternative, in practice, the SDF remained dominated by YPG command structures and reliant on a core of PKK-trained fighters.[93] Seven US bases were established in PYD-controlled areas of northern Syria near Qamishli, Kobani, Ain al-Issa, Hasakah

---

[90] Ibid., 05/03/2017.

[91] Talal Silo defected to Turkey in November 2017. Kino Gabriel was then appointed spokesperson of the SDF. See Reuters 15/11/2017: 'Senior official in US-backed Syria forces defects to Turkey-rebels', *Reuters*, https://www.reuters.com/article/us-mideast-crisis-syria-defection/senior-official-in-us-ba cked-syria-forces-defects-to-turkey-rebels-idUSKBN1DF29Q (last accessed 11/05/2018).

[92] IIST interview: Talal Silo, SDF spokesperson, 25/04/2016.

[93] International Crisis Group, 28/04/2017: 'Fighting ISIS: The road to and beyond Raqqa', International Crisis Group, https://www.crisisgroup.org/middle-east-north-africa/eastern-mediterranean/syria/ b053-fighting-isis-road-and-beyond-raqqa (last accessed 22/05/2017).

and Tal Abyad[94] tasked with training local SDF forces and providing logistical support to coalition soldiers involved in operations in Raqqah and Manbij.[95] The SDF successes against ISIS and its capture of large areas of territory in major military campaigns were also supported on the ground by Western Special Forces units, from the United Kingdom, the United States and France.[96]

The Donald Trump administration, elected in November 2016, increased US assistance to the YPG/SDF: between January and March 2017 additional armoured vehicles and as many as a thousand US ground troops were sent to support SDF operations in Raqqah.[97] The US investment in the YPG and SDF forces helped develop effective military alliances and increased the agency of local actors, particularly the YPG/PYD, against ISIS. In the political field, this translated into greater PYD agency locally and regionally, despite the absence of official US support for decentralization and DAA governance.

For the PYD and the Administration, the support of coalition forces during and after the battle for Kobani was critical to its survival. Its ability to uphold its regional agency and its importance to international agendas in Syria depended largely on its ability to continue to successfully challenge and defeat ISIS in Syria. Important questions remained, however, about US policy following a defeat of ISIS in Syria. In the short term these focused on what the United States would do once key operations against ISIS were completed and what that would mean for the PYD. The US ground forces commander in Iraq, Lt. Gen. Stephen Townsend, said in March 2017 that the YPG would not retain a presence in Raqqah after the removal of ISIS but leave governance to locals and 'move on' and he claimed that the Kurds, at 'less than 10 percent of the population', could not 'rule or dictate what happens in northern Syria'.[98] US diplomat Robert Ford also believed it was

[94] Fars News 24/09/2016: 'US Deploying Forces in 7 bases in Northern Syria', *Fars News*, http://en.farsn ews.com/newstext.aspx?nn=13950703001196 (last accessed 29/03/2017).

[95] Thomas Gibbons-Neff 15/03/2017: 'U.S. military likely to send as many as 1,000 more ground troops into Syria ahead of Raqqa offensive, officials say', *Washington Post*, https://www.washingtonpost.com/news/ checkpoint/wp/2017/03/15/u-s-military-probably-sending-as-many-as-1000-more-ground-troops-into -syria-ahead-of-raqqa-offensive-officials-say/?utm_term=.a7c015039551 (last accessed 29/03/2017).

[96] Nancy Yousef and Wladimir van Wilgenburg 27/05/2016: 'U.S. troops 18 miles from IZIS capital', *The Daily Beast*, http://www.thedailybeast.com/articles/2016/05/26/u-s-troops-18-miles-from-isis-c apital.html (last accessed 14/03/2017).

[97] Tom Perry 31/01/2017: 'Syrian militias get more U.S. support for IS fight, plan new phase', *Reuters*, http://www.reuters.com/article/us-mideast-crisis-syria-arms-idUSKBN15F15S (last accessed 23/03/2017); Thomas Gibbons-Neff 15/03/2017: 'U.S. military likely to send as many as 1,000 more ground troops into Syria ahead of Raqqa offensive, officials say', *Washington Post*, https://www.was hingtonpost.com/news/checkpoint/wp/2017/03/15/u-s-military-probably-sending-as-many-as-100 0-more-ground-troops-into-syria-ahead-of-raqqa-offensive-officials-say/?utm_term=.a7c01503 9551 (last accessed 29/03/2017).

[98] Defense.gov 28/03/2017: 'Department of Defense Briefing by Gen. Townsend via Telephone from Baghdad, Iraq', *US Department of Defense*, https://www.defense.gov/News/Transcripts/Transcrip t-View/Article/1133033/department-of-defense-briefing-by-gen-townsend-via-telephone-from-b aghdad-iraq (last accessed 20/03/2017).

unlikely that the US administration would defend the Kurds in the future: 'I have no any sense from my contacts in DC that they will try to defend the Syrian Kurds, as they did with the Iraqi Kurds.' He added 'When I was in Iraq, we made it clear more than once to the government in Baghdad that the Iraqi Kurds are recognized and should not be attacked. I don't think we would do that in Rojava.'[99] The duality of US military and political policies in Syria regarding the YPG/PYD was predicted to persist beyond ISIS. Short-term military cooperation between the YPG and the United States, to prevent the re-emergence of ISIS in eastern Syria and to eliminate remaining ISIS cells, appeared likely. More long-term cooperation and US political support to the Administration appeared unrealistic.

> The military folks will want to protect them. The SDF is their child. The political folks don't yet have an agreed upon policy for what to do with Syria after ISIS. (Washington-based analyst Nicholas A. Heras)[100]

The announcement in December 2018 that US troops would be withdrawn from Syria came as a shock to many within the Trump administration and parties outside it. Although ISIS had been rolled back significantly, talk of 'defeat' was still controversial and the presence of pockets of territory and ISIS cells in Syria was still given as a basis for extending a US military presence there. The future of the SDF military alliance, however, was uncertain and maintaining a non-state military group beyond the mandate for intervention that ISIS provided the United States was fraught with risks. For the Kurds, the consequence of this dual policy left the future of Kurdish autonomy in Syria open to bidders. The two forces most likely or capable of maintaining and securing a PYD-led Kurdish self-rule were the Syrian government and Russia. Their willingness to support it, however, was still intrinsically linked to their relations with Ankara – the most vehement opponent of PYD dominance in northern Syria and crucial NATO ally to the United States, and whose military was encroaching on YPG-held territories in northern Syria.

Russia

Russia's position on Syria, its unwavering support for the Assad government and intrigue in Kurdish issues was set within the context of Moscow's historical tensions with the United States and its competition for resources and influence in the Middle

[99] IIST interview: Robert Ford, 15/03/2017.
[100] IIST interview: Nicholas A. Heras, Middle East Security Fellow, Center for a New American Security, 25/03/2017.

East. Moscow leant support to the PKK until the end of the Cold War, during which the relation offered it a strategic lever against and influence over the domestic policy of Turkey. Russia's renewal of relations with the PKK/PYD during the Syrian conflict were directly connected to Moscow's long-standing relations with the Assad government and the deterioration of its relations with Ankara, which worsened considerably following Russian intervention in Syria in November 2015.

Moscow's intervention in Syria sought to secure Russian power and influence over its northern border. The US influence over the PYD/YPG/SDF in northern Syria and the implementation of Russian, Iranian and Turkish guardianship of de-escalation zones promised to divide Syria between US and Russian spheres of influence. Amid these tensions, the PYD had been able to engage both sides. Russia, unlike other international powers, had not classified the PKK as a terrorist organization and, although relations between Russia and Turkey had improved through trade agreement brokered after 2008, Ankara's decisive support for the Syrian insurgency against Bashar al-Assad in 2011 renewed hostilities between Moscow and Ankara. Within these regional tensions, the rise of the PYD in Syria presented Moscow with a card that could be played tactically against Ankara.

The PYD met with Russian officials several times: for example, Russian Deputy Foreign Minister Mikhail Bogdanov met with the leaders of the PYD as early as 2012.[101] Relations developed further after Turkey's downing of a Russian fighter jet in November 2015. Following this incident, Ankara accused Moscow of providing anti-aircraft weaponry and rockets to the PKK and air support to the YPG near Azaz.[102] Although unconfirmed, these accusations reflected both the increase in communication between the PYD/YPG and Russia and the worsening of relations between Ankara and Moscow. The PYD itself opened an administrative office in Moscow on 11 February 2016. PYD representative Khaled Issa commented: 'Russia is a big power and knows that without the Kurdish people there isn't any stability and peace in Syria.'[103] For their part, Russian officials also mediated between the Kurds and the Syrian government

[101] Mohammed Ballout 06/08/2012: 'Russia, Turkey quietly spar over Syrian Kurdistan', *Al Monitor*, http://www.al-monitor.com/pulse/politics/2012/08/the-un-adopts-saudi-arabias-non.html#ixzz4ciqZdnQY (last accessed 20/03/2017); Wladimir van Wilgenburg 30/10/2015: 'The Kurdish predicament in Syria: Balancing Russia, Turkey and the United States', *Jamestown Foundation*, https://jamestown.org/program/the-kurdish-predicament-in-syria-balancing-russia-turkey-and-the-united-states/ (last accessed 14/03/2017).

[102] Orhan Coskun and Ece Toksabay 30/05/2016: 'Turkey's Erdogan accuses Russia of arming PKK militants', *Newsweek*, http://www.newsweek.com/turkeys-erdogan-accuses-russia-arming-kurdish-militants-464989 (last accessed 14/03/2017); *Daily Sabah* 29/11/2017: 'Russia supports PKK-affiliate YPG with airstrikes in Azaz, Aleppo', *Daily Sabah*, https://www.dailysabah.com/politics/2015/11/30/russia-supports-pkk-affiliate-ypg-with-airstrikes-in-azaz-aleppo (last accessed 14/03/2017).

[103] IIST interview: Khaled Issa, PYD France representative, 13/08/2016.

when clashes erupted in Qamishli on 20 April 2016, and intervened again on 24 August of the same year following a week of conflict.[104] Russian military presence in Syria steadily grew after 2015 and, in April 2017, military bases intended to prevent Turkish attacks on northern Syria were established in the Afrin region, only 19 kilometres from Afrin city.

Russian assistance to the YPG and PYD was viewed by Ankara as a direct threat to its own security. Yet, Ankara's attempts to prevent the unification of the Kurdish cantons were hindered by continuing hostilities between the two countries. 'With support from Russia, the PYD is trying to capture land between Jarablus and Azaz, going west of the Euphrates. We will never accept this', an anonymous Turkish official was reported to have said in October 2015.[105] Relations slowly improved after 27 June 2016, when the Turkish president apologized for downing the Russian jet, and developed further following the failed military coup d'etat in Turkey on 15 July. Putin's personal phone call to Erdogan was said to have given the government advance warning of the 2016 attempted coup and Russia was one of the first countries to condemn it. Despite improvement in relations between Russia and Turkey, Moscow continued to champion PYD representation in the Geneva peace talks and engaged with the party following the Astana talks in January 2017. In March, both Russian and US troops were deployed in Manbij to deter Turkish aggression and to prevent Turkey from obstructing the SDF offensive around Raqqah. After the Turkish military captured the town of al-Bab on 23 February and threatened to take Manbij from SDF forces, Russia again mediated a deal between the Syrian government and the Kurds to hand over control of a number of villages on the outskirts of Manbij to the Syrian Army.[106] Iran, Russia, the United States and the Syrian government all opposed the extension of the Turkish-led Euphrates Shield operation further than al-Bab and their efforts to block Turkish advancement within Syria opened the possibility of the PYD establishing a corridor, or road, between Kobani and Afrin traversing government-held territory around Manbij.

Although Russia had given Ankara a green light to intervene north of Aleppo, it did not relinquish its Kurdish card and sought to limit the Turkish

---

[104] Wladimir van Wilgenburg 20/04/2016: 'Clashes erupt between Syrian regime and Kurdish forces in Qamishli', *ARA News*, http://aranews.net/2016/04/clashes-erupt-syrian-regime-kurdish-forces-qamishli/ (last accessed 14/03/2017); ARA News 24/08/2016: 'Hasakah: Truce reached between Syrian regime, Kurds after Russian mediation', *ARA News*, http://aranews.net/2016/08/hasakah-truce-reached-syrian-regime-kurds-russian-mediation/ (last accessed 14/03/2017).

[105] Orhan Coskun 13/10/2015: 'Turkey warns U.S., Russia against backing Kurdish militia in Syria', *Reuters*, http://www.reuters.com/article/us-mideast-crisis-syria-turkey-idUSKCN0S71BF20151013 (last accessed 14/03/2017).

[106] Wladimir van Wilgenburg 05/03/2017: 'A Kurdish-Russian deal against Turkey!' *ARA News*, http://aranews.net/2017/03/russian-general-confirms-a-kurdish-russian-deal-against-turkey/ (last accessed 28/03/2017).

presence and influence in the region, which could potentially threaten the Assad government. The Russian presence in the Afrin region, to deter Turkish attacks, also reflected its continued categorization of Ankara as a power hostile to the Syrian government's interests. In 2018, however, Russia did not oppose Ankara's occupation of Afrin when Kurds refused to hand the region to the Syrian government. Kurdish officials maintained that Russia had sold Afrin in an alleged deal with Turkey over Idlib.[107] This increased tension between Washington and Ankara over continued US support for the SDF, with Ankara demanding an end to cooperation and the handover of Manbij to Turkish-backed proxies.[108]

Through its intervention in Syria, Russian influence and presence in the Middle East restored and increased. Long-term agreements, signed in January 2017, looked set to enlarge Russia's military presence in the country, extending its naval and air bases as well as its defence systems. Cooperation between Moscow, the Syrian government and the Kurds had contained and balanced Turkey and the US influence in northern Syria could have provided some opportunity for the PYD to address its weak political position. But after Ankara's intervention in Afrin and in Idlib, the SDF-held areas in eastern Syria fell almost completely under US influence and Russia became more critical of SDF rule and of SDF cooperation with the United States. Donald Trump's troop withdrawal announcement in December 2018, however, revived Kurdish-Russian communications and joint Russian-SDF checkpoints were established around Manbij in early 2019.

It remained to be seen how relations between these different actors would develop after ISIS was defeated in Syria: if the Syrian rebels were defeated by Assad, if pockets of rebel-held territories remained in Syria, if the United States decreased its military presence or reached an agreement with Turkey to limit the YPG influence, and if and when Assad attempted to regain control of northern Syria, a deal might also be struck with Turkey to unpick Kurdish autonomy. In this latter case, the cooperation of Moscow, Ankara and Damascus against the Kurds would strangle the nascent autonomy. What powers might come to its assistance? Would Kurdish bonds of ethnicity unite the deeply divided Kurdish polity or would such a scenario be exploited by parties such as the KDP and KNC to weaken the PYD/PKK? There was no sign that any such scenario was

---

[107] ANF 21/02/2018: 'Today in the attack on Afrin launched with Russia's permission', *ANF*, https://anfenglish.com/rojava/today-in-the-attack-on-afrin-launched-with-russia-s-permission-24310 (last accessed 06/05/2018).

[108] Chase Winter 31/03/2018: 'US, Turkey on collision course in Syria's Manbij', *DW*, http://www.dw.com/en/us-turkey-on-collision-course-in-syrias-manbij/a-43207419 (last accessed 06/05/2018).

imminent, but without domestic, regional or international recognition and legitimacy the PYD-led autonomy and democratic autonomy project in northern Syria appeared particularly vulnerable.

The implications of regional and international involvement in Syria and in the Kurdish issue there, directly or indirectly, were considerable. Historically, great powers shaped the Middle East and were instrumental in forging and supporting power relations that had denied Kurdish representation. The part they played within regional attempts to redefine those power relations and in the upheaval that the 'Arab spring' had unleashed, was no less momentous. The involvement of regional and international powers in Syria and the influence that it gave them over the future of Kurdish representation increased uncertainties among the Kurds and required local actors and sub-state organizations to negotiate regional and international power relations as well as local ones. The PYD proved masterful, initially, at addressing these challenges: the decisive agency of the PYD-led administration and security efforts had in many ways countered or, at least, balanced the negative influences of Turkish interests in Syria. Yet, Ankara remained a decisive figure in the future of Kurdish self-rule in Syria and in the agency and influence that the PYD could retain. This was demonstrated clearly by Turkey's Operation Olive Branch in early 2018 and the weak response from Washington in defence of a military ally. The YPG had initially secured international support from both the United States and Russia which had decisively increased its power on the ground in Syria, but it extended military struggles beyond a popular mandate defined by Kurdish national identity. The PYD negotiated territorial isolation through developing wider regional relations with Iraq and Iran while it simultaneously exploited inter-Kurdish tensions, the PKK presence in the KRI and relations with the PUK to its advantage in Sinjar. But the extension of these tensions into KRI territory had already strained relations between the main Iraqi Kurdish parties, pitting these parties against each other and undermining the government of the KRI. Maintaining channels of communication with the Syrian government while remaining mostly neutral in the fight between Syrian rebels and the government, the PYD established a negotiating position on future governance, should the Syrian government survive. As the Assad government regained control of greater areas of territory from rebel forces, and as coordination between Damascus, Moscow and Ankara increased, an impending reckoning on northern Syria, (involving the Syrian government, Syrian rebel forces, Russia, Turkey, the United States, Iran, the KDP, the PUK and the PKK and, of course, the PYD,) appeared to be drawing closer.

6

The Prospects of Kurdish Self-Representation and Self-Governance

In drawing conclusions about the prospects of self-representation and self-government for the Kurds and the future of the unitary state, it is essential to return first to the realities of the war in Syria. The unitary state of Syria existed primarily in name and in the understandings that were driving the authoritarian government, the Syrian opposition, ISIS and the PYD. The models and expectations of what Syria should become or return to were strikingly different. Although the Syrian civil protest movement that developed in March 2011 was driven initially by a call for democracy and basic equalities and freedoms in Syria, the country became host to a myriad of conflicts and competing and antithetical agendas and interests. On the ground, autonomous areas of control under self-made governments rose and gained varying degrees of strength and legitimacy. Areas of Syria became testing grounds for the implementation of radical ideologies. During the research for and writing of this book, ISIS had gained and retained control over significant territory in Syria and its method of government, based on extreme understandings of Islamic doctrines, had produced an international military campaign aimed at driving it out of Syria and Iraq. Its erosion of formal borders between Iraq and Syria had challenged a world order based on sovereign territories and the permanency of the post First World War regional order. In other areas of Syria, *Hay'at Tahrir al-Sham* (formed in January 2017, originally the Syrian affiliate of Al Qaida, *Jabhat al-Nusra*, which was renamed *Jabhat Fateh al-Sham* in July 2016) had encroached on rebel-held areas, especially in Idlib, taking over provision of services and, thus, increasing dependence of locals upon its religiously driven form of government.[1] Sharia law had replaced civil law in many areas outside government control, with the

---

[1]   See, for example, Yasir Abbas 10/05/2016: 'How al Qaeda is winning in Syria', *War on the Rocks*, http://warontherocks.com/2016/05/how-al-qaeda-is-winning-in-syria/ (last accessed 16/09/2016).

notable exception of Kurdish-controlled regions. In the 'Rojava' region, the PYD's ideology of radical democracy also involved encroaching on and capturing civil and political space. The PYD and the democratic autonomy project challenged understandings of sovereignty and national identity, established parallel trans- and sub-state structures of representation and nationhood and gained agency through its foreign relations. Being secular in character and heavily touting feminist ideals, this form of governance gained much Western sympathy, not condemnation, despite Turkey's vehement objection to it. The YPJ, in particular, presented to the world 'an appealing face of the guerrillas – an image of women battling as equals with male comrades against an appallingly misogynist enemy'.[2]

Meanwhile, the Syrian government, much reduced to a hard core of loyalists and others benefiting from continued stability in some government-held areas, had gained ground against rebel groups across Syria as a result of heavy Russian and Iranian intervention, while the United States focused on ISIS. This increased the likelihood that this once doomed government would emerge triumphant and that the shift in the balance of international and local powers would give it increased leverage in any settlement of the conflict. Nonetheless, the presence of small fiefdoms and local militia, with only nominal loyalty to Assad and significant degrees of political independence from Damascus heightened uncertainties about what remained of the Assad government, the real level of government control in these areas[3] and the nature of central authority in a future Syria.

Regional and international involvement in the Syrian quagmire raised the stakes of local tensions, adding layer upon layer of complexity and intrigue to what began as a popular domestic challenge to an authoritarian government. Competition for resources between local groups escalated and translated into power plays between competing international and regional powers. Turkish military intervention in Syria, through the Euphrates Shield operation in August 2016, the Olive Branch operation in Afrin in January–March 2018 and agreements on safe-zones, suggested that the territory could also end up a patchwork of militarized zones of influence that maintained and entrenched

---

[2] Mat Bradley and Joe Parkinson 24/07/2015: 'America's Marxist allies against ISIS', *Wall Street Journal*, http://www.wsj.com/articles/americas-marxist-allies-against-isis-1437747949 (last accessed 01/05/2017).

[3] Tobias Schneider 31/08/2016: 'The decay of the Syrian regime is much worse than you think', *War on the Rocks*, http://warontherocks.com/2016/08/the-decay-of-the-syrian-regime-is-much-wor se-than-you-think/ (last accessed 16/09/2016); Jihad Yazigi, September 2016: 'No going back: Why decentralisation is the future of Syria', *European Council on Foreign Relations*, Policy Brief (online). PDF available on: http://www.ecfr.eu/page/-/ECFR185_-_NO_GOING_BACK_-_WHY_DECE NTRALISATION_IS_THE_FUTURE_FOR_SYRIA.pdf (last accessed 16/09/2016).

existing divisions. This myriad of overlapping and conflicting interests and areas of territorial control that chequered Syria, and the volatility of the situation, meant that making nuanced predictions about the future of Kurdish areas and the DAA system, while also avoiding biases or commitments to one or the other possible outcome, was problematic. What was possible at this point, however, was to return to the Syrian arena to outline gains made in representation and freedoms of identity, and to highlight the obstacles to their preservation and to the development of representative self-governance on the level of the state, within the area of northern Syria and among the Kurdish communities themselves.

The state context: Representation and identity

The prospects of Kurdish self-government and self-representation were bound intrinsically to the fate of the Syrian government and, in particular, to constitutional definitions of citizenship, future governance structures and control of strategic resources. Although the country had fragmented and its reunification under a central government looked far removed from realities on the ground in Syria, its sovereignty remained intact and, in the international and regional order, the government's status remained recognized, either as a rightful ruler or as a pariah power.

The Syrian government had denounced and rejected Kurdish calls for federal decentralization and the devolution of political decision-making powers to the Kurdish regions. The SNC had similarly rejected all but administrative decentralization and favoured addressing Kurdish demands after Assad's removal from government. Regardless of questions concerning the exact character of the political system, power structures and relations that would govern a post-conflict Syria, the unprecedented prominence of the Kurdish issue in Syria made explicit the basic need to rethink Syrian state identity to adequately represent the ethnic, religious and cultural diversity within its territory. As shown in Chapter 1, the historic attachment of sovereignty and citizenship to ethnicity in state formation and legitimacy led the Arab identity to be enshrined in the Syrian constitution and in its laws. This exclusion and denial of Kurdish identity, and other ethnic identities, from rights and representation equal to those of the ethnic majority caused them to be problematized collectively as a threat to the integrity of the state. The presence and historical legacy of the Kurds in Syria, however, was not removed or diminished by the decades of attempts by Syrian governments to deny their identity, forcibly assimilate or to physically remove them from Syria.

The Kurds maintained their significant presence in Syria, regardless of persistent disputes about their numbers and origins and, with the twists and turns of history, that presence became all the more visible and assertive. Nationalistic pan-state Kurdish identity and popular attachment and belonging grew in Syria, as it did in Iraq, Turkey and Iran. In parallel, understandings of political and social options available to this group deepened and diversified.

During the Syrian crisis the Kurdish struggle for representation and democratic pluralism became bound up with general calls for democratization, with the civil war, regional proxy wars, the international coalition's fight against ISIS, in addition to inter-Kurdish rivalries and divisions. In 2011, demonstrations in Kurdish areas echoed Syrian national civil protests and general calls for democratization. Like in other areas of Syria these calls were lost beneath the aggressive reactions of the Assad government and the devastation caused by the wider militarization of the civil protest movement in 2012. Yet, the question of how those basic rights and democratic representation should be gained and what they would look like in a future Syria remained a barrier between and within different opposition groups, social groups and the government itself. Even among the Syrian Kurds, widely differing personal and collective definitions of identity and choices about models of representation, examined in Chapters 1 and 4, divided the population and prevented the development of truly representative structures in the governance vacuum that formed in June 2012.

The strength of identification based on (Kurdish) ethnicity and community had increased further through the conflict.[4] The mobilization of close social and local networks, particularly under threat from groups identifiable by sectarian or ethnic characteristics, increased reliance on and development of reciprocity norms based around ethnic identity and political coalitions formed on those lines. Building a unitary environment in which central state institutions and practices provided protection and security against harm and exploitation by other groupings, appeared distant after years of conflict that had involved increasingly micro level and sectarian alliances, brutal state suppression of rebel groups and civilian infrastructures and the rise of Islamist and Jihadist groups.

The crisis in Syria and the deepening of sectarian alliances and conflicts had, for many, made imagining that communal Syrian identity and the political and social processes that could rebuild it more difficult.[5] Advances made by Kurdish YPG forces in northern Syria sparked increased allegations of Kurdish separatism

---

[4] IIST surveys 2016.
[5] IIST surveys showed an acknowledgement that understandings of self-identity among Syrian Kurds had changed as a result of the crisis, the conflict with ISIS and the gains made by the PYD Administration.

from individuals within the main Syrian opposition groups and exposed the enduring importance of ethnic and religious identity to political ambitions of groups and individuals within them. Gains made in terms of ethnic rights and representation within Kurdish majority areas under PYD control also increased the need to defend those new freedoms from potential threats emanating from the Syrian government and from dominant political and social forces. While the Assad government was an obvious threat to these rights, an equally organized radical Arabist and Islamic opposition grouping vehemently opposed Kurdish self-rule and continued to characterize Kurdish ambitions as a threat to the state.

The PYD's democratic autonomy project had established a de facto self-administration in northern Syria, which the majority of the external forces looked powerless to dislodge. While the government maintained influence and was still able to extend its powers into this territory, the PYD and DAA controlled the majority of services, local resources, infrastructure, as well as the use of force. This had allowed the DAA to widen its authority territorially, increase its agency in regional affairs and slowly replace government institutions. Relations with foreign powers and their investment in the YPG and SDF to combat ISIS in Syria were seized upon as political capital and interpreted as an assurance that gains made in Kurdish self-administration would sustain opposition from the SNC and from the Assad government, at least while ISIS remained incumbent in many areas. The extension of this external support and the protection it had offered against Ankara also informed the SDF's decision to fight ISIS in Raqqah and Deir al-Zour. The intrinsic connection of international support to the campaign against ISIS, however, left many unanswered questions about the security of the administration post-ISIS and its ability to maintain military support, alliances and the territory that extended the project beyond the Kurdish demography.

Various scenarios for the future of Syria presented themselves. However unlikely, considering the balance of powers and control in the country, it was still a remote possibility that international pressure could secure a political settlement that installed an interim government based on the existing SNC coalitions. Such a government would be reasonably likely to include KNC representation. Political decentralization to Kurdish regions, however, would become a point of tension that would encourage the KNC to pursue devolution independently of the SNC. Alternatively a softening of relations between Ankara and the government, already underway with the government on the ascendant, would create a powerful alliance against Kurdish autonomy in Syria, particularly one dominated by the PYD. The withdrawal of US military personnel after a defeat of ISIS in Syria (a prospect tabled in December 2018) would significantly weaken the PYD/YPG's capacity to confront external challenges to its control. Russian and US assistance against ISIS prevented Turkey from attacking Manbij in March 2017, but in January 2018 the Russian position changed when Moscow gave way to Ankara to attack Afrin, and Turkey's military was poised to challenge PYD control further east, through direct confrontation or through the establishment of a US supported 'safe-zone' along the Syrian-Turkish border. Details of control over any proposed safe-zone encompassing Kurdish majority areas (to be established following the US withdrawal) and the nature of any protection it might offer the Kurds were, however, also contested. What was also likely at this juncture, however, was that the Assad government would regain control over the majority of Syrian territory, despite international pressures, and that remaining rebel forces and the opposition would be imprisoned, forced into exile in Turkey, entrenched in isolated pockets of resistance or isolated within the zones controlled by Turkey. Such a scenario held the possibility that an understanding between the government and the PYD could be reached that would enable it to maintain a monopoly over Kurdish politics in Syria and continue its social programme, while also making concessions to the Assad government. This would also serve to contain and isolate Turkish-backed rebel-controlled territories north of Aleppo. In this scenario, other Kurdish parties connected to the KNC would be further marginalized and forced to remain in exile in the KRI. An understanding between the PYD and Baghdad could decrease the isolation of the Administrations if the DAAs were connected to Iraqi government territory through Sinjar or through the Syrian border. This would further undermine the KDP and Turkey regionally and increase the PYD/PKK agency in regional affairs.

A further scenario, and one that Kurds had been at pains to avoid, was inter-Kurdish conflict between the PYD and the KNC and/or between the PKK and the KDP in Syria or in Sinjar. Accordingly, KRG president Masoud Barzani had sought compromise and agreement between the PYD and the KNC and, despite fractures in Kurdish politics regionally, the possibility of a successful agreement between the KNC and PYD could not be ruled out completely. All possible scenarios posed challenges to the PYD and the DAAs, but mostly to the KNC. In any scenario, it seemed, the KNC would face continued marginalization and arrests and, although the PYD retained options because of its agency and diverse alliances, the balance of powers in the Middle East region remained crucial to its survival, as did some degree of cooperation or agreement with the Syrian government.

As the government gained ground after the Russian military intervention in Syria, the question of how and when the government would address the Kurdish issue became more pressing. It maintained some hold and influence in DAA regions through mayoral offices and identity documents issued from Damascus or Aleppo, as well as through its small pockets of territory within DAA areas (notably in those in Hasakah and Qamishli and the Qamishli airport). Some trade from DAA areas also depended on transit through or sale within government-controlled areas and the state intelligence services still managed to operate within some DAA areas despite appearances to the contrary.[6] Although the a quasi-autonomous region had been developed, its independence from the central government and its ability to attain self-sufficiency were hindered by a reliance on these government services and on the state infrastructure, as well as by its problematic relations with Turkey and the KDP. The rights and institutions created by the PYD and DAA also existed in parallel to state laws and institutions. In the unitary state, the role of ethnicity, the Kurdish language, the rights of women and control over local resources were still to be negotiated. Both the Syrian opposition and the Syrian government rejected any form of self-governance for the Kurds and, although acceptance of Kurdish cultural rights was implied in negotiations, the Syrian government had not changed or removed laws that discriminated against and excluded Kurds.[7] For the Administration to sustain its quasi-state powers post-ISIS, clear borders defining jurisdiction and security would have to be established. The PYD/DAAs would then risk consolidating its state-like powers and further undermining the participatory foundations of its administration.

The hold of the government on DAA areas and Russian inroads into the Afrin region raised questions about the possible extension of central control. Since 2012, the DAA and the government had observed tacit non-interference agreements similar to those the PYD developed with the Syrian rebels around Aleppo. For the embattled state, unable to provide services and provisions to much of its territory, there were obvious benefits in entering into a mutually convenient informal relationship with the Administration, a non-state group, acting with state-like powers. Not least among these were the pacification of Kurdish areas as well as the negative effect that the non-aggression pacts had on the wider Syrian opposition. As in any such tacit arrangement the PYD also benefited. Much of the power and authority that the PYD gained was because the government withdrew from Kurdish territories against the backdrop of militarization of the Syrian crisis and the increased vociferation of Ankara

---

[6] Local respondents reported that security services were able to enter Amude and question the family of a refugee on his activities. IIST communications February 2017.

[7] In January 2017 a draft constitution for the Syrian Republic was presented to the Syrian opposition as a basis for negotiation in the 23–4 January 2017 Astana Talks. According to news reports, the word 'Arab' would be dropped from name of the state, it promised greater Kurdish self-administration (cultural autonomy) and the equal use of Kurdish and Arabic languages in these areas.

against the Syrian government. The withdrawal allowed the PYD to assert control and its parallel governance structures facilitated the graduated extension of PYD authority. With time and further consolidation of DAA control the role of the government was lessened and its power to manipulate and influence the DAA and the PYD weakened. The support of the US-led coalition to the SDF also precipitated this by increasing the agency of the PYD and the YPG. Security, laws, services and 'shadow citizenship' created by non-state organization and local acceptance of much of what it represented (especially ethnic rights, local governance, local control over resources and services, protection from discrimination and persecution) allowed the DAAs to assume state-like powers.

Nevertheless, as shown in Chapter 5, alliances forged by the Syrian government remained powerful determining factors in the future status of the northern Syria. Assad's alliance with both Russia and Iran added both military strength to its army and international influence over future settlements in Syria. Both powers had a history of exploiting Kurdish issues and using the PKK to weaken Ankara's hand both domestically and regionally. Alongside this, the US government's focus on its immediate goals of defeating ISIS in Syria and Iraq assisted the entrenchment of the DAA and its military in Syria and increased US investment in Kurdish autonomy there, equally at Turkey's expense. US support for the DAA's political organizations and arrangements, however, had not been offered and remained a scenario fraught with political landmines for the United States and was far less certain in a post-ISIS arena. Indeed, a post-ISIS landscape was defined more by traditional international and regional political alliances than by those within Syria.

Locally, control of resources and revenues was likely to remain a crucial point of tension, both between the DAA and the Syrian government (as shown by clashes in Deir al-Zour over oil fields) and within the DAA between factions, particularly between the Kurdish and Arab areas. There was a constant threat to resources and territory from the Syrian government, from ISIS, from Syrian rebel forces, as well as from other groups within northern Syria that allied with or opposed the PYD/YPG. Maintaining these resources, revenues and control over territory to which the Kurds had an historical claim was a source of legitimacy that was critical to the DAA ability to govern unchallenged by local populations.

The control of councils in non-Kurdish majority areas within the DAA system, by pro-Assad tribes or militias, also provided a possible avenue for the Syrian government to increase its influence over northern Syria and to contract the territory held by the PYD. An overlap in interests was already evident in the intersections of control of the SDF and government forces in some villages around Manbij. Joint interest in preventing Turkish interference in northern Syria also provided a basis for future agreements on decentralization of some governance powers to PYD authorities, either officially, or more likely, implicitly through government toleration of PYD dominance in exchange for the pacification and management of the Kurdish areas, similar to previous arrangements with the PKK. This would preserve PYD self-governance at the expense of KNC parties.

The northern Syria context

The prospects of maintaining the self-governance of the DAAs were tied intrinsically to alliances made with other ethnic and religious groupings and to the successful maintenance of pluralistic representative structures. Under the prevailing circumstances of war and uncertainty the democratic autonomy project offered successful strategies for coping with security issues, economic chaos and internal disunity and dispersal. Empowerment of people, in particular of women, and the involvement of people in local decision-making had encouraged local social changes, which many would describe as progressive.[8] The development of cooperative economic activities had encouraged self-sufficiency and maintained productivity within a civil war situation, enabling people to better sustain living standards and slow the tides of economically driven outward migration. Despite criticisms about partisanship and the absence of political pluralism and freedoms, organization within communes had facilitated the distribution of limited goods and services and had organized communities to cooperate effectively in the absence of state institutions. For many, the provision of services, security, civil order and the development of economic opportunity and institutionalization of rights were recognized as successes that shielded much of the population from the worst of the conflict in Syria.[9] The Administration also offered a vision of a future system of government and social organization that went beyond those practical solutions to the governance vacuum. Here its successes were less clear, where it met most criticism and diverged from political and nationalist beliefs held by many Syrian Kurds and other social groupings in northern Syria. It was in this context that the Administration remained vulnerable to armed and political opposition from groups backed by Turkey; to the pro-regime Arab and Christian grouping; the KNC; to a rise in localized Kurdish unrest; and to tribes that maintained strong alternative allegiances based on distinct identities and political interests.

---

[8] IIST surveys.
[9] Ibid.

It was unclear how, and if, the PYD could avoid the trappings of vanguard authority that its internal evaluation processes sought to overcome. Only by removing opposition to its ideological doctrine and revolutionary project could the project actually succeed in fulfilling its objectives. In theory this should occur naturally as part of the 'revolution'. While that 'revolution' was incomplete, however, the issue of opposition and dissent remained an active, albeit controlled, obstacle to the completion of the revolution itself and to the development of democratic autonomy. Clearly many Syrian Kurds were committed to the PYD. to the social project and democratic autonomy, and the crisis in Syria had encouraged greater numbers (which included non-Kurds) to participate in it. Evidence suggested that much of the population, however, temporarily tolerated inadequacies of the Administration and the domination of the PYD because of the war and the lack of alternatives available to them.[10] The security, public services and semblance of normal life that it provided encouraged acceptance of the DAA system and, as ISIS had become an external threat, a congruence of interests was secured rather than a shared ideology.[11]

As detailed in Chapters 3 and 5, the YPG forged strategic military alliances with non-Kurdish groups within areas under its control which both extended its territory and neutralized possible threats to PYD/DAA rule. Although attempts were made to de-ethnicize the DAA, the association of these governance structures with 'Kurdish rule' had not been shed easily. The continued association of the DAAs with the PYD increased the prospects of potential challenges against its dominance, particularly from within non-Kurdish majority areas. Backing from either the Syrian government or from Turkey could provide incentive for attempts to alter local balances of power. At the time of writing and while the government and rebels remained embattled, alliances with military groups and minority communities, defined against these external threats and limited territorially, posed only minimal threat to the wider governance structures of the DAA in eastern Syria. However, this remained a latent fault line open to future manipulation by either the Assad government or the Turkish-backed Syrian rebels. The opposition of Ankara to a Syrian-Kurdish region on its borders, its intervention in Syrian territory around in northern Aleppo and Afrin, and the continuation of its domestic war with the PKK, all provided the PYD with an ideological narrative and socio-political complex of existential threat to Kurdish identity and representation. In the absence of meaningful rapprochement

---

[10] IIST interviews and surveys.
[11] There are exceptions to this, such as the Assyrian Soharto group which had, for many years, cooperated with the PKK and adopted its ideological doctrine.

between Ankara and Damascus or between Ankara and Washington, and the continued use of Syria's northern border to the strategic advantage of Syria and Russia, it was possible that the PYD would remain entrenched in areas of northern Syria. Rebel factions exiled in Turkey or in Turkish-controlled areas of northern Syria could provide Ankara with a counter-card to the PYD, shifting the front lines of the Syrian conflict to the Syrian–Turkish military and land borders. Here, however, those tensions and hostilities would be bound integrally to inter-state relations and to regional and international balances of power.

The DAA's ability to accommodate other ethnic and religious social groupings in northern Syria had been demonstrated by the alliances it forged, the power-sharing mechanisms it developed and by its ability to relinquish power to local councils and non-Kurdish leaders. Within the Kurdish society, however, its ability to accommodate other political models or ideologies and organizations was impaired. The *Rojava Peshmerga* and the KNC – rooted in the same ethnic and territorial base – could not be accommodated by DAA governance structures without, at the same time, fundamentally undermining the democratic autonomy project itself.

Kurdish society

Relations within Kurdish regions – among the Kurds and between the different political factions – remained a continuous and fundamental challenge for the PYD, as well as for the Assad government. While external threats to Kurdish rule existed per se, the primary systemic challenge to the PYD came from within Kurdish society and from other Kurdish political parties that resisted the ideological transformations and compromises to representation that the democratic autonomy project was believed to entail. If the PYD would fail to deliver 'democracy' in a form that represented different sectors of Kurdish society and, instead, maintain the dominance of its governance system and a modus vivendi with the Assad government, what form and character might opposition and resistance to PYD rule take? This, again, depended largely on the future of the central government and the relationship forged between it and the northern regions, and on whether draconian security measures, similar to those in pre-2011 Syria, would dominate and restrict rival political organization. It remained to be seen whether other Kurdish parties would return to a practice of managing an unfavourable status quo in order to prevent inter-Kurdish conflict or whether their politics and environment would develop in a manner that would enable them to challenge, peacefully, those power relations. Military confrontation between the two groups had been avoided but it remained a possible scenario that would damage the legitimacy claims of both blocs. The cold conflict between the PKK and the KDP, marked by a seemingly unbridgeable fissure in Kurdish politics and played out largely within Syria, could still ignite.

The circumstances surrounding and opportunities available to the PYD and the KNC were remarkably different: almost as if they were operating in different states. The PYD and DAA operated and developed within a governance vacuum within which it had carved out governance and representation structures and local alliances. It held powers of governance and monopolies over security, resources and services necessary to maintain that power. The political space it created offered representation to a 'moral society' that was still in the making. The KNC, in comparison, continued to operate in an environment in which political freedoms were restricted and democratic rights to representation were not available. Its organization was restricted, its symbols destroyed and its activists arrested. The increase in restrictions on KNC activity within the DAA regions in March 2017 deepened divisions within Syria and within the wider regional Kurdish political arena, between the PKK and the KDP. Both the KDP and the PKK cracked down the other's activities in their respective zones of influence, while the PUK provided the PKK and PYD with a safe zone to operate in and from which to send foreign volunteers to Syria. Examples of the suppression of activists and political parties critical of it suggested that the PYD might intervene more within decision-making processes should organized grass-roots opposition to it emerge. With the KNC weakened further within Syria's borders, local channels of representation available to Syrian Kurds were increasingly limited. The respective politics of the PYD and the KNC reflected and responded to these different environments and opportunities but were located within the structures of Kurdish society, much of which were rooted in traditional socio-economic relations. The PYD was accused of dominating representation in northern Syria and uprooting those traditional structures. The KNC was accused of narrow nationalism incapable of representing the diverse identities in northern Syria and for refusing to accept the local administrations. Yet, both these political blocs operated in Syria, which despite its fragmentation during the conflict, remained a sovereign state with an expanding central government that would eventually turn its attention to addressing Kurdish autonomy. The prospects of both were clouded by the interests of foreign powers and set within popular conceptualizations of identity and choices about representation.

For Syrian Kurds, questions of identity and representation in the future Syria, whatever that would look like, remained as pertinent as ever. The DAA experiment had made clear that the practical application of identity rights was not sufficient to satisfy popular demands for representation and democratic governance. Research in Syria showed that the conflict had increased adherence to the Kurdish identity among Syrian Kurds. In other parts of Syria, sectarian, local, ethnic and religious identities were similarly strengthened. Kurdish society itself had been grappling with tensions between modernity and traditional structures: a struggle that manifest within Kurdish political parties in their attempts at nation-building and in their relations to Kurdish society, in particular the youth.[12] The consequences of war, the transformations in local governance and the revolution that democratic autonomy envisaged also added uncertainties to established social, political and economic structures and put pressure on pre-existing sub-state social and representative networks.

Divisions between Kurdish political parties appeared all the more intractable when one factored in the deeper social fissures that underlay their attempts to form policy on identity and representation. As detailed in Chapter 1, 'Kurdishness' included and overlapped with a multitude of cultural identities and loyalties. While Kurdish political parties had developed from interpretations and understandings of that identity and how it could be represented, accepting the diversity within it and permitting change and/or consolidation of aspects of it remained a challenge for all parties. This complex diversity, even within the Kurdish population, required governance structures capable of supporting them and preventing conflict between them. The revolutionary model of the PYD offered change and transformation of society and, with that, it sought to break down the traditional hierarchies that many Kurds identified with and sought representation through. To do so it offered a reconceptualization of the nation, which was expanded beyond Kurdish ethnicity and the contradictory nationalisms grounded within historical tradition and experiences. The KNC parties adhered to a nationalism rooted in its historical development and existing social structures but was rejected by many for appearing to support the elite and failing to adapt to social changes. Although political reform occurred and a middle ground between these two models was developing through youth movements and through the development of political programmes and policy, neither the PYD nor KNC model of representation appeared to adequately

---

[12] See Allsopp, *The Kurds of Syria*.

respond to the interests, concerns and criticisms of the general Kurdish population.

The demography of Kurdish areas always posed a problem for conceptualizations of political control and decentralization. The division of Syrian territory into ethnically defined areas of control was highly problematic, not least because of territorial overlaps between different groups that formed an ethnic and religious mosaic within Syria. The crisis itself increased both ethno-nationalism in Kurdish areas and the rate of demographic change. IDPs from other areas of Syria increased diversity in areas that could once be defined ethnically or religiously, and Kurdish migration out of Syria also affected ethnic density. The autonomy from the central government that was gained by the Kurds in Kurdish majority areas was welcomed by most, despite the reluctance by many to accept the domination of one particular political party and ideology. But equally, the promotion of ethnic and religious pluralism and a democratic political system was generally supported by the population.

The continuation of political tensions between the Kurdish and Arab opposition groupings did not inspire confidence that Kurdish identity and the variety of social and political organizations present in Kurdish areas would gain adequate representation through either a political system dominated by an interim government based on the SNC or the Baath Party regaining control over Syria's territory. Similarly, the continued distinction between Kurdish political groupings and the focus on negotiating representation of Kurds with either the PYD bloc or the KNC, rather than dealing with the Kurdish issue as one of representation itself, suggested that ethnicity and the entrenchment of distinctions between ethnic groups in Syria would be further politicized. Unless the Kurdish identity itself was depoliticized, through changes in laws and in understandings of state citizenship, politics for Kurds was likely to remain defined by their ethnic identity (to greater or lesser extents) and by a political spectrum based on different definitions that identity: whether the Kurds should be represented as a 'minority' or a 'national' group, or whether liberation of Kurdish identity through the breakdown of hierarchical relationships must precede representation.

Models of federalism proposed by Kurdish political parties in the KNC relied on the recognition of a Kurdish majority region. The non-contiguous demographic spread of the Kurds in northern Syria and large populations outside this area presented challenges to the formulation of democratic governance solutions. The PYD model of democratic autonomy purported to overcome this problem by de-ethnicizing governance. The model, as applied in northern

Syria, was not without problems. In addition to the persistence of parallel local organizations based on ethnicity, religion, and tribe, the decision-making and representation across the DAA's governance was dominated by the PYD. While there was potential for this to change if free elections were held, the issues of social reform and security remained areas through which heavy intervention of the PYD in society and government could be justified.

With the exception of the Afrin region, in which PYD control was most absolute before Turkish intervention, the areas under its control were mixed ethnically and religiously. It was possible that alliances forged by the administration and participation of non-Kurdish groups in it would unravel in peacetime if and when militarized front lines dissipated and traditional sub-state loyalties and interests revived. With the removal of external threats, such as that posed by ISIS, new power struggles could arise between the centre and periphery, as well as local struggles for control and domination. The continued domination of the PYD over political processes meant that some level of dissent was inevitable, particularly from other Kurdish parties or by other non-Kurdish communities backed by either Ankara or Damascus. Under the prevailing circumstances, however, the space for dissent inside northern Syria was restricted. The focus of the population on local civil society organization and the administrative divisions between regions and communities, distanced the people from political decision-making. It was possible that this disjuncture between political and civil action and the elevation of political decision-making beyond the democratic processes that the general population could participate in was a temporary consequence of the crisis, which would be remedied in peacetime. The removal of ISIS could alter alliances with ethnic and religious minorities in the regions as the need for strategic alliances decreased. As it was, however, PYD claims to popular legitimacy were weakened by its extension beyond the territory connected to, and beyond dominant understandings of, Kurdish national identity. The control it had gained over society, education, and representation, however, could still bring about the widespread ontological changes that the system required to survive without it resorting to vanguard power.

Research in Syria suggested that many Kurds who opposed the PYD were, nonetheless, fearful of the consequences of resisting it, and/or that they did not possess the necessary resources to mobilize, and/or that they were not organized in a manner that could generate successful opposition. Although media reports from within Kurdish areas and interviews confirmed that acts of opposition to PYD rule continued to occur – in the form of demonstrations and local actions against conscription – expression of political dissent against the governance structures and its agents remained limited. Nevertheless, research indicated that democracy and representation, for most Kurds, included a level of political pluralism that was, at the time of writing, underdeveloped within the Kurdish areas. Although the DAAs had held local elections, competition or participation of rival parties in these elections had been limited. Latent and suppressed political dissent remained a challenge to the DAA that would arise when conditions allowed it; unless, however unlikely, the KNC recognized the local self-administration and its ideological project in exchange for concessions on power-sharing.

Sub-state socio-economic relations were both reinforced and damaged by the conflict in Syria. The migration of thousands of Kurds out of Syria negatively affected what remained of the tribal system in Kurdish areas, especially in Kobani, where the siege on the town led to widespread destruction and exodus. It had similarly negatively affected social mobilization in opposition to the DAA. By comparison, it had facilitated the PYD/DAA attempts to develop alternative systems of sub-state, regional and central representative structures and social organizations that would replace pre-existing social networks rather than accommodate them. This ideological current encountered resistance from within Kurdish communities, including non-participation in the commune system, particularly in the Jazirah. The degree of integration of traditional social hierarchies into the DAA system, evident from field research, also suggested that the system still offered an avenue for protecting traditional hierarchies where they overlapped with hierarchies of commitment and loyalty to the democratic autonomy project.

The permanency of DAA's self-governance was not guaranteed and the level and sheer diversity of threats posed to it meant that to survive it should continue to adapt and morph to its external environment or rely on its armed forces. The structures of self-governance were vulnerable to changes to the alliances it had forged, the encroachment by the Assad government, the attacks from Turkey and to popular dissent and opposition from rival Kurdish parties. The maintenance of rights related to diversity in identity were easier to maintain than the democratic autonomy project itself and could be achieved by different actors and scenarios connected to the Syrian arena and international resolutions.

Uncertainty

Despite extensive research and investigation, still more questions about the DAA arose than could be answered. Its governance was part of a larger process and project and it adapted continuously not only to fulfil and maintain its own political agenda but in response also to its complex external and internal environments and challenges. Questions remained about whether this revolution and form of democracy could be realistically achieved without the participation of the majority, or whether the majority would gradually internalize the PYD ideology and necessary social transformations would occur and normalize these structures and re-conceptualizations of identity. How would, or could, those participating in this alternative social paradigm coexist with pre-existing social and political structures without conflict or resort to vanguard authority? How could local self-defence coexist with state security apparatus? Where did local law stop and state law begin? At the time of writing the Administration held state-like powers in eastern Syria: this fact itself a paradox. It controlled the economy of the region and the security, and it enacted laws that it considers binding to all residents within the territory it controlled, and it enforced them. Without separation from Syria, which was not on the cards and was impractical, how would parallel legal systems and laws exist within a given state? How could the Administration explain and define its territorial dimension and control of resources within Syria without conflict with central authorities?

Questions remained about the response of the Administration to requests made by the people that went against the fundamental ideological forces of the revolutionary movement; and about the status of those within the territories held by the YPG but who chose not to participate in the ideological system. Authority was invested in social change and in revolution; however, the primary drivers of this revolution were not the people at the grass roots. Many participated in it, but its drivers were political organizations imbued with an ideological blueprint for self-governed democratic society that traced back to one political party, supported by a military.

The future of the autonomous administration in Syria still hung in the balance of international and regional relations and in communal relations among the Kurds. The domination of Russia over Syrian affairs and its defence of existing government appeared a realistic scenario for the future, while US interest in pursuing democracy in Syria had extended only as far as its official rhetoric. Russian influence presented ever greater obstacles to US foreign policy objectives beyond ISIS. For Turkey, the Kurdish issue remained central to its regional strategic and domestic security concerns. It remained a card that could be easily played by the Assad government, Russia, or Iran against Turkish interest and regional ambitions. The Kurds remained caught between hostile actors.

Over the course of the crisis in Syria Kurdish political parties became committed to developing a federal solution to the Kurdish issue in Syria. Overwhelmingly, participants in surveys and political parties supported 'federalism' as a system for future representation. Negative experiences of central governance, the history of Kurdish political organization and the more recent provision of ethnic and religious freedoms by the Administration all stimulated support for a decentralized political system as a means of protecting identity and securing representation of interests associated with it. Although the Syrian government continued to hold on to power, its reach over its people and territory had been broken. It was unlikely that the government would be able to regain that control without some degree of decentralization or without resorting to further authoritarian practices and bloodshed. Yet, the degree of decentralization to YPG/SDF-held Kurdish and Arab areas remained a sticking point and it was an issue around which identity politics, nationalism and years of latent prejudice re-emerged on the state sphere. Opposition to political decentralization – to federalism – was one point on which the government and the dominant opposition groupings converged.

This book has demonstrated the complexity involved in defining Kurdish identity itself, in pinning down the priorities of the Kurdish population, and in understanding existing and emerging forms of representation and how they met or fell short of expectations. The intricacy of identity politics in Syria, and even within a Kurdish neighbourhood, made it almost impossible to generalize about Kurdish identity despite the broad political blocs that engulf it. The development of a multi-party, pluralistic democracy that could accommodate and represent Kurdish identity, in all its variations, remains an active and ongoing process with many obstacles to its achievement. Significant practical changes had occurred in Kurdish areas of Syria as a result of the implementation of rights and freedoms of expression. While these rights could be preserved through agreements between the PYD and the KNC, the PYD and the government, or the KNC and the SNC, the course of developing democratic and representative governance in Kurdish areas, and in Syria as a whole, was long and complex. Local actors, regional ones and the international community contributed to the continuing crisis as well as to paving a path out of it. Divergent interests and agendas tangled together within the territory promised to make the political processes of settling the many disputes and conflicts in Syria and in the Kurdish areas equally long and complex. In any event, the Kurds were likely to resist external threats in order to retain the rights of ethnic representation, expression and language, including progress made in women's rights and local administration, that they had gained. But while deep fissures between the two political blocs of the PYD/PKK and the KNC/KDP remained unbridgeable, securing these rights would be all the more problematic. Representation of Syrian Kurds remained a battlefield in itself.

Yet, if one could speak generally about the Kurds of Syria, regardless of the political fissures that opened up in northern Syria and among the great complexities and uncertainties of the war, it would be to say that the Kurds in Syria had stepped up decisively onto the local, regional and international arenas and that the Kurdish position on the world stage had shifted, irreversibly.

Bibliography

Ahmed, Muhammad Mullah 2000: *Jamaʿiahat Khoybun wa al-ʿAlaqat al-Kurdiyah Armaniyah*, KAWA, Bonn.

Akkaya, Ahmet Hamdi and Joost Jongerden 2012: 'Reassembling the political: The PKK and the project of radical democracy', *European Journal of Turkish Studies*, Vol. 14, available on http://ejts.revues.org/4615 (last accessed 18/05/2016).

Ali, Massoud 2010: *Years of Drought: A Report on the Effects of Years of Drought on the Syrian Peninsular, Heinrich-Böll-Stiftung - Middle East Office*, https://lb.boell.org/site s/default/files/uploads/2010/12/drought_in_syria_en.pdf (last accessed 14/10/2016).

Allsopp, Harriet 2014: *The Kurds of Syria: Political Parties and Identity in the Middle East*, I. B Tauris, London.

Almohamad, Hussein and Andreas Dittmann 20/05/2016: 'Oil in Syria between terrorism and dictatorship', *Social Science*, Vol. 5, Issue 2, http://www.mdpi. com/2076-0760/5/2/20/htm (last accessed 04/04/2017).

Bateson, Florence, Toon Dirkx, Georg Frerks, Donna Middelkoop and Noralie Tukker 2016: *Gendered Alternatives: Exploring Women's Roles in Peace and Security in Self-administered Areas of Northern Syria*. Utrecht University and the Women's Commission of Rojava, https://www.kpsrl.org/sites/default/files/publications/files/ gendered_alternatives_policy_report_1.pdf (last accessed 18/12/2018).

Cagaptay, Soner 05/04/2012: 'Syria and Turkey: The PKK dimension', *The Washington Institute*, http://www.washingtoninstitute.org/policy-analysis/view/syria-and-turk ey-the-pkk-dimension (last accessed 06/05/2017).

Cagaptay, Soner, and Andrew J. Tabler 23/10/2015: 'The U.S-PYD-Turkey Puzzle', Washington Institute, Policy Analysis, Policywatch 2510, http://www.washingtoninst itute.org/policy-analysis/view/the-u.s.-pyd-turkey-puzzle (last accessed 21/04/2016).

Cagaptay, Soner, and Coskun Unal 26/02/2014: 'Leadership reshuffle – PKK makes changes in its ranks', IHS Jane's, available on http://www.washingtoninstitute.org/ uploads/Documents/opeds/Cagaptay20140226-Janes.pdf (last accessed 07/07/2017).

Collelo, Thomas, ed. 1987: *Syria: A Country Study*. Washington: GPO for the Library of Congress, available on http://countrystudies.us/syria/23.htm (last accessed 15/04/2016).

Egret, Eliza, and Tom Anderson, May 2016: *Struggles for Autonomy in Kurdistan and Corporate Complicity in the Representation of Social movements in Rojava and Bakur.* Corporate Watch, (Online) available on https://corporatewatch.org/sites/default/file s/Struggles%20for%20autonomy%20in%20Kurdistan.pdf and https://cooperativee conomy.info/a-conversation-with-tev-dems-bedran-gia-kurd/ (last accessed 05/05/2017).

Fares, Qais 08/05/2014: 'The Syrian constitution: Syria's magic wand', *Carnegie Middle East Centre*, available on http://carnegie-mec.org/diwan/55541?lang=en (last accessed 14/09/2016).

Grojean, Olivier 2014: 'The production of the new man within the PKK', *European Journal of Turkish Studies*, (online) available on http://ejts.revues.org/4825 (last accessed 14/09/2014).

Halliday, Fred 2006: 'Can we write a modernist history of Kurdish nationalism?', in Faleh A. Jabar and Hosham Dawod (eds), *The Kurds: Nationalism and Politics*, Saqi, London, 11–20.

de Jong, Alex 18/03/2016: 'The new-old PKK', *Jacobin*, https://www.jacobinmag.co m/2016/03/pkk-ocalan-kurdistan-isis-murray-bookchin/ (last accessed 10/10/2016).

Knapp, Michael (translated by *Richard Braude*) 06/02/2015: 'Rojava – the formation of an economic alternative: Private property in the service of all', Peace in Kurdistan Campaign, https://peaceinkurdistancampaign.com/2015/02/06/rojava-the-format ion-of-an-economic-alternative-private-property-in-the-service-of-all/ (originally published by Kurdistan Report: http://www.kurdistan-report.de/index.php/arch iv/2014/171/13-privateigentum-im-dienste-aller).

Knapp, Michael, Anja Flach and Ercan Ayboga 2016: *Revolution in Rojava*, Pluto Press, London.

Lowe, Robert 2014: 'The emergence of Western Kurdistan and the future of Syria', in David Romano and Mehmet Gurses (eds), *Conflict, Democratisation and the Kurds in the Middle East*, Palgrave Macmillan, London, 241.

Lowe, Robert, August 2016: 'Rojava at 4: Examining the experiment in western Kurdistan: workshop proceedings', LSE, available on http://eprints.lse.ac.uk/67515/1/ Rojavaat4.pdf (last accessed 23/03/2017).

Lynch, Maureen, and Perveen Ali, January 2006: 'Buried Alive', Refugees International, London, available on http://www.refworld.org/docid/47a6eba80.html (accessed 10/06/2016).

McDowall, David 2000: *A Modern History of the Kurds*, I. B. Tauris, London.

McGee, Thomas, June 2016: 'Statelessness displaced: Update on Syria's stateless Kurds', *Institute on Statelessness and Inclusion,* The Netherlands, available on http://www. institutesi.org/WP2016_02.pdf, 1 (last accessed 20/06/2016).

McQuinn, Jason 31/07/2016: 'Lessons from Rojava: Democracy and Commune; this and that', *Modern Slavery*, http://modernslavery.calpress.org/?tag=tev-dem (last accessed 05/05/2017).

Montgomery, Harriet 2005: *The Kurds of Syria: An Existence Denied*, Europäisches Zentrum für Kurdische Studien, Berlin.

Ocalan, Abdullah 2009: *War and Peace in Kurdistan*, International Initiative Edition in Cooperation with Mesopotamian Publishers, Neuss.

Ocalan, Abdullah 2011: *Democratic Confederalism*, Transmedia Publishing Ltd, London.

Ocalan, Abdullah 2013: *Liberating Life: Women's Revolution*. International Initiative Edition in Cooperation with Mesopotamian Publishers, Neuss.

Ozoglu, Hakan 2007: 'Impact of Islam on Kurdish identity formation', in Muhammad Ahmed and Michael Gunter (eds), *The Evolution of Kurdish Nationalism*, Mazda Publishers, California, 18–35.

Phillips, Christopher, May 2011: '*Turkey and Syria*', in Turkey's Global Strategy, LSE IDEAS, LSE, London, available on http://www.lse.ac.uk/IDEAS/publications/repor ts/pdf/SR007/syria.pdf (last accessed 06/05/2017).

Romano, David 2006: *The Kurdish Nationalist Movement: Opportunity, Mobilisation and Identity*, Cambridge University Press, Cambridge.

Rondot, Pierre 1939: '*Les Kurdes de Syrie*', La France Mediterranee et Africaine, Vol. II, No. 1 (Lib. Sirey, Paris): 88–126.

Roussinos, Aris 2015: *Rebels: My Life Behind Enemy Lines with Warlords, Fanatics and Not-so-friendly Fire*, Random House, London.

Soz, Jiwan 22/03/2016: 'Isolation of the Kurds in Syria', *Atlantic Council*, (online) http://www.atlanticcouncil.org/blogs/syriasource/isolation-of-the-kurds-in-syria (last accessed 16/01/2017).

Stein, Aaron, and Michelle Foley 26/01/2016: 'The YPG-PKK connection', *Atlantic Council*, http://www.atlanticcouncil.org/blogs/menasource/the-ypg-pkk-connection (last accessed 13/01/2017).

Tejel, Jordi 2009: *Syria's Kurds: History, Politics and Society*, Routledge, London.

Vali, Abbas 2006: 'The Kurds and their "others": Fragmented identity and fragmented politics', in Faleh A. Jabar and Hosham Dawod (eds), *The Kurds: Nationalism and Politics*, Saqi, London, 49–78.

Ware, Alan 1999: *Political Parties and Party Systems*, Oxford University Press, Oxford.

Organisations/think tanks (online)

Unpublished Western NGO report: September 2015: Youth Labour Market Assessment, Northeast Syria.

Amnesty International

13/10/2015: 'Syria: US ally's razing of villages amounts to war crimes', *Amnesty International*, https://www.amnesty.org/en/press-releases/2015/10/syria-us-allys-razing-of-villages-amounts-to-war-crimes/ (last accessed 27/03/2017).

13/10/2015: 'We had nowhere else to go': Forced displacement and demolitions in northern Syria', available on https://www.amnesty.org/en/documents/mde24/25 03/2015/en/ (last accessed 30/03/2017).

Danish Immigration Service 26/02/2015: 'Syria: Military service, mandatory self-defence duty and recruitment to the YPG', *Danish Immigration Service*, Copenhagen, available on http://www.refworld.org/pdfid/54fd6c884.pdf (last accessed 05/05/2017).

Chatham house

Butter, David, June 2015: 'Syria's economy: Picking up the pieces', Chatham House Research Paper, Chatham House, London, https://www.chathamhouse.org/sites/files/chathamhouse/field/field_document/20150623SyriaEconomyButter.pdf (last accessed 13/01/2017).

Khalaf, Rana 08/12/2016: 'Governing Rojava: Layers of legitimacy in Syria', Chatham House Research Papers, Chatham House, London, https://www.chathamhouse.org/sites/files/chathamhouse/publications/research/2016-12-08-governing-rojava-khalaf.pdf (last accessed 24/03/2017).

Sari, Ghadi, September 2016: 'Kurdish self-governance in Syria: Survival and ambition', Chatham House Research Paper, Chatham House, London, https://www.chathamhouse.org/sites/files/chathamhouse/publications/research/2016-09-15-kurdish-self-governance-syria-sary_0.pdf (last accessed 29/09/2016).

Syrian Observatory for Human Rights 19/12/2015: 'Sheikh Maqsood neighborhood is witnessing an agreement between YPG and Fath Aleppo operations room', *SOHR*, http://www.syriahr.com/en/?p=40690 (last accessed 18/06/2017).

Human rights watch (HRW)

HRW 10/11/2009: 'On vulnerable ground: Violence against minority communities in Nineveh Province's disputed territories', available on https://www.hrw.org/report/2009/11/10/vulnerable-ground/violence-against-minority-communities-nineveh-provinces-disputed (last accessed 04/10/2016).

HRW 18/06/2014, 'Syria: Abuses in Kurdish-run Enclaves', *Human Rights Watch*, https://www.hrw.org/news/2014/06/18/syria-abuses-kurdish-run-enclaves (last accessed 05/04/2017).

HRW 19/06/2014: *Under Kurdish Rule: Abuses in PYD-run Enclaves of Syria*, https://www.hrw.org/report/2014/06/19/under-kurdish-rule/abuses-pyd-run-enclaves-syria (last accessed 01/02/2017).

HRW 15/07/2015: 'Syria: Kurdish forces violating child soldier ban', https://www.hrw.org/news/2015/07/10/syria-kurdish-forces-violating-child-soldier-ban-0 (last accessed 24/03/2017).

HRW 04/08/2016: 'Iraq: KRG restrictions harm Yezidi recovery', *Human Rights Watch*, https://www.hrw.org/news/2016/12/04/iraq-krg-restrictions-harm-yezidi-recovery (last accessed 16/03/2017).

HRW 25/08/2016: 'Iraqi Kurdistan: Kurdish journalist abducted, killed', *Human Rights Watch*, https://www.hrw.org/news/2016/08/25/iraqi-kurdistan-kurdish-journalist-abducted-killed (last accessed 03/06/2017).

HRW 26/10/2016: 'Syria: Improvised mines kill, injure hundreds in Manbij', *Human Rights Watch*, https://www.hrw.org/news/2016/10/26/syria-improvised-mines-kill-i njure-hundreds-manbij (last accessed 04/04/2017).

HRW 04/12/2016: 'Iraq: KRG restrictions harm Yezidi recovery', *Human Rights Watch*, https://www.hrw.org/news/2016/12/04/iraq-krg-restrictions-harm-yezidi-recovery (last accessed 31/03/2017).

HRW 16/03/2017: 'Kurdistan region of Iraq: 32 arrested at peaceful protest', *Human Rights Watch*, https://www.hrw.org/news/2017/03/16/kurdistan-region-iraq-32-arre sted-peaceful-protest (last accessed 11/03/2017).

International crisis group

Joost Hilterman 19/05/2016: 'The Kurds: A divided future?' *International Crisis Group*, https://www.crisisgroup.org/middle-east-north-africa/gulf-and-arabian-peninsula/ iraq/kurds-divided-future (last accessed 14/03/2017).

28/04/2017: 'Fighting ISIS: The road to and beyond Raqqa', *International Crisis Group*, https://www.crisisgroup.org/middle-east-north-africa/eastern-mediterranean/syria/ b053-fighting-isis-road-and-beyond-raqqa (last accessed 22/05/2017).

04/05/2017: 'The PKK's fateful choice in Northern Syria', *International Crisis Group*, https://www.crisisgroup.org/middle-east-north-africa/eastern-mediterranean/syria /176-pkk-s-fateful-choice-northern-syria (last accessed 09/06/2017).

KurdWatch

KurdWatch n.d: *Cities: KurdWatch*, http://www.kurdwatch.org/index.php?cid=183&z= en (last accessed 15/04/2016).

KurdWatch 02/06/2012: 'Afrin: Free Syrian Army attacks PYD and regime', http://www .kurdwatch.org/index.php?aid=2547&z=en (last accessed 15/05/2017).

KurdWatch 11/06/2012(a): 'Afrin: Participants in a meeting of the Kurdish National Council kidnapped by the PYD', *KurdWatch*, http://www.kurdwatch.org/index.php? aid=2554&z=en&cure=245 (last accessed 15/05/2017).

KurdWatch 11/06/2012(b): 'Afrin: PYD forces the construction of a checkpoint by kidnapping activists', *KurdWatch*, http://www.kurdwatch.org/index.php?aid=2552&z =en (last accessed 15/05/2017).

KurdWatch 11/06/2012(c): 'Afrin: PYD establishes courts', *KurdWatch*, http://www.kurd watch.org/index.php?aid=2553&z=en (last accessed 15/05/2017).

KurdWatch 12/06/2012: 'Al-Qamishli: Further demonstrations—for the first time, the PYD constructs check points in alQamishli', *KurdWatch*, http://www.kurdwatch.org/ index.php?aid=2555&z=en (last accessed 15/05/2017).

KurdWatch, 15/11/2012: 'Afrin: PYD concludes an agreement with the Free Syrian Army', *Kurdwatch*, http://kurdwatch.org/?aid=2687&z=en (last accessed 17/03/2017).

KurdWatch 30/11/2012: 'Amude: Yekiti forms armed battalion', *KurdWatch*, http://kurdwatch.org/?aid=2703&z=en (last accessed 05/01/2017).

KurdWatch 21/12/2012: 'Al-Qamishli: Armed attack on PYDcheckpoint', *KurdWatch*, http://www.kurdwatch.org/index.php?aid=2587&z=en (last accessed 15/05/2017).

KurdWatch interview with Salih Muslim 04/01/2013: 'Salih Muslim Muhammad, chairman of the PYD: "We are free and independent, and we are pursuing our own strategy"', *Kurdwatch*, http://www.kurdwatch.org/?e2853 (last accessed 25/04/2017).

KurdWatch 30/06/2013: 'New press law for the Jazirah Canton', *KurdWatch*, http://kurdwatch.org/?e3885 (last accessed 05/05/2017).

KurdWatch 14/04/2014: 'Erbil: New party founded', *KurdWatch*, http://kurdwatch.org/?aid=3069&z=en (last accessed 15/05/2017).

KurdWatch 30/09/2014: 'Rojava, Kurdish autonomy and peace-building efforts in Syria: Report from a roundtable discussion', *KurdWatch*, http://kurdwatch.org/?cid=185&z=en (last accessed 04/04/2017).

KurdWatch 30/10/2014: 'Future movement founds military wing', *KurdWatch*, http://www.kurdwatch.org/?aid=3260 (last accessed 11/01/2017).

KurdWatch 26/03/2015: 'Amudah: Results of local elections are announced', *KurdWatch*, http://www.kurdwatch.org/%20pdf/KurdWatch_D038_de_ar.pdf?aid=3384&z=en (last accessed 25/03/2017).

KurdWatch 01/06/2015: 'Kurdish National Council accepts new members', *KurdWatch*, http://www.kurdwatch.org/?aid=3448&z=en (last accessed 26/06/2016).

KurdWatch 17/09/2015: 'Afrin: Following elections all co-chair positions on the municipal councils are to be filled by TEVDEM', *KurdWatch*, http://www.kurdwatch.org/?e3600 (last accessed 04/04/2017).

KurdWatch 30/09/2015: 'Al-Qamishli: PYD takes possession of refugees' property', *KurdWatch*, http://kurdwatch.org/?e3605 (last accessed 30/03/2017).

KurdWatch 15/10/2015: 'Damascus: PYD negotiates with Assad and the Russian military', *KurdWatch*, http://www.kurdwatch.org/?e3631 (last accessed 30/06/2015).

KurdWatch 23/02/2016: 'A new party alliance formed', *KurdWatch*, http://www.kurdwatch.org/?e3754 (last accessed 16/01/2016).

KurdWatch 06/05/2016: 'al-Hawl: Residents return to the city', *KurdWatch*, http://kurdwatch.org/?e3826 (last accessed 04/04/2017).

KurdWatch 30/06/2016: 'New document: Press Law for the Jazirah Canton', *KurdWatch*, http://kurdwatch.org/?e3885 (last accessed 04/04/2017).

Society for Threatened Peoples (STP) June 2016: 'Rojava – a "protection zone" for religious and ethnic minorities in northern Syria? Report on a research trip', *Society for Threatened Peoples*, https://www.gfbv.de/fileadmin/redaktion/Reporte_Memoran den/2016/Northern-Syria-research-trip-2016.compressed.pdf (last accessed 20/08/2017).

Orsam

Bilgay Duman 26/06/2015: 'What PYD leader Muslim's Baghdad visit means', *Orsam*,
URL: http://www.orsam.org.tr/index.php/Content/Analiz/4432?s=orsam%7Cenglis
h (last accessed 14/03/2017).

Orsam 04/04/2017: 'Federalism in Syria, PYD and ambivalent Position of Iran', *Orsam*
(online) http://www.orsam.org.tr/index.php/Content/Analiz/5094?s=orsam%7Ce
nglish (last accessed 08/07/2017).

Washington Institute

Fabrice Balanche 24/08/2016: 'Rojava's sustainability and the PKK's regional
strategy', *Washington Institute*, http://www.washingtoninstitute.org/policy-ana
lysis/view/rojavas-sustainability-and-the-pkks-regional-strategy (last accessed
04/04/2017).

Political party publications

PYD / Administration Documents

Afrin Canton 19/05/2015:'Law of self-defence is taking place in Afrin canton with
global unique advantages', *Afrin Canton*, http://cantonafrin.com/en/news/view/1050
.law-of-self--defense--is-taking-place-in-afrin-canton-with-global-unique-advant
ages.html (last accessed 16/06/2017).

The Charter of the Social Contract of the Rojava Cantons 29/01/2014: available in HRW
June 2014: 'Under Kurdish Rule', Appendix I, p. 54, https://www.hrw.org/sites/defa
ult/files/reports/syria0614_kurds_ForUpload.pdf (last accessed 20/08/2017).

Democratic Self-Administration Executive Council for the Kobanî Canton Committee
of Defense and Self-Protection 02/06/2016: *Memo, Democratic Self-Administration
KurdWatch*, http://kurdwatch.org/pdf/KurdWatch_D040_en_ar.pdf (last accessed
16/06/2017).

Draft Social Contract of the Democratic Federal System of Northern Syria, available on
http://hawarnews.com/ا-الفيدرالية-للعقد-الاجتماعي-العقد-عن-الكشف/ (last accessed 07/07/2017).

Foreign Relations body of Democratic Self-rule Administration – Rojava, n.d. 2014:
'The Democratic Self-Rule Administration's Response to the Report of Human
Rights Watch Organization', published by *Human Rights Watch*, https://www.hrw.
org/sites/default/files/related_material/The%20Democratic%20SelfRule%20Adm
inistration%E2%80%99s%20Response%20to%20the%20Report%20of%20Human
%20Rights%20Watch%20Organization.pdf (last accessed 04/04/2017).

The Independent Board for the Reconstruction of Kobanî, Dr. Musallam Talas
18/12/2014: 'The declaration of the independent board for the reconstruction of

Kobanî', available on *Yekiti Media*, http://en.yekiti-media.org/declaration-indepe ndent-board-reconstruction-kobani/ (last accessed 05/05/2017).

KNK May 2014: 'Canton based democratic autonomy of Rojava (Western Kurdistan – Northern Syria)', *Peace in Kurdistan Campaign*, https://peaceinkurdistancampai gn.files.wordpress.com/2011/11/rojava-info-may-2014.pdf (last accessed 05/05/2017).

Kurdistan National Congress (KNK) 07/03/2014: 'Briefly history of Syria and Rojava', *KNK*, http://www.kongrakurdistan.net/en/briefly-history-of-syria-and-rojava/ (last accessed 05/05/2017).

Organizational Charter of the Kurdish Community in Western Kurdistan KCK-Rojava, first edition 2007 (last accessed 15/07/2016).

The Social Contract of the Democratic Federalism of Northern Syria (draft) 29/12/2016: 'Rules of Procedure of the Democratic Union Party (PYD)' (Internal Code) 2015, *PYD Rojava*, available on http://en.pydrojava.com/index.php/2016/02/25/internal-s ystem/ (last accessed 20/08/2017).

TEV-DEM 16/02/2015: 'The project of a Democratic Syria', available on *Peace in Kurdistan Campaign*, website: https://peaceinkurdistancampaign.com/resources/roj ava/the-project-of-a-democratic-syria/ (last accessed 24/03/2017).

YPG: 'About the Peoples Protection Units (YPG)', *YPG Rojava*, https://www.ypgrojava. org/About-Us

YPG: 'Rules of Procedure', 2013, available in Appendix II of HRW 2014: *Under Kurdish Rule: Abuses in PYD-run Enclaves of Syria*, https://www.hrw.org/report/2014/06/19/ under-kurdish-rule/abuses-pyd-run-enclaves-syria (last accessed 01/02/2017). Available also in Arabic on https://www.hrw.org/sites/default/files/reports/syria06 14ar_kurds_ForUpload.pdf (last accessed 01/02/2017).

YPG International n.d: 'Support YPG in Rojava', available on *YPG International*, https:// ypginternational.blackblogs.org/ (last accessed 15/-5/2017).

The Syrian Arab Republic

The Constitution of the Syrian Arab Republic 1973, available on http://www.icla.up.ac.za/ images/un/use-of-force/asia-pacific/SyrianArabRepublic/Constitution%20Syria n%20Arab%20Republic%201973.pdf (last accessed 20/08/2017).

The Constitution of the Syrian Arab Republic 2012, available on http://www.ilo.org/w cmsp5/groups/public/---ed_protect/---protrav/---ilo_aids/documents/legaldoc ument/wcms_125885.pdf (last accessed 20/08/2017).

Decree No. 49, 2008, available on http://www.kurdwatch.org/pdf/kurdwatch_dekret 49_en.pdf (last accessed 20/08/2017).

SANA (Syrian Arab News Agency) 06/12/2015: 'President al-Assad: Britain and France have neither the will nor the vision on how to defeat terrorism', *SANA*, http://sana. sy/en/?p=63558 (last accessed 16/06/2017).

Syrian Nationality Law, Legislative Decree 276, 24/11/1969, available on http://www.
refworld.org/pdfid/4d81e7b12.pdf (last accessed 20/08/2017).

The Kurdish Yekiti party in Syria

The Political Programme, 2009, translation available on http://yekiti-media.org/archive/
nuce.php?z=&id=33&z=en (accessed 19/10/2016).
Yekiti Media 06/01/2017: '*Mawq'a Rudaw yanshr dustur Kurdistan suriya alathi
iqtaraHihi al-majlis al-watani al-Kurdi*', *Yekiti Media*, http://ara.yekiti-media.org/
موقع-روداو-ينشر-دستور-كردستان-سوريا-ال/ (last accessed 16/06/2017).

Kurdish National Council

KNC 05/07/2016: 'Position of the Kurdish National Council on Political
Decentralisation, Federalism and Local Governance', http://knc-geneva.org/wp-
content/uploads/2016/07/KNC-Federalism-and-Decentralisation.pdf (last accessed
11/07/2017).

KNC 18/11/2016: 'Amude – Along the lines of Stalinism: PYD security forces
shut down another radio and raid Yekiti office', available on http://knc-geneva.
org/?p=795&lang=en (last accessed 29/11/2016).
KNC 16/03/2017: 'PYD's repression of the KNC reaches new climax', http://
knc-geneva.org/?p=1059&lang=en KNC Geneva (last accessed 10/03/2017).
KNC 16/08/2016: 'President of the KNC abducted and deported by the PYD',
http://knc-geneva.org/?p=657&lang=en (last accessed 07/07/2017).

IIST Interviews

Abdul Karim Omer, foreign relations head of Cizere canton, Qamishli, 11/05/2016.
Abdulhakim Bashar, senior official in KDP-S, Erbil, 15/02/2016.
Abdulhamid Darwish, head of the Kurdish Democratic Progressive Party,
Sulaymaniyah, 13/02/2016.
Abdulkarim Saroxan, president of Executive Council in Cizere canton, 19/04/2016.
Abdullah al-Aziz Begi, co-head of Shehid Rezan commune in Amude, 02/05/2016.
Abdulsalam Mohammed, Kurdish language teacher, Qamishli, 16/02/2017.
Abdulselam Ahmed, senior TEV-DEM official, Qamishli, 20/07/2016.
Abdulsamad Xalaf Biro, member of the political bureau of the Yekiti party, 19/04/2016.
Adib Abdulmajid, founder and lead editor of ARA News, 02/02/2017.
Agid Kalari, PKK commander in Sinjar city, 15/04/2016.

Ahmad Sulaiman, member of the political bureau of the Kurdish Democratic
    Progressive Party in Syria, 06/05/2016.
Ahmed Sulaiman, leading member of Progressive Party, Qamishli, 06/05/2016.
Alan Mohtadi. Head of T&S consulting, 14/05/2017.
Aldar Xelil, Executive Committee Member of the Democratic Movement Society
    (TEV-DEM) in Syria, Amude, 02/05/2016.
Amjad Othman, head reform party, member of Syrian Democratic Council, Qamishli,
    07/05/2016.
Anwar Muslim, head of the Kobani canton, 26/05/2016.
Arshek Baravi, founder of the Kurdish education system, Amude, 12/05/2016.
Ayse Efendi, co-chair of the People's Assembly of Kobanê Canton, Kobani,
    17/06/2017.
Ayten Ferhat, co-head of the Asayish, Qamishli, 28/03/2014.
Aziz Biro, former member of Yekiti Party, Qamishli, 11/05/2016.
Bahjat Bashir, member of the KNC, Erbil, 14/03/2016.
Bandar al-Humaydi, head of the Sanadid Militia, Tal Alo village, 30/04/2016.
Canaan Barakat, co-president of Cizere canton, interior minister, 18/04/2016.
Ciwan Ramadan Hussein Abdullah, member of the Rojava Peshmerga, Erbil,
    28/02/2016.
D. Sanharib Barsom, co-head of the Syriac Union Party, Qamishli, 13/05/2016.
Dicle Sulaiman, co-president of the Amude municipality, 02/05/2016.
Dilsaah Haji Younes, co-head of the Shehid Rezan commune in Amude, 02/05/2016.
Faysal Yusuf, chairman of the Kurdish Reform Movement 2013 Syria, 14/03/2016.
Gello Isa, member of the Syrian Democratic Kurdish Party, 04/08/2016.
Hakim Gulo, co-president of the legislative council, Cizere canton, 24/04/2016.
Hamdan al-Abad, Tal Abyad council co-head, Tal Abyad, 30/05/2016.
Hassan Salih, senior official of Yekiti party, Qamishli, 04/05/2016.
Hediya Yousef, co-head of the federal system, 21/04/2016.
Heval Jiyan, a foreign fighter in YPG base close to Ayn al Issa, 17/10/2015.
Heybar Othman, former head of Kurdistan 24 office, 18/02/2017.
Hussein Azzam, vice-president of executive council of Cizere canton, 19/04/2016.
Hussein Badr, member of al-Wahda Party, Qamishli, 18/04/2016.
Ibrahim Biro, head of KNC, Erbil, 13/03/2016.
Ibrahim al-Hassan, deputy co-chair of Syrian Democratic Council (SDC) and head of
    judicial council in Tal Abyad, 31/05/2016.
Ibrahim Kurdo, head of foreign relations Kobani, 01/06/2016.
Idris Nassan, former vice Minister of Foreign Affairs in Kobani, 11/10/2015.
Ilham Ahmed, co-head of the Syrian Democratic Council, Sulaymaniyah, 14/06/2017.
Ismet Sheikh, head of Defense Ministry, 24/05/2016.
Kamiran Haj Abdo, member of foreign relations of KNC, by Skype, 10/03/2016.
Khaled Issa, PYD France representative Khaled Issa, 13/08/2016.
Layla Mohammed, co-head of Tal Abyad Council, 30/06/2016.

Leyla Hamza, co-president of the Martyr Diyar commune in Amude, 02/05/2016.

Majdal Dalil, Yekiti, Qamishli, 01/03/2017.

Majdal Delli, senior Yekiti member, 12/04/2017.

Manaan Kajjo, teacher in Amude, 05/10/2015.

Mansour Saloum, the Arab co-head of the federal Rojava Region, Ramalan, 21/04/2016.

Midya Mahmud, pharmacist and former KNC member, 10/05/2016.

Mizgin Amed, senior TEV-DEM official, Amude, 19/04/2016.

Mohammed Hassan, Russian Today journalist, 06/05/2016.

Mohammed Ismail, senior KDP-S official, Qamishli, 10/05/2016.

Mohammed Said Wadi, KDP-S Qamishli, 06/05/2016.

Mohammed Salih Abdo, co-chair of education commission, Qamishli, 11/05/2016.

Mohammed Shemo (54), a teacher in Amude, 02/10/ 2015.

Mustafa Kino, member of the *al-Wahda* Party, 05/06/2016.

Mustafa Sino, member of the national and foreign relations committee in the KNC, Geneva by Skype, 13/03/2016.

Nicholas A. Heras, Middle East Security Fellow, Center for a New American Security, 25/03/2017.

Ni'mat Dawud, head of the Kurdish Democratic Equality Party in Syria (KNC leader), 21/5/2016.

Perwin Mohammed Amin, member of the legislative council, deputy of the co-president, 19/04/2016.

Reshan Shakr (25), history teacher at the Mesopotamia Academy, Qamishli, 12/05/2016.

Rezan Gullo, head of defense, Cizere canton, 24/07/2016.

Riyaad Heme, member *al-Wahda* Party, Erbil, Tuesday, 05/04/2016.

Riyaad Temmo, Left Party, 12/06/ 2016.

Robert Ford, former US ambassador to Syria, by Skype, 15/03/2017.

Rody Naso, ARTA FM radio manager Amude, 04/05/2016.

Saadon F Sino; Rojava Peshmerga, 11/03/2016.

Salih Didi, co-head of the Shehid Viyan commune in Kobani, 15/06/2016.

Salih Gheddo, leader of the Kurdish Democratic Left Party, Qamishli, 11/05/2016.

Salih Muslim, co-head of the PYD, Kobani, 26/05/2016.

Sihanok Dibo, presidential advisor PYD, Qamishlo, 02/05/2016.

Sharvan Darwish, spokesperson for SDF, near Kobani, 27/05/2016.

Sheikh Ali Jamili from the Jarablus Council, 29/05/2016.

Sheikh Mohamed Qadri, head religious affairs Cizere canton, 23/04/2016.

Sheruan Hussein, representative Rojava administration in the Netherlands, 16/02/2017.

Siham Yousef Kyo, member of Syriac Union Party, co-head of foreign relations Cizre canton, 12/05/2016.

Sinem Mohammed, senior official and representative of the Rojava cantons in Europe, 10/10/2016.

Sipan Seyda, former member of Syrian opposition, Erbil, 11/03/2016.

Tahir Saʾdun Sifuk, chairman Kurdish Democratic Patriotic Party in Syria (KNC leader), 21/05/2016.
Talal Mohamed, co-president of the Kurdistan Democratic Peace Party, part of TEV-DEM, 08/05/2016.
Talal Silo, spokesperson of SDF forces, Hasaka, 25/04/2016.
Walter Posch, National Defense Academy (Vienna, Austria) by e-mail, 24/03/2017.

Anonymous interviews

Afrin resident, 17/09/2016.
Afrin resident (telephone), 28/02/2017.
Afrin residents, 08/10/2016.
Anonymous conscript from Kobani, 18/02/2017.
Anonymous KNC politician, 15/02/2016.
Anonymous Peshmerga member of the CTG forces in Erbil, 16/03/2017.
Anonymous PYD official, 15/02/2017.
Anonymous US official, 12/02/2017 and 05/03/2017.
Anonymous YPG fighters in Tal Abyad, 17/10/2015.
Anonymous YPG foreign fighter, 23/03/2017.
Anonymous YPG official, 16/02/2017.
Former US volunteer YPG forces, 11/02/2017.
Kurdish civilian, Qamishli, 26/06/2016.
Shop owner in Qamishli, Sunday, 26/06/2016.
Tal Abyad, city council members, 30/05/2016.

Index

NOTE: Page references in *italics* refer to maps.